Words of Praise

"Having previewed the book, I can say that the reader will be encouraged and blessed. Not only by the wisdom but by the writers own personal experience. It is based in sound biblical knowledge with a sensitivity from one who has traveled life's road and found God's unchanging love."

—Jay Gallimore, former president, Michigan Conference of
Seventh-day Adventists

"I knew Phyllis for almost forty years and she was one of the most genuine Christians I've ever had the privilege of knowing. She loved people and it was her heart's desire to share the love of Jesus with everyone. She was generous with her time and talents and she had a special quality about her in that she could sense when others were in need of a little extra love. Phyllis was not one to be stingy with hugs or a shoulder to cry on. She had an adventurous spirit and loved life and endeavored to live it to its fullest. Phyllis was a student of the Word and she was a teacher at heart which you will discover as you journey through this book."

—Nadine Whitacre, Retired Nurse

I0135336

The Devil Made Me Do It

Choose Love Over The Lie

Phyllis Gruesbeck

TEACH Services, Inc.
PUBLISHING
www.TEACHServices.com • (800) 367-1844

Copyright © 2022 Phyllis Gruesbeck
Copyright © 2022 TEACH Services, Inc.
ISBN-13: 978-1-4796-1052-5 (Paperback)
ISBN-13: 978-1-4796-1053-2 (ePub)
Library of Congress Control Number: 2022909715

All scripture quotations, unless otherwise indicated, are taken from the King James Version (KJV) Public domain.

Scripture quotations marked NKJV are taken from the New King James Version®. Copyright © 1982 by Thomas Nelson. Used by permission. All rights reserved.

Scripture quotations marked NASB are taken from the New American Standard Bible (NASB) Copyright © 1960, 1962, 1963, 1968, 1971, 1972, 1973, 1975, 1977, 1995 by The Lockman Foundation.

Published by

TEACH Services, Inc.
P U B L I S H I N G
www.TEACHServices.com • (800) 367-1844

Table of Contents

The

Devil

Made Me

Do

It!

Are You Gullible?

Do you realize that the

title of this Book,

The Devil Made Me Do It,

IS

A BALD-FACED LIE?

Well, it is!

Come and see why!

But it got your attention—didn't it?

Come find out

who it is

that tells us that lie every day.

Who is God?

Do you really know Him?

Wouldn't you like to know Him better?

He knows you

and

He greatly loves you!

Yes,

He loves you very much!

Come and meet Him!

This is how much He Loves You!
He let His Only Son

DIE

Just for You

Now! That's Amazing Grace!

But what is grace?

The Bible—God's Word—says:

Grace is the kind of love God only gives to sinners! It's as simple as that!

Yes! It is an undeserved gift of love.

And what love it is!

God only gives it to sinners—because they are the only ones who need it.

If you haven't sinned—you don't need to be saved from sin.

But do you realize that God says,

"All Have Sinned"

So! the biggest question is—Do we really love Him?

Yes! I said "we."

We are all in this together!

Come and see why!

Introduction

Caution!

This is a love story!

It's not mushy!

So if you were hoping for the mushy kind!

Don't read this book!

It's all about God—He truly is love!

I'd like to know Him better.

If you want to know Him better too—come with me.

Bring your Bible so you can check me out to see if I am agreeing with God's Word!

But! Are you sure you know what love is? God lets us in on a gorgeous truth. Here it is! It tells us it is **God, who is love.** Isn't that beautiful? This book is all about God—the most loving Being who ever lived. My Bible tells me knowing Him is the most important thing any of us can do. You see! I believe with all my heart if we really know Him we will love Him. They, God, are real lovers! There is absolutely nothing fake or two-faced about them. Not anything!

Yes, I said, "They"! We'll learn more about Their oneness later on. They love everyone! But God has an enemy. They even gave their enemy, the devil, freedom of choice—a choice to be good or bad. He is the most unlikeable fellow there is. Lucifer became the most cruel being who was ever created. And no! God did not make him unloving, and no again, the devil is not dead. Not yet!

Unfortunately, he is still very much alive. He only looks out for himself. And he even does a rotten job of that. He's the most disgusting character who has ever existed. There are two words that describe him well—selfish and proud!

Those two words describe his character to a tee. He puts up an amazing front. He lies and tries to make himself look very good. But! He's a deceitful, slick trickster. He lies to each one of us daily. That is why we need God in our life every moment.

So watch out!

He wants to make you miserable. He hates you! Why? Because God loves you! The devil hates everyone who loves God. In fact, he just hates us because we were made by Jesus, God's Son. He thinks God the Father was unfair to him. We will talk more about why he feels that way and how he became so vengeful and angry. God wants us to know all about Satan so we can make wise choices when we have to deal with him. And, yes, we definitely will have to face him. He, the devil, will see to that. We also will find out why God allows bad things to happen to us. He, the devil, made himself an enemy to God. He thinks he should have been the creator! He especially considers us his enemy if we truly love God.

That is why we need to know God really well! And in that knowing, the Bible tells us why and how this beautiful angel became His enemy. So, I think it is important to put knowing God in first before knowing about the devil. Why? Because that knowledge will fortify our minds and help us make wise choices concerning our relationship with God. We need Him to protect us from the wickedness of the devil. So let's get to know God better first.

How do we get to know our wonderful God better? It is very simple! Just read the Bible. It's God's love letter to us. Talk to Him in prayer. Have a personal relationship with Him. God needs to be the most important Being on our agenda. Our life depends on it. God is our most important and reliable source of protection against the devil. We have everything to gain and nothing to lose, except the things that would destroy us, and I certainly want to lose those. So, come, take this trip with me.

God is always available. He wants to teach us how to stay safe from Satan's evil plans for us. Knowing this is a life and death matter. So come, if you so desire, and find out the truth about our worst enemy—the devil. And keep in mind that he is a user. He uses all of us. How? He deceives us and tricks us into doing his dirty work. That's why we need to know everything about him; so we don't innocently become his helper to destroy both us, our family, and our friends—even those who do not like us.

There are many ideas about who the devil is. Always keep this in mind! If someone tells you something that does not agree with the Bible, just realize what they are saying is not from God and is untrue. But also remember all of us are frail human beings. We should not shun someone just because they do not agree with us. We all need each other. We should help one another. And realize if what they are saying doesn't agree with the Bible, they have been deceived by the devil. We all fall into that category. If you know, then show them what God says. Then it is their choice to accept or reject either the devil or God. They have freedom of choice. Who are we to try to take this freedom away from them? Place them in God's care. Ask the Holy Spirit to speak to them. He's the one we all need to go to.

Remember! We are all sinners. That means all of us have been tricked by the devil. We need them, and they need us. We are all in this together. Each of us can learn things about both God and Satan. No one knows everything. We are not God. He's the only one who knows everything. All of us have limited knowledge. It is impossible for us to have all knowledge. All of us are often tricked by the devil. He tricks all of us into believing his lies. He may have tricked either them or us into believing him. The devil is the one who tries to get us to act and feel like know-it-alls. Run from him! Quickly run to God minute by minute! He is always available. You can talk to Him any time.

He never says, "I can't talk now, or I don't have time!" Not even if it's in the middle of the night! That means we can go to Him when we are happy, sad, or at a moment's notice—even when we are scared to death! Now that's some God! So, before we talk more about God's enemy—the devil—what do you say we take a closer look at God—the most loving Being who has ever existed.

There's nothing to stop you except your freedom of choice! Yes, I said choice! Love is all about choice—that freedom is given to us by God Himself—our real lover. He always gives us freedom to make our own choices in life, and He always will. In fact—there can be no love without the gift of freedom of choice. So grab your Bible. Check out what I have said for yourself as we take this walk through the Bible together! And rely only on God. He is the only truly trustworthy Holy Being there is. The Word of God—our Bible, is the **only** place where we can be sure to find honest answers for any and all of our questions. God is perfectly worthy; no one else is worthy of such trust. Absolutely no one!

We humans might think we are giving honest answers, but we often misunderstand what we read in God's Word. So our answers must be compared with God's answers. The Bible gives true, honest answers to all of our questions. No one but God can give us answers like that! As you become more acquainted with your Bible, you will find it is like a jigsaw puzzle. So just as you do with a puzzle, you need to do with your Bible.

You need to find as many pieces of information on the same subject as you can.

Isn't that just like a puzzle? You begin by finding all of the edge pieces. When you piece them together, you have your picture framed. You know where the trees will be, etc. Then you sort the pieces into separate areas— sky, trees, or water, etc., by looking at the picture on the box. The Bible is our box. Place each one in a certain place alongside your frame. Water with water, and so on. Then you must put them together to see the whole picture. It is the same when you study the Bible. You get a concordance and look up the verses on a certain subject. As you do that, the picture begins to emerge. You get a more complete image of the whole truth on that subject. It's fun.

Caution! If you read your Bible, you just might fall head over heels in love with God. I did! But it really takes a lifetime to do this. Do you realize when you read your Bible, you are telling God how much you love Him? And at the same time, it is telling you how much He loves you. Love is always a two-way street. And, when you love someone, you want to spend lots of time with them. Spending time with God, learning who He is, what He is like, and talking with Him through prayer really strengthens one's love relationship with Him. The Bible also tells us how to love our ene- mies. Are you shocked? That's just who God is. This is why He can love us even when we sin against Him. Jesus walked the walk the devil tries to make us walk. He took that walk for us. He's so wonderful. That means Jesus has experienced everything that lies ahead of us in this world. In His Word, He leaves His footprints. Yes—a trail for us to follow. The actions of Jesus, His Father, and the Holy Spirit; truly reveal what godly love is all about. And in this way, God shows us how that great love can be our love too. They love each one of us. Now that's what you call personalized love. You can't do better than that!

So! Come! Learn to love Him more, and let's learn how to love our fellowmen more, too, even our enemies. The more, the merrier—it's more fun that way. Part of the reason for taking this walk through the Bible is to size up our enemy. The devil certainly is our enemy. We really need to know what he is like. He lies and tells us God is not trust- worthy. The Bible is the only place where we can learn how dreadfully deceitful he is. He's our worst enemy. He fills our minds with errors. In the Bible God exposes the devil's lies and teaches us how to recognize his voice, so we can say no to him and run into God's arms for protec- tion. The more we listen to God, the more we will recognize the voice of the Holy Spirit. That's special! You'll never be sorry you learned the truth. Anything that is untrue comes from the devil. That is how we can find out who is speaking to us. Be careful! He always mixes truth and error together.

In fact, our act of confidence is another way to tell God we love Him. Jesus told His disciples, *"If ye love Me, keep my commandments. And I will pray the Father, and he shall give you another Comforter, that he may abide with you for ever; Even the Spirit of truth; whom the world cannot receive, because it seeth Him not, neither knoweth Him: but ye know Him; for He dwelleth with you, and shall be in you" (John 14:15–17)*. What a beautiful promise. And I have experienced it. It is true. But! For me, every time I committed myself to the Lord this way, the devil came at me full force. Everything went wrong; that is because the devil couldn't stand to let me totally trust and obey God. He hangs onto us for dear life. He thinks he can shun hell that way. He thinks he can save himself and trick God. How wrong he is. So if that is your experience, too, just keep doing what you are doing, trusting and obeying God's Word. But! Always remember! There may be more Bible verses to make the picture more complete. Let's search for them.

God always keeps His promises, and life on this earth will never be a piece of cake. But! The cake is coming. With lots of frosting on top. We just need to keep our eyes on God's promises. He will be with us through thick and thin. Just look at this beautiful promise. *"I will never leave thee, nor forsake thee. So that we may boldly say, The Lord is my helper, and I will not fear what man shall do unto me" (Heb. 13:5–6)*. Notice who it is that does bad things to us. Not God—but men! We just blame God because we think He should have controlled the men and kept them from harming us. God will not remove their freedom to be wicked. We must trust Him. We can't make it on our own. That's what faith is all about. His comfort is wonderful. I can't live without it. No one can! He helps me go through all the meanness from the wicked. When I do that, my faith grows.

God provides all of us with this information and help because He greatly loves us. He is love in action. The freedom to make our own choices is what real love is all about, for without it, there is no love at all. The Bible tells us why. It looks like it very soon will be too late to come to Him. Then this special privilege of getting to know God better will be gone. That time is rapidly approaching! The Bible tells us it is almost time for Jesus to come and take us on that glorious trip.

**But! Are we ready? Yes! Again, I said we!
Our life depends on it. It's a life-and-death matter.
For you and for me!**

1

If You Truly Know God You Will Love, Trust, and Obey Him

So! Are you ready to begin this walk with me through the Bible on this topic from its beginning to its very end? Learning about God is the most important wisdom we can attain. Best of all, we will be learning what God wants us to know. Reading the Bible with the help of the Holy Spirit will shine a light on our enemy and expose his lies. It will make the love and truthfulness of our God stand out in sharp contrast to the devil's lies and hatred. So bear with me as we acquire a basis for understanding how truly evil the devil is. But! I believe with all my heart we need to look at God's love first before we learn more about our enemy, the devil. Why? Because knowing and loving God will fortify our minds against his lies. If we do not have a good picture of God's love, the devil can easily deceive us. Why? Because sometimes God has to use tough love, and it can easily be misunderstood as not love at all. That's only one reason why knowing God is so very important!

God always needs to be first, last, best, and most important to us. The Bible introduces us to the Spirit of God—the Holy Spirit—early in the Creation story. He is the one who leads us to Jesus and guides us in all of our human endeavors. I believe God thought the Holy Spirit was so important that He had the writer begin the Bible by telling us about Him. And notice that God didn't just introduce the Holy Spirit in the very first chapter, but He introduced Him in the second verse in the Bible.

Wow! You can't beat that. To me, that shows us how important the Holy Spirit really is to us. And I can't over-stress the fact that each one of us needs to search and see for ourselves what God is like! It is the Holy Spirit who helps us know God. Never forget—all of us are human. We all make mistakes. And all of us have a tendency to think we are **not** wrong. But how wrong we are many times! The Bible tells us right up front: *"All have sinned, and come short of the glory of God" (Rom. 3:23).* That includes you and me too. This is true whether we like it or not. Even our pastors, popes, priests, masters, and whatever other word our church uses for their title, are sinners! So this verse includes them too. No one can take God's place. Jesus alone was God in human flesh to be sin for us. He alone of those who are made of human flesh is truly holy. He alone is the only one down here who has never sinned. But it is different in heaven. All of the created beings who are in heaven have never sinned except those taken to heaven by Jesus through translation or resurrection. But notice! They are not God either. Their holiness is on a different level, for God says, talking about Jesus *"And they sing the song of Moses the servant of God, and the song of the Lamb, saying, Great and marvelous are thy works, Lord God Almighty; just and true are thy ways, thou King of saints. Who shall not fear thee, O Lord, and glorify thy name? for thou alone art holy" (Rev. 15:3–4).* The Father wants us to know without a doubt that Jesus is the only human who is holy and totally God.

That's right! Jesus was totally God and totally man when He came to this earth in human flesh. He, alone among men, **never** made a mistake. So He is the One we need to listen to. Look what else God claims: He says, *"To the law and to the testimony: if they speak not according to this word, it is because there is no light in them" (Isa. 8:20).* What is God talking about? It is the Bible God is talking about. God says we can trust every word which comes from His mouth. He says, *"Man doth not live by bread only, but by every word that proceedeth out of the mouth of the LORD doth man live" (Deut. 8:3).* **EVERY WORD OF THE BIBLE IS TRUE!** But let me caution you. Many men have misquoted the Bible and changed it. Many have done so innocently. So this is only true if the Bible has not been tampered with. God told the children of Israel, *"Ye shall not add unto the word which I command you, neither shall ye diminish ought from it, that ye may keep the commandments of the LORD your God which I command you" (Deut. 4:2).* This verse is talking about the Ten Commandments. He is our God too. He is the God of all the people of our world if they choose Him to be. If we are trusting another human, we are **not** trusting God. Everything we trust must be backed up with God's words. I am not telling you not to listen to what others say. They might be more knowledgeable because they have spent more time studying their Bible. But no matter how knowledgeable they are, they make mistakes. They are not God. The Bible must have the final say.

We need to ask God to open our eyes to the truth. Remember, Jesus said, *"It is written, Man shall not live by bread alone, but by every word that proceedeth out of the mouth of God" (Matt. 4:4).* God also tells us to ask the Holy Spirit to help us be willing to follow His say-so in His Word. We need to check out each truth for ourselves in the Bible and through the guidance of the Holy Spirit. The Spirit of God will always agree with the Bible. The Holy Spirit certainly did get front and center stage! He is always available. We need His guidance every moment of our life. Without Him, we cannot be saved! He teaches us about salvation. He is willing to help us when we are in trouble. The Bible begins with these words: *"In the beginning God created the heaven and the earth" (Gen. 1:1)*. Then the writer said: *"And the Spirit of God moved upon the face of the waters" (Gen. 1:2)*. Scholars believe it was Moses who wrote the first five books of the Bible. The Holy Spirit is the one who inspired him and other men of God to write His words down. God says so! Here they are: *"No prophecy of scripture is of any private interpretation. For the prophecy came not in old time by the will of man: but holy men of God spake as they were moved by the Holy Ghost" (2 Peter 1:20–21)*. So we have God's Word itself telling us the Bible contains the only words we can trust. The Bible is honest, and it tells us everything we need to know about God. The Holy Spirit inspired those holy men of God. Then those holy men of God wrote the message in their own words using human language. You can't get better than that! Don't you agree?

What anyone else writes must agree with the Bible to be true. We must choose wisely what Bible we read. It cannot be one that has been tampered with by mankind. It must be a carefully translated Bible, like the King James Version, New King James Version, and The American Standard Version. But Bibles can be updated with modern words that mean the exact same thing. From old English to new English. Words that do not change the meaning of what God told His prophet.

From time to time, we do need to make language changes. Words are always taking on new meaning from one generation to another. This makes updating necessary, so people in our day can know what God is saying. It is good to update the Bible once in a while. The King James Version has been updated this way. They have removed words like "thee" and "thou" that make the Bible difficult to understand. Removing those words and using words like "you" and "me" to take their place makes it easier to understand. The translating is done by a panel of Bible-believing scholars, represented by many of the Christian churches.

Their goal must **not** be to change the meaning of what God said or delete words because they think they don't agree with what God said. The changes must match the words of the prophets and agree with God's original words, for remember! And this is so important that I feel I must repeat it—God says if they do not agree with His Word, there is no light in them. Absolutely none! If the changes do not agree with the original Bible, they are not the words of God. If there are additions that contradict the Bible, those additions are false. Man falsifies the Bible when he adds things to it.

Throughout his lifetime, Moses watched the Holy Spirit work on the hearts of the children of Israel. The Spirit of God is the One who guides us in every aspect of our life today too. If we ask Him, He will speak to us through our thoughts as we read God's Word. He will help us understand what the Bible is telling us. God wants us to know the truth about Them and the truth about everything else. Why? So we will know what God is telling us about salvation. Who gives us the Holy Spirit? *"If ye then, being evil, know how to give good gifts unto your children: how much more shall your heavenly Father give the Holy Spirit to them that ask him"* (Luke 11:13). The Father never forces us to accept the help of the Holy Spirit. But once we know God and who the Holy Spirit is, we will want Him in our life. He is willing and able to help us in every situation in life. When you really know, love, and trust Him, then the comfort He gives us will be a wonderful gift.

> **"**
> *It is extremely important to study our Bible, so the Holy Spirit can bring God's words to us to help us.*
> **"**

Mark cautions us not to be deceived. He gives us a long list of bad things that will happen just before Jesus comes back to earth to take us to heaven with Him! God encourages us by saying, *"When they shall lead you, and deliver you up, take no thought beforehand what ye shall speak, neither do ye premeditate: but whatsoever shall be given you in that hour, that speak ye:"* Why? *"For it is not ye that speak, but the Holy Ghost"* (Mark 13:11). But, if we have not read the Bible, there won't be anything for the Holy Spirit to bring to our memory. It is extremely important to study our Bible, so the Holy Spirit can bring God's words to us to help us. When we witness for Christ, the Father sends the Holy Spirit to us, but we must ask for the Spirit! He will not just take over as Satan does. God never forces His will on anyone! Isn't that wonderful! And neither should we try to force our will on anyone either.

That is where intercessory prayer comes in. God alone knows a person's heart. So, when a person does not realize they are in error, we need to intercede for them. God wants us to ask the Holy Spirit to teach them what God wants them to know. Ask Him to give them a heart to know God. He alone can do this heart work because He alone knows everyone's heart. Thank You, God, for the blessed gift of the Holy Spirit and for intercessory prayer. Thank You for giving us the privilege of working with You. It is so comforting that You will do this for everyone who will accept it. Do you realize all three of the Beings who are our One God are Spirit? God says so! *"God is a Spirit: and they that worship him must worship him in spirit and in truth" (John 4:24).* Then, talking about Jesus, Paul said, *"Now the Lord is that Spirit: and where the Spirit of the Lord is, there is liberty"* (freedom of choice) *(2 Cor. 3:17).* Yes, the Lord Jesus is Spirit too. It is so very important that our information comes from God. And I am so glad God lets us know *"All Scripture is given by inspiration of God" (2 Tim. 3:16).* It is so comforting to know every last bit of it comes from God alone. All the thoughts in the Bible are what God impressed those holy men to write. And God says they are *"profitable for doctrine, for reproof, for correction, for instruction in righteousness" (2 Tim. 3:16).*

For what purpose? So *"That the man of God may be perfect, thoroughly furnished unto all good works" (2 Tim. 3:17).* If that isn't good news, I don't know what is! We need to listen to God alone! All of our answers need to come from Him. So when someone tells you something, don't feel funny about asking them to back up what they say with a Bible verse. So, why should we depend totally on the Bible? First of all, it is because it is God Himself talking to us. He is the One we meet through its pages. He is the One who told those holy men to write it.

Another reason is that the Bible tells the truth. God says through His disciple John: *"Thy word is truth" (John 17:17).* I like it when someone is truthful with me. And I bet you do too. Just listen to what Jesus says the truth in God's Word will do for us. *"If ye continue in my word, then ye are my disciples indeed" (John 8:31).* I like that too. I want to be a follower of God. I want to be His disciple. I love Jesus. I bet you do too. Therefore, I really like the next verse. It also is good news. It says, *"And ye shall know the truth, and the truth shall make you free" (John 8:32).* And *"If the Son therefore shall make you free, ye shall be free indeed" John 8:36).* You can't find anything better than that. But who does the Bible say sets you free? It is Jesus! He really is the only one who can set us free from sin and everything else which is false. He paid an extremely high price to set us free. He died the most cruel death possible to pay for our sins. What a heavy load He bore. More than any man. Thank You, precious Savior. Remember! Jesus likened reading our Bible to eating. No one can live without eating. I used the first part of the verse earlier. Now let's look at all of what Jesus said. He tells us what else we need in order to live. He says we need *"Every word that proceedeth out the mouth of God" (Matt. 4:4 last part).*

If we don't eat, we die physically. The same is true spiritually. If we do not know God's words, we will die spiritually. I don't want to die spiritually, and neither do I want to die the second death. I want to live with God and go home with Him when He comes to take us to heaven with Him at His second coming. I bet you do too. It looks like His coming will be very soon. What can we do about it? We can eat the words of the Bible. We can read them, and they will become part of us, just as our food becomes part of us when we eat it. God's words are like a delicious dessert, for God's words are sweet.

Isn't that an interesting analogy Jesus gave Satan after the devil tempted Him to turn stones into bread? Many times every day, the devil tries to trick us into believing lies like this. I don't think anyone can find a better reason to read it. We need God's words to fortify us when the devil tempts us to do things God does not want us to do. Everything we do must agree with God's Word. It will never tell us to do something God does not approve of. It can and will prepare us to meet the Father, Son, and the Holy Spirit if we allow the Spirit of God to guide us as we read and then obey Him. I find that thrilling. So, each time before I read my Bible, I ask the Holy Spirit to guide me while I read. That's one of the Spirit's jobs. So, I suggest each of us personally, if we desire, pause right now, bow our heads, and ask God for His guidance. Thank You, Holy Spirit, for Your answer to each of our prayers. The Bible says, through the writing of Paul, concerning the Holy Spirit,

> *I, brethren, when I came to you, came not with excellency of speech or of wisdom, declaring unto you the testimony of God. For I determined not to know any thing among you, save Jesus Christ, and him crucified. And I was with you in weakness, and in fear, and in much trembling. And my speech and my preaching was not with enticing words of man's wisdom, but in demonstration of the Spirit and of power: That your faith should not stand in the wisdom of men, but in the power of God. Howbeit we speak wisdom among them that are perfect: yet not the wisdom of this world, nor of the princes of this world, that come to*

nought: But we speak the wisdom of God in a mystery, even the hidden wisdom, which God ordained before the world unto our glory: which none of the princes of this world knew: for had they known it, they would not have crucified the Lord of glory. (1 Cor. 2:1–8)

I encourage you to read the rest of the chapter and also chapter three of First Corinthians. It continues to talk about the Holy Spirit. He tells us our body is the temple of God and that when we obey God, we belong to Him. *"What? Know ye not that your body is the temple of the Holy Ghost which is in you, which ye have of God, and ye are not your own? For ye are bought with a price: therefore glorify God in your body, and in your spirit, which are God's" (1 Cor. 6:19–20).* And Paul says further, concerning the Holy Spirit, *"Wherefore I give you to understand, that no man speaking by the Spirit of God calleth Jesus accursed: and that no man can say that Jesus is the Lord, but by the Holy Ghost" (1 Cor. 12:3).* Definitely, we need to be led by the Holy Spirit. We need Him to be our guide and comforter.

Jesus said to his disciples, *"I will pray the Father, and he shall give you another Comforter, that he may abide with you for ever; Even the Spirit of truth; whom the world cannot receive, because it seeth him not, neither knoweth him: but ye know him; for he dwelleth with you, and shall be in you. I will not leave you comfortless: I will come to you" (John 14:16–18. "These things have I spoken unto you, being yet present with you. But the Comforter, which is the Holy Ghost, whom the Father will send in my name, he shall teach you all things, and bring all things to your remembrance, whatsoever I have said unto you. Peace I leave with you, my peace I give unto you: not as the world giveth, give I unto you. Let not your heart be troubled, neither let it be afraid" (John 14:25–27).* I think those are some of the most beautiful promises in the whole Bible. Jesus gives them to us. Even if we have never been told about the Holy Spirit before, He has impressed us unless we told Him not to. When we study the Bible, we find out how marvelous God is, and we see the tremendous amount of love He showers on us every day. The words of those men of old always agree because all of their information came from our One True God. Every single word in the Bible was inspired by God unless the writer said it was his own personal viewpoint as Paul did at least one time. I am so glad God confirmed that the whole Bible is true and that it was God who impressed Paul to let us know it was him talking when he put his own two cents into the pot. It was very important Paul tell us that those few words were not from God. This means we can get a true answer from the Bible for any question we ask.

The answers are there so we can know God. It is so comforting that they are honest answers, straight from God. But we must search for the whole truth on each particular subject, not just use one or two verses. That is why you need to read your Bible for yourself and come up with additional Bible verses on each subject. A *Strong's Concordance* is a good tool for finding more verses on a certain subject. I encourage you to get one.

If we fill our minds with truth, we will recognize when something is false. The truth will stand out in sharp contrast to Satan's lies. The Bible not only shows us when we are wrong, but most importantly, it tells us how to do things God's way—the right way. Oh, how it makes Him hurt in each generation when they disobey Him. What a God! Jesus died for all of us even though He knew what each of us would do. He is waiting until everyone who will come to Him has come. He is so longsuffering. The Bible says He *"is longsuffering to us-ward, not willing that any should perish, but that all should come to repentance" (2 Peter 3:9).* Not one single person is left out. Oh, how I love Him! God help us to not stumble, and if we do, please woo us back to You through the Holy Spirit. Thank You, Lord. Jesus opens our eyes by saying, *"Blessed are ye, when men shall hate you, and when they shall separate you from their company, and shall reproach you, and cast out your name as evil, for the Son of Man's sake. Rejoice ye in that day, and leap for joy: for, behold, your reward is great in heaven: for in the like manner did their fathers unto the prophets (Luke 6:22–23).* Jesus is the Son of Man. He trod that path before us. Oh, how wonderful He is. He didn't have to do it. He chose to do it.

God also says, *"Woe to you that are full! for ye shall hunger. Woe unto you that laugh now! for ye shall mourn and weep. Woe unto you, when all men shall speak well of you! for so did their fathers to the false prophets. But I say unto you … Love your enemies, do good to them which hate you, Bless them that curse you, and pray for them which despitefully use you" (Luke 6:25–28). "And as ye would that men should do to you, do ye also to them likewise. For if ye love them which love you, what thank have ye? for sinners also love those that love them" (Luke 6:31–32). "But love ye your enemies, and do good, and lend, hoping for nothing again; and your reward shall be great, and ye shall be the children of the Highest: for He is kind unto the unthankful and to the evil. Be ye therefore merciful, as your Father also is merciful" (Luke 6:35–36).* That's why the enemy does not want us to read the Bible. And when we read something we don't understand, we have the privilege of asking the Holy Spirit to help us trust what God said. Someday, we will look back and understand why God had us do some of the things the way He did. Just like He did with me when I was bitten by the pit bull. Someday He will tell me why He did that, and I will be glad.

God never allows us to go through anything traumatic like that without a good reason. Every one of us is special to Him, and He knows just what trials we need, so our journey in life will end with us in His arms. When we are tempted to put off reading and studying the Bible, we know who is responsible for those temptations. It is the devil! When we talk about our anxieties and selfish desires, we help him, for he hears us and uses our fears and obvious selfishness to destroy and bully us. The devil will always make following God appear fearful or following him enticing, which is on the other end of the spectrum. He is the bully of bullies! He has many fears and enticements. But, remember! We are the ones who find enticing the wrong Satan places in our minds. That's right! We play a part in our own sins. But he is a bully! And that's the way bullies are—cowards! Remember the children of Israel when they stood on the banks of the Red Sea? We, too, will have to turn our eyes away from the raging water or whatever is causing our fear. With the help of the Holy Spirit, we, too, can say, *"The LORD is my strength and song, and he is become my salvation: he is my God, and I will prepare Him an habitation; my father's God, and I will exalt Him" (Ex.15:2).* No, it's not ever easy to buck the devil. It never will be. It will be anything but easy! But God will send the Holy Spirit to each of us if we ask Him to. God knows it won't be easy. It certainly wasn't easy for Jesus or His Father. What father would ever want their child to take on such a burden? Especially God the Father! When we have fear, God will take care of it. He gives us such beautiful promises. And we will find that, *"There is no fear in love; but perfect love casteth out fear: because fear hath torment. He that feareth is not made perfect in love" (1 John 4:18).* God repeatedly said to the children of Israel, and these words are for us too: *"Be strong and of a good courage, fear not, nor be afraid of them: for the LORD thy God, he it is that doth go with thee; he will not fail thee, neither forsake thee" (Deut.31:6). "And the LORD, he it is that doth go before thee; he will be with thee, He will not fail thee, neither forsake thee: fear not, neither be dismayed" (Deut. 31:8).* Obviously, God considered these words extremely important for them because He repeated them. Right when we are in the throes of the test, God will take care of our fear. I experienced this when I was bitten by the pit bull. God was there. He took my fear away.

It was marvelous. You can read about it in my book titled *The Lost Thread of God's Love*. That is unless we are being tested by the devil as Job was. We will look at his story later. God just wants to hear us say, "I am willing to do whatever You want me to do, Lord." Then He will take care of our fear unless He is putting us through a test like Job went through when the devil was egging God to prove that Job would stay true to Him. It was marvelous how Job stood up for God during all of that unfair treatment. It is amazing how Job's faith and trust in God grew from that trial. The pain Job suffered was horrendous. He truly was born of the Spirit. It was obvious that the Spirit of God lived in him. For Job said; *"Though He slay me, yet will I trust Him" (Job 13:15).* Fear is all about Satan's antics to destroy those of us who innocently follow in his footsteps. You might want to read the whole book of Job. Satan accused God of protecting Job, and the devil goaded God, saying, *"Put forth thine hand now, and touch all that he hath, and he will curse thee to thy face" (Job 1:11).*

But Job stayed true to God. Satan is still doing things like that to God's people. God wants us to know what Satan is doing behind the scenes. God knew Job's heart! He knew Job would come out fabulously on His side. Job was a very faithful witness, an example God could use to show us how sinful Satan is. You can bet Satan will pick and choose what harm he can do to us too. Then we can be glad we know Job's story and how God honored Job for his loyalty. Knowing what God did for Job can help us understand what might be going on behind the scene between God and Satan, and us, too. Our fears will not be taken care of until we have said yes to God and are obeying Him no matter what is happening to us. Some of us—like John the Baptist and Peter—may have to give up our life here to follow God. It is Satan who causes these troubles—not God. We must leave such things totally in His hands. If God asks us to do something fearful, our part is to keep obeying Him regardless of what is taking place. It is not us who is wrong; it is the devil who is wrong and is scaring us, so we will be like him. If we are placed in a spot like that, then we can follow the example of others who have been hassled by the devil.

But! We must read our Bibles, so we will know we are not just obeying the enemy out of fear. Job had no control over what the devil was doing to him. His only comfort came through his obedience to God's law. Many times it may be that way for us. We have the same options Job and others had when they obeyed God. God only asks us to know and obey His Ten Commandments. Those laws, along with the guidance of the Holy Spirit, must be our guide. Those who obey Satan will be totally destroyed in the fire prepared for the devil and his angels. Those fires are not prepared for any person on earth. It was Jesus who said, *"Then shall He say also unto them on the left hand, Depart from me, ye cursed, into everlasting fire,* *prepared fo*r *the devil and His angels" (Matt. 25:41).* We need to keep our eyes on the future that God has promised His people and know what God wants us to do so that we can have the beautiful future He has planned for us. Knowledge about it is available to us—yes, every last one of us. When we obey God, we are walking in Jesus' footprints. Look at the great number of people who learned about God through the three Hebrew boys' refusal to bow to the great image *(see Dan. 3:1–28).* Most of the people of his whole kingdom were present. Wow!

Those men of God did not cave in because of fear; instead, they trusted God. The Bible says, *"God hath not given us the spirit of fear; but of power, and of love, and of a sound mind. Be not thou therefore ashamed of the testimony of our Lord, nor of me his prisoner: but be thou partaker of the afflictions of the gospel according to the power of God; who hath saved us, and called us with an holy calling, not according to our works, but according to His own purpose and grace, which was given us in Christ Jesus before the world began" (2 Tim. 1:7–9).* What comforting words these were Paul wrote to Timothy! They are comforting for anyone who is being afflicted. Satan doesn't like it when we obey God. Did it sink in for you what Paul told Timothy? I find it exciting! He tells us we were saved (mankind, that is, as a whole, when we were given the privilege of salvation) even before our world was created. We will talk about that in another chapter, a very important one, on freedom of choice. God tells us about it in His Word, so each of us will know we are free to choose whether we want to obey God or Satan.

I cringe just thinking about treating God the way many have treated Him. They were following the guidance of their leaders who did not accept Jesus as their Savior. We may face like situations from the leaders of our churches too. Just remember; no matter who you are, the Lord Jesus Christ is your Savior if you choose Him to be. Satan deceived the Jewish people too, and they believed the devil's lies concerning Jesus being God. We need to decide not to allow anyone to deceive us. Christian versus non-Christian, no matter our nationality, no matter how our parents raised us—none of that can keep Jesus from saving us! All of us may be *"Justified freely by His grace through the redemption that is in Christ Jesus" (Rom. 3:24).* For *"ye are all one in Christ Jesus" (Gal. 3:28).* Those are such beautiful words. Our choice to serve or not serve God is our own personal responsibility. No one can make that choice for us. I am so glad it is that way that God makes freedom of choice available for every single person, no matter who or where they are. God has done so much for each of us.

We need to pray that all of the Jews alive today will learn that Jesus is their Savior. God's ears are still open to their cries just as He is to ours, the Gentiles. There are many Jews accepting Jesus as their Savior today.

The Jewish Seventh-day Adventists have a Jews for Jesus program. And many are coming to know Jesus. God tells us what it is that makes the difference. It was what God did for us when They created us, and then Jesus died on the cross to pay for our sins. Each holy Being, who is our One God, made it possible for any and all of us to have freedom of choice. And then Jesus chose to die to pay for our sins so that all sinners could be saved. It was Jesus' choice. And that choice is available for each of us. No one can make that choice for us. Each of us must choose whether to have God on our side. God says through Paul, *"There is therefore now no condemnation to them which are in Christ Jesus, who walk not after the flesh, but after the Spirit. For the law of the Spirit of life in Christ Jesus hath made me free from the law of sin and death. For what the law couldn't do, in that it was weak through the* flesh, *God sending His own Son in the likeness of sinful flesh, and for sin, condemned sin in the flesh: That the righteousness of the law might be fulfilled in us, who walk not after the flesh, but after the Spirit" (Rom. 8:1–4).* Never forget that every one of us has walked after the flesh. We are all guilty.

Did you notice what the Father's part was? He made salvation possible through His Son Jesus and through the Holy Spirit. The Father is over all. And He is the one who makes all things possible. How does He do that? He did it by giving everyone freedom of choice and thereby leaving us free to be created in His image. At Creation, we were created that way. It is our choice whether we keep that image or deface it. What a gift that is. Thank You, Father, Son, and Holy Spirit, that You worked together. Thus, we can ask the Holy Spirit to help us, and He will show us Your love so that we can make a wise choice. And thank You for not turning Your back on us when we make wrong choices.

You are so wonderful—You make it so hard to commit the unpardonable sin. Even when we are afraid we have committed sin, that very fear is proof that we have not committed the unpardonable sin. Thank You so much, Lord. Fear comes from the devil, but You are talking about a holy fear. Fear of hurting You. Satan is the one who wants us to think we have committed the unpardonable sin. That kind of fear is not the fear of the Lord. My heart is filled with gratitude at the thought of spending eternity with the Ones who love me that much. *"But is now made manifest by the appearing of our Savior Jesus Christ, who hath abolished death,"*

WOW! *"and hath brought life and immortality to light through the gospel"* *(2 Tim. 1:10)*. We need to tenaciously keep hanging onto His hand and never let go of it no matter what the devil or any person says to us. God will see us through! Look up these verses and enjoy them; they tell us how to emulate Jesus. He is our example. Matthew 7:12; Galatians 6:2; Matthew 16:24–26; 1 Peter 3:3–4; 1 Corinthians 10:31; 1 Peter 2:11–12. Listen to James. He says, *"Blessed is the man that endureth temptation"* *(James 1:12)*. *"Let no man say when he is tempted, I am tempted of God:"* Why! *"for God cannot be tempted with evil, neither tempteth He any man"*(-*James 1:13)*. Those are some of the most encouraging words in the Bible. So, who besides the devil tempts us? Our God is straightforward with us. He tells us the truth.

He says, *"But every man is tempted, when he is drawn away of his own lust, and enticed"* *(James 1:14)*. And praise God; He does not leave us when we fail. Rather, He pleads with us to come back to Him. Read what God did for Israel. They were serving idols.

> And He said, *Yet the Lord testified against Israel, and against Judah, by all the prophets, and by all the seers, saying, Turn ye from your evil ways, and keep my commandments and My statutes, according to all the law which I commanded your fathers, and which I sent to you by my servants the prophets. Notwithstanding they would not hear, but hardened their necks, like to the neck of their fathers, that did not believe in the Lord their God. (2 Kings 17:13–14)*

God will do no less with us. Read the next three verses. Just be sure you have not mistaken who is speaking to you. So, if we lose out on eternal life, we have no one to blame but ourselves. God has certainly made it clear that He does not want to destroy anyone who will honor His laws. He is always willing to forgive us if we repent of our sin and choose to not sin anymore. He is always ready and willing to forgive us. But we must admit our wrongs and be willing to change our ways. Just think! God is always willing to send the Holy Spirit to help us. We are the ones who are stubborn and refuse to clean up our act. What a God! He is so long-suffering. Isn't it amazing that the Holy Spirit speaks to every one of us personally? How grateful I am that God does not leave us in the dark. He loves us so much He let His Son die for us! Now, if that's not a WOW, I don't know what is. That is why God tells us how longsuffering He is and how terrible the devil is. Don't believe the devil when he tells you that you are lost.

On the other hand, we often choose to be evil. That's right. It is our own choice. So we can't blame anyone else! That sounds just like Satan's sins—pride and selfishness. We, too, just like him, want to be our own boss. But each one of us can obey God and win over our evil desires with the help of the Holy Spirit. We just need to ask Him. God says it's a life-long journey. Thank You, God! This means we are wrong if we say, "the devil made me do it." The sorry truth is, we choose to do it! Always remember, God is only a prayer away. Look what Job says God did for him when he was in a hard situation. God fights for us. He does not want us to be lost. That's why Jesus died.

Job said, "*Then He openeth the ears of men, and sealeth their instruction, that He may withdraw man from his purpose, and hide pride from man. He keepeth back his soul from the pit, and his life from perishing by the sword*" (*Job 33:16–18*). It is my prayer that these words may do this very thing for all of us who read them and for those who may think they have committed the unpardonable sin so that they will realize it is the devil telling them a lie. God wants each of us to know we can still give our hearts totally to Him. He does it over and over for us as we slip and fall and have to ask forgiveness again and again. That is God's will for the life of every human being who was ever born. May God bless you. He still loves you.

All of us, at some time or other, have played the blame game. We really are chips off the old block. Remember, Eve started that game in the Garden of Eden when she ate the forbidden fruit. It's hard to hear that we are our own worst enemy. But it's true. So can we really blame it on the devil? The answer is **no**! We just have to remember we have freedom of choice. God does a good job of what He does. We really can be winners with His help. He is always ready to help us just for the asking. Yes, it's as simple as that! But this does not mean we won't have to suffer. We will suffer! So, may I ask? Would you really want to lose your freedom of choice? I wouldn't! I don't want anyone bossing me around. Not even God. And He won't. What a loving and wise God He is.

Remember! Without the privilege of choice, there is no love—only total control. We need to know what and who our common enemy is like so that we can recognize when he is forcing his way into our life. Sometimes we are our own worst enemy. We allow the enemy of our souls to force his own ideas and desires into our sometimes gullible and sometimes selfish hearts. But we are always free to actively reject them. God gives us that privilege. It's totally up to us. So don't let anyone force you to do something against your will. That choice, asking God for help, and then sticking with it is the only thing we have to do. It is our safety net.

The Holy Spirit is present to guide us always. Just listen to these words from God. He is still grieving, desiring, and saying about His people today. *"O that there were such an heart in them, that they would fear Me, and keep all of My commandments."* Take note of God's next word. *"Always."* Oh yes! God wishes that we would always want to keep His commandments. Listen as He tells us why. *"That it might be well with them, and with their children for ever" (Deut. 5:29).* Getting acquainted with God helps us recognize our enemy when he comes sneaking around. He is absolutely nothing like God.

Do you realize Jesus says the devil is a god, (Notice I used a small "g," and I said "a" god.) Listen to these words Jesus said to John. *"And now I have told you before it come to pass, that, when it is come to pass, ye might believe. Hereafter I will not talk much with you: for the prince of this world cometh, and hath nothing in me. But that the world may know that I love the Father; and as the Father gave me commandment, even so I do" (John 14:29–31).* Knowing God is the best way to recognize the enemy. When Jesus was down here on earth wrapped in human flesh, He told John, *"I am the light of the world: he that followeth Me shall not walk in darkness, but shall have the light of life" (John 8:12).* Jesus and His enemy, the devil, are as different as night is from day. Jesus is light and honesty. The devil is darkness, lies, and deceit. Jesus and His Father are longing for us to accept the light.

That is the True Light—Our Lord and Savior Jesus Christ

I want to walk in Jesus' footprints, wherever they take me. Coming with me? It's exciting to tell others that Jesus loves them. The best way to tell them is through our obedience to God. Yes, through our own actions. If we really love God, we will obey Him and be like Him. Loving, forgiving, and cheerful! God is love. He loves us to death! His death! How can we stand to not love Him back?

We show our love for Him

by

our actions

toward each other.

God bless you as you read.

2

We Have an Awesome God; They Are Love in Action

Yes! Again, I said "They." They, God, have many characteristics which belong only to Them! I stand in awe before Them and fall to my knees in gratitude and appreciation for what They have done, are doing right now, and what They plan to do for us in the future. They created us, and They created this world; it was teamwork, if you please. They worked together and co-operated with one another.

Even we humans work together in unity—many hands make the work load lighter and much more enjoyable. Below is a picture of them in the form of a math problem.

1 Father + 1 Son (Jesus) + 1 Holy Spirit = 3 holy Beings = 1 Holy God

Yes, God is One—not One Being—but One God.

It is Together that They are One God.

The disciple John says, *"For there are three that bear record in heaven, the Father, the Word, and the Holy Ghost: and these three are one" (1 John 5:7).* Yes, Jesus is both the written Word—the Bible and also the Word in the form of flesh. *"And the Word was made flesh, and dwelt among us, (and we beheld his glory, the glory as of the only begotten of the Father,) full of grace and truth" (John 1:14).* John also quotes Jesus as saying, *"I and my Father are one" (John 10:30).* Learning this truth will help us see how all-wise and all-caring our God really is. They agree with each other. And all three are working together for our salvation. Their love for each other is one of the ways They are One. They are love in action. The apostle Paul agrees with John that *"God is one" (Gal. 3:20).*

In the creation story, after the Bible writer told us God was the One who created this world, he shared this with us. He said, "Let Us." Did you hear that? It is One of the Beings who are God who is talking, and He used the word "Us." But that's not all! He said more! Here is His whole statement. *"Let us make man in our image, after our likeness" (Gen. 1:26).* This means the three of Them have the same image; they are alike. But how? They worked together as One God when They created us and the world we live in.

Physically, there definitely are three holy Beings who are One God. They also are one in that They cooperate with one another. But that's only the beginning of the things that make Them One. Before there was Planet Earth, and before there was a Bible, there was God. But you must not believe me; you must only believe what our wonderful God tells us. It is very important that we only believe Him! When Paul talked about God, he gave us a good reason why God is the only One we can trust. Paul said, *"In hope of eternal life, which God, that cannot lie, promised before the world began" (Titus 1:2).* And Moses said, *"God is not a man, that He should lie" (Num. 23:19).* That's right! God cannot lie and still be the loving God He is. And God is our only Savior! That's an extra special reason. God's love is worth everything! We'll talk more about Their love later on.

> **"**
> **Before there was Planet Earth, and before there was a Bible, there was God.**
> **"**

Just think about how it was before there was sin. I like to compare sinlessness with inhaling a breath of fresh air. It would be fresher than any air we will ever breathe on this earth. God had holy men write the Bible under His inspiration. That means the Bible does not tell lies because God is its author. People know us by our words, too, whether we tell the truth or lie. We are only as good as our word—the words we say! The thoughts we think! That's some of the reasons why, when John told us about Jesus, he called Him *"the Word" (John 1:14).*

Since Jesus is God, let's briefly look at His life while He was here on earth in human flesh. Look at this revelation. John was talking about Jesus after He was born of Mary. Yes, and after He was created in human flesh so that He could be like us for the purpose of saving us. The Bible also says Jesus *"Is the image of the invisible God, the firstborn of every creature" (Col. 1:15).* One of the definitions for these words, *"the firstborn of every creature,"* is that Jesus was the most important person who was ever born. Jesus was just like His heavenly Father. He looked like Him. And that likeness was in His character, too, not just His appearance. Yes, *"God created man in His own image" (Gen. 1:27)*. And then, after man sinned, He created His Son in His own image in human flesh. If that isn't a Wow! I don't know what is. So, in the beginning, Adam and Eve had perfect characters, for they were made in the image of God. They had God's perfect character and looks. How blessed we are. And again, God said, *"God created man, in the likeness of God" (Gen. 5:1)*.

Just listen to this: David said, *"As for me, I will behold thy face in righteousness: I shall be satisfied, when I awake, with thy likeness" (Ps. 17:15)*. He certainly felt blessed. He believed that when God wakes him up from the sleep of death, he will be in God's likeness, that he will look like Him and act like Him. I am looking forward to that day. How about you? I've heard it said that copying someone is the greatest form of love and praise. I certainly want to love and praise God—all three of them. When Jesus was born down here, He, too, was made in the image of His heavenly Father. This verse helps us see that part of the likeness in God's character. What gives me license to say this? The Father does! For He said, *"When we shall see Him, there is no beauty that we should desire Him" (Isa. 53:2)*. This has to be talking about Jesus' outward appearance in His human form. Jesus acted like God; His actions were like the Father because He was and still is God. You could say, He's the spittin' image of His Father, just like Him in character. Never forget that we were created in the image of God too. What a privilege!

The Bible also says, *"[He] was made in the likeness of men" (Phil 2:7)*. He looked like us, and He was free to keep the character His heavenly Father gave Him. But, He was also free to follow in the footsteps of His earthly father. Yes, Jesus was born with freedom of choice, just like Adam and Eve were. Jesus could have no advantage we do not have, and it still be fair and just. He looked like us. And just as we were tempted, so was He. God says so! He *"Was in all points tempted like as we are, yet without sin" (Heb. 4:15)*. WOW!

If He had not been tempted like we are, the test wouldn't have been fair. Jesus came to prove that no one has to sin. Even though He came to earth in human flesh, He never sinned. What a victory! But that's just the way God is. Perfect! What love! That He would come to earth bundled in human flesh and allow Himself to be subjected to sin! The Bible says,

And being found in fashion as a man, He humbled Himself, and became obedient unto death, even the death of the cross. Wherefore God also hath highly exalted Him, and given Him a name which is

above every name: That at the name of Jesus every knee should bow, of things in heaven, and things in earth, and things under the earth; And that every tongue should confess that Jesus Christ is Lord, to the glory of God the Father. (Phil. 2:8–11)

We need to do that too, but we can't because we were born sinful. That's why Jesus came down here and died to pay for our sins. Adam and Eve were created perfect; they could have stayed that way. What a marvelous gift God gave us. We, like them, must make a choice to serve or not serve God. I am so thankful God makes salvation possible. Thank You, God—all three of You. Jesus, His Father, and the Holy Spirit help us make those choices. They each have their part. Without the gift of any one of Them, it would not work. Each one is very important. Together They save us.

Just look how special Jesus is. Go back and read the verses again. Notice that Jesus glorified His Father! Just consider for a moment—what love They had for each other. Now, contemplate the love They have for us. Consider how hard it would be for any human father to see something like this happen to their son, and then consider how a Father who is love would feel so much deeper for a Son who had done no wrong to be dying the death Jesus died. It's impossible to compare the two, for there is no comparison. Thank You, Father. You are so wonderful. Adam and Eve were created in the likeness of God. God Himself says so! He wanted them to know He was their Creator *"So God created man in his own image, in the image of God created he him; male and female created he them" (Gen. 1:27).* But they certainly did not walk in Jesus' footsteps. Paul said, about Jesus, *"He is before all things, and by him all things consist" (Col.1:17).* Thus, the Bible verifies that before there was anything else, there was God, and that included Jesus. So I encourage you to think in those terms about God—The Father, Jesus the Son, and the Holy Spirit. They! Yes, all three of Them were in existence before our world was created. There is no doubt about it; They, together, were our Creators.

Remember, God the Holy Spirit was the second Holy Being the Bible introduced us to. We met Him in the second verse of Genesis. He also is called God. It was when God, the three of Them, created our world that we met the Holy Spirit. All three of the Beings, who are our One God, had no beginning. And They will never cease to exist. There will **never** be an end to Their life. Jesus only chose to lay down His life for three days to pay for our sins. Jesus said, *"As the Father knoweth me,* *even so know I the Father: and I lay down my life for the sheep" (John 10:15).* Those who love Him are His sheep. Jesus told His disciples this very thing. Here are His words. They were asking Him to show them the Father. Read, and listen to Jesus' reply for yourself in John 14:9–17. As we read the Bible, we will uncover Their massive trustworthiness. That trust will go a long way toward helping us trust that They have been in existence forever. In this world, everything has a beginning and end. So a forever existence is foreign to us. Our finite minds can't grasp it. That's why we must accept it by faith. Faith is merely total trust and belief in something or someone. They, God, are the only Ones who are worthy of that kind of trust.

The fact that the very first verses in the Bible specifically talk about the Holy Spirit just helps verify that all three of Them, the Father, the Son, and Holy Spirit, were together as one God when our world was created and before. This truth is certainly a mystery to us. It is a truth we may never totally understand. Why? Because everything we know has a beginning and an end. It's just one of the amazing traits that is special to God alone. I've heard it said, "truth is stranger than fiction." This is one of those truths. *"God is love" (1 John 4:8).* Love is totally Them! It is Their character to love. A person's character is who they are. According to the dictionary, a characteristic is a distinctive trait. For God, love is His distinctive trait. It is who He is. I'm sure you have heard someone say, "he or she is quite a character." They were speaking of what that person is really like. A person's words and actions tell us who they are. God really is love!

What a beautiful God He is. Have you ever thought about and realized that the Ten Commandments are a transcript of His character? God's Law reveals His love. Each command tells us a different way He is love. Let's review it since it is a picture of God Himself. Only God is 100 percent Love. I am so thrilled that He is more than willing to help us be more like Him. What a privilege. We can't go wrong by emulating our Savior. He's the best teacher in the world! Also, do you realize that the only reason *"We love Him,"* is *"because He first loved us" (1 John 4:19)?*

That sounds selfish, doesn't it? But maybe it isn't! For how can we love someone before we know them? If God had not loved us, we wouldn't know what love is. Mere words are incapable of expressing the expanse of His love. He is so much more than human word or thought can express. If you feel this picture of God shows only a faint glimmer of His glory, you are correct. So let's look at His law of love—His character. Let's pray as we read each command and ask the Holy Spirit to guide our minds and create a true picture of God in our thoughts and heart. He is so much more than anyone can ever express. The commandments perfectly mirror God's character of love. They are a transcript of it.

3

God's Ten-Commandment Law Teaches Us How to Love

One of the definitions of the word "character" is "mark. The mark or characteristic of that person tells us what they are like." It is a quality that makes them uniquely them. Each person's special characteristics are what make them who they really are. Each person's special characteristics are different from anyone else. Each person has many such marks that define who they are and what they are like. The combination of all of these specific qualities make them who they are: Jane, or Mary, or John.

God's law, the Ten Commandments, are a list of God's special characteristics, and each one of them points out a different trait to us, a different special way He is love. His law and His charac-

> **66**
>
> *Each commandment defines a different attribute of His love.*
>
> **99**

ter match each other. It tells us who He is and what He is like. Each commandment defines a different attribute of His love. So let's find out what each one tells us about Him. Yes! Each commandment describes a special way God is love. Together they provide a gorgeous picture of Him. Love is beautiful! God is beautiful! His first command says:

1 *Thou shalt have no other gods before Me. (Exod. 20:3)*

Why does He ask us **not** to have any other gods? Devotion is a very special attribute. He gives us His devotion. It means He gives us first place and wants us to give Him first place in our life. God always must be first, best, and last in our affections and praise, plus everything else. We must worship Him and only Him. Because He is perfect, Jesus is the only being in human flesh who is worthy of our devotion, worship, and praise. The Bible says so!

*And I saw in the right hand of him that sat on the throne a book
written within and on the backside, sealed with seven seals. ... Who
is worthy to open the book, and to loose the seals thereof? And no
man in heaven, nor in earth, neither under the earth, was able to
open the book, neither to look thereon. (Rev. 5:1–3) And I beheld,
and I heard the voice of many angels round about the throne and
the beasts and elders: and the number of them was ten thousand
times ten thousand, and thousands of thousands; Saying with a
loud voice, Worthy is the Lamb that was slain to receive power, and
riches, and wisdom, and strength, and honour, and glory, and blessing. And every creature which is in heaven, and on the earth, and
under the earth, and such as are in the sea, and all that are in them,
heard I saying, Blessing, and honour, and glory, and power, be unto
him that sitteth upon the throne, and unto the Lamb for ever and
ever. (11–13)*

He is the epitome of love; therefore, His character shows us what love
is like. They are, and yes, again I said "They," They are the only Beings
who are totally love. So why would we want to put some other god ahead
of Them? There is no other "true" god. Any so-called god we place before
or ahead of Them is imperfect in its love. Thus, our triune God alone is
love. That means the other gods are inferior to our perfect God of love.
There really is only One God who is love. I think you will agree that God's
reason for not wanting us to worship those other gods is extremely important. In fact, it is a matter of life and death, as we shall see. Why in the
world would we want a god who is inferior; when we can have a God who
is perfect.

But it's even bigger than that! Our God's love is perfect. There's nothing better than that. Do you realize choosing some other being to be our
God minimizes our true God and destroys us? No wonder God doesn't
want us to choose any other god ahead of Him. We would be putting ourselves in jeopardy and spurning Him at the same time. He loves us so
much He warns us of our danger. That's real love! Yes, there is someone
who wants to steal love from the one and only true God. That's who this
book is all about. Come and see who it is! But let's honor our God of love
by finding out more about Him first. Let's find out who He really is. Then
we will recognize the false gods when they come around to bully us. Are
you game? Did I hear you say yes? Great! Let's search our Bible to find
the truth about our God.

God's people of old knew when the commandment said, "before Me," it was telling them not to place any other god ahead of their God in any way. In truth there is no other god who can take His place. All others are imposters and traitors. So! Why would we want to accept one who is not truly God when we can have One who is the best God there is—the only God who has a character of love. He alone is the only true God!

I certainly don't want some other so-called god when I can have the true One. Certainly, I do not want to obey anyone who wants to be ahead of and/or in place of the true God. Someone who is a traitor! If the other god is before our God, then he is our God's enemy and certainly not the true God. Thus, I consider him my enemy too. He is a being I want to stay as far away from as I can. He is antichrist—someone who is usurping God's honor and glory—someone who places himself in God's place. There have been many of them down through the ages. Lucifer was only the first of a long line of them. They are all following in his footsteps. He is their leader and guide. Do you know anyone who claims to be Christ on earth? Remember! There are many. Just like their leader, they claim God's worship for themselves. They want us to worship them. They want us to confess our sins to them. The truth is, they can't forgive sins. Only God can do that. Jesus is the One who can claim God's honor and glory.

So come! Let's look at the rest of our God's commands. They are the laws of His government. They are easy to understand, and they tell us how to love God and everyone else and even love all the other creatures He created. There really is no other true and legitimate God. All other beings who call themselves "God" are impostors. Lucifer was the first impostor, the first antichrist, the one who put himself ahead of and in place of God. He stole worship that belonged only to God. That makes him a thief. In fact, Jesus said to the people who honored Lucifer, *"Ye are of your father the devil, and the lusts of your father ye will do. He was a murderer from the beginning, and abode not in the truth, because there is no truth in him. When he speaketh a lie, he speaketh of his own: for he is a liar, and the father of it"* *(John 8:44)*. Now that's pretty bad. Those are very strong words.

God very carefully shows us how important His law is both to Him and to us. The law itself makes it very clear how extremely important it is to not worship any other God. He definitely wants us to know worshiping someone or something else other than Them is seriously wrong. Actually, when someone tries to get us to put something or someone else first, they are either worshiping themselves, or they are worshiping a false god. The Bible tells us that "god," the one spelled with a lower case "g," is the god of this world, the devil or a follower of his. I sure don't want to worship him, but if we are not worshiping the one and only true God, we are worshiping the devil. We are the ones who choose to do that because we want to do as we please. Yes, we choose to be lost so that we can have our own way. God says, *"But if our gospel be hid, it is hid to them that are lost: in whom the god of this world hath blinded the minds of them which believe not, lest the light of the glorious gospel of Christ, who is the image of God, should shine on them" (2 Cor. 4:3–4).* That's right! We worship him because we don't want to obey one of God's commands. The devil keeps the light of the true God from shining on those who are worshiping him.

Who and what makes Lucifer the devil, the god of this world? He can't be a god without someone calling him god. The truth is, anyone who chooses to serve him is giving him license to be the god of this world. If no one worshipped him as a god, he would not have a kingdom. Since each commandment is an expression of God's love, God's first command tells us we are not to worship any other being as God. There is someone out there who will steal God's love from us. What kind of God would our true God be if He did not notify us of the danger we are in. Not our God! He is right up front. He tells us what is at stake before anything can happen to us. I'm so glad we can serve the one and only God of love.

Remember! Never forget! The god of this world is the father of lies. Anyone who bows to him or anyone else claiming to be "God" is in extreme danger. Satan is the instigator of all the lies his followers whisper in our ear, and he is the one who pushes us to serve other gods. Yes, there are other gods; all of them are Lucifer's slaves. Whenever we serve them, we are in grave danger. We, too, become a slave of the devil if we worship him. Our only hope is through our God's love. He is willing to forgive anyone and everyone. He says, *"If we say that we have no sin, we deceive ourselves, and the truth is not in us. If we confess our sins, he is faithful and just to forgive us our sins, and to cleanse us from all unrighteousness" (1 John 1:8–9).* Isn't that wonderful? Anyone who asks to be forgiven will be forgiven. But we must ask God to forgive us, and we must ask the one we sinned against to forgive us too. And then we must turn away from the evil one we were following.

What a forgiving God He is. He loves every single person who has ever been born. If you discover that you have been disobeying God, and you didn't realize you were sinning, won't you go to Him right now and tell Him you want to be His child? The same holds true for those of us who have deliberately chosen to worship a false god. Really, when we are honest with ourselves, all of us have chosen to serve the wrong god at times, for we are told all have sinned. What it really boils down to is that all of us are selfish. We are seeing what we can get out of it. Me—me—me! He loves you very much. I don't care who you are! That is true for every single person who has ever lived. The devil is our common enemy, no matter who we are. The Creator of heaven and earth is the God of everything in existence. Now, if that doesn't awe you, nothing will. There is no other true God. This is still very true today. And it will be true forever. Satan is feverishly anxious to take complete control of this world. I'm so glad our God has declared Himself to be the winner of the battle between good and evil. He alone can and will help us win it if we let Him. But He will never force us to bow to Him. He truly is the most loving, caring Being who has ever lived.

Do you want to know other reasons why God does not want us to have any other gods and why He wants to occupy first place in our hearts? Again, it is because He loves us so much! It's as simple as that! It's just who He is. If someone claims to be God with a capital "G," they are lying and obeying that serpent of old. It is the devil who claims to be God! Nothing is further from the truth. When anyone claims to be "God," they are obeying the devil. This book is being created to expose the devil's lies and shine a light on all others who falsely claim to be God and identify them. The Bible calls him *"the dragon, that old serpent, which is the Devil, and Satan" (Rev. 20:2).* I am so glad God is so very straightforward with us. And that He does not leave us wondering what He wants us to do and why He wants us to do it. Neither does He lie as those so-called gods do. I don't know why anyone would want to put anything or anyone ahead of our true God. This book is all about WHY! Come with me as God shows us the truth from His Word. He doesn't leave us wondering. But I can tell you this! It's all about God's love. Come and see for yourself. Don't just believe me. I'm just a sinner like everyone else.

God's love includes every person who has ever been born. The Father chose to allow His Son to willingly lay down His life to rescue us from our enemy, the devil. Jesus said, *"Greater love hath no man than this, that a man lay down his life for his friends. Ye are My friends, if ye do what I command you" (John 15:13–14).* Jesus, with His Father's and the Spirit's consent, chose to give His life for us. If the Father had said "no," Jesus would have obeyed Him. We know because Jesus told John, *"If ye keep my commandments, ye shall abide in my love; just as*

I have kept my Father's commandments, and abide in his love" (John 15:11). Jesus knew He didn't have anything to worry about. He knew His Father would stay true.

> **2** *Thou shalt not make unto thee any given image, or any likeness of any thing that is in heaven above, or that is in the earth beneath, or that is in the water under the earth. Thou shalt not bow down thyself to them, nor serve them: for I the LORD thy God am a jealous God, visiting the iniquity of the fathers upon the children unto the third and fourth generation of them that hate me; and shewing mercy unto thousands of them that love me, and keep my commandments. (Exod. 20:4–6)*

In this second command, God tells us He is a jealous lover. That doesn't sound very good, does it? But really it is good. This command tells me God loves me so much He does not want me to be lured away from Him by a false god who does not love me. He wouldn't be a loving God if He didn't protect me this way. His protection shows me His deep love. True lovers are always protective of the one they love.

We will hear all about the very first jealous lover. It was Lucifer! That is if you want to call him a lover. I don't. He is the one I said loves only himself, but he really doesn't even love himself, or he wouldn't have disobeyed God's law! Why do I say this? It is because disobedience to God's law is leading him to his death. That doesn't seem like a very nice thing to do to anyone, especially someone you love. No, he really doesn't even love himself.

> **"**
> *Love always honors freedom of choice.*
> **"**

You can decide how you feel about it as you read. God doesn't want a divided love. He wants all of our love. Now that doesn't mean God is selfish in the way we usually think of selfishness, either. Oh, no! You see, God knows many things we would never know without Him telling us. First of all, there are many so-called gods. Notice that I set these gods apart by using a lower case "g" as I did with others. To make something into a god, we have to obey it. I choose to only obey God. I choose to not obey the lies Satan whispers in my ear. I don't really want what he entices me to think I want. I want to keep the freedom to obey God.

We obey God because He really does love us. That means He will not control us. Love always honors freedom of choice. He does not dictate what we can or can't do or say. God's love leaves us free to choose to love Him or not love Him. This is done moment by moment. We are constantly making these very important life-and-death decisions. And unfortunately, many times, our choices end up being fly-by-night decisions. Whew! I'm so glad He knows I'm just a kindergartener in the school of sin. God is rock-solid. Remember! Jesus is called the *"Rock" (1 Cor. 10:4)*. He never changes. His love is solid like a rock. Also, it is like a breath of fresh spring air compared to the so-called love of those other gods! They are nothing but trouble!

All others do not love us at all. Instead, they love themselves—just like their master, Satan, does. Their love is a selfish love. It is nothing but selfish jealousy. They want to use us and control us. Their goal is to lead us away from God. That's because they know it really hurts God when we choose to not love Him. The devil is jealous of Jesus' position. He wants to be God. But he can't be God, so he is angry with Jesus. Nothing makes him happier than doing things that hurt Him. So if he can steal us away from God, that makes his day. He truly is a sorry mess.

True love never controls. God leaves all beings free to choose either to love or withhold love. Now, that doesn't mean there are no consequences for not loving Him. There are consequences no matter what or who you are. Each being's choices determine their own consequences. I sure do prefer ending up in heaven versus ending up in hell. God would never choose hell for anyone! The devil did! I choose to go to heaven with God. The only reason someone doesn't make that choice is that they believe the devil's lies, when he tells them bowing to idols is much nicer because ? ? ? ! But! Notice what the real issue is for the devil. He wants to steal the throne from God. How would you like to live in his world forever? I sure wouldn't. That is why God doesn't want us to put anyone or anything ahead of or in place of Him.

Most Christians realize idols or graven images are made out of something which already exists—something Jesus created. But all of us have bowed to other images. There are other things that become images, too, and take their place. An image is whatever keeps us from communing with, worshipping, and obeying the true God. They are the time-consumers. Here are a few. See if you agree. We bow to television, parties, shopping, etc., when it robs us of time to worship God. We each have our own personally-chosen idols that steal the time we have devoted to God. Sometimes we know what the idol is, and sometimes we don't even realize we have an idol.

Often, we are alerted to our failure to worship Him when we realize we are not spending time with Him. Did you notice that the first commandment was also talking about worshipping false gods? Those who do not really love God and don't know it are worshipping other people or other gods. A lot of times, this happens because they do not realize they are not obeying God. But His commandments are very understandable. It's just that many times our parents didn't know they were not worshipping God either. They are innocent of their disobedience.

A god is merely someone or something we put ahead of or in place of God. We give it first place in our affections. That makes it very difficult to change because now it has taken first place in our priorities. It has become a habit. We are creatures of habit. Most of us want to cling to our old ways. It is hard to change. Our only hope is that God is willing to help us change and ask for forgiveness. But we have faith in that god, and we love it or them. We spend time with the one person or thing we love. Then it becomes our god because we let it tell us what to do and when to do it. We lust after it, crave it, and idolize it because of the pleasure we receive from doing it. Actually, we let it control our life. We let things such as television control us and keep us from reading our Bible or going to church on God's day of worship. God wants us to know His Son Jesus as our Lord, Savior, and friend. To do that, we must walk in His footsteps, do what He did, and obey God's Word.

Remember what the devil did to Jesus? As you read these next verses, try to put yourself in Jesus' place. *"Again, the devil taketh him up into an exceeding high mountain, and sheweth Him all the kingdoms of the world, and the glory of them; And saith unto Him, All these things will I give thee, if thou wilt fall down and worship me" (Matt. 4:8–9).* Aha! The devil tried to pull this trick on Jesus. He wanted Jesus to worship him. He wasn't very smart to use that trick on God Himself. He desired to take God's throne from Jesus. That was uppermost in his mind. He's a thief and a liar! This world does not belong to him. He can't give it to us. We do see wicked people giving things to other people that they stole from someone. They are walking a tightrope the devil puts them on. They need our prayers. They are believing his lies. How sad!

Just listen to Jesus' reply. *"Then Jesus saith unto him, Get thee hence, Satan:"* Please notice what Jesus used to help Him with His answer! It is the same thing we can and should use when the devil temps us to do something wrong. Jesus said, *"it is written, Thou shalt worship the Lord thy God, and Him only shalt thou serve" (Matt. 4:10).* It is the Word of God who wrote this verse. Yes, it was Jesus Himself. He is the "Word" who became flesh and dwelt among us. Do you see how the Father, Son, and Holy Spirit are all involved? They are the only Beings who are to be worshipped. Jesus loved His Father. He read His Bible when He was down here housed in human flesh. He read the scrolls of the Old Testament. The New Testament hadn't been written yet. The first book in the New Testament was written about seventy years after Jesus went to heaven. Jesus called the devil's bluff! And what did the devil do next? The Bible says, *"Then the devil leaveth Him, and, behold, angels came and ministered unto Him" (Matt. 4:11).* The devil ran like the coward and bully he is. Praise the Lord! And God's helpers came and helped Jesus.

I really believe God took care of the pit bull who bit me too. When a pit bull bites, they often hang on and really tear the person apart. I believe God intervened on my behalf. As it was, for six months, it was painful for me to sit. I was doing God's work. He had given me the go-ahead to take the books to the people in that neighborhood. I obeyed Him, and He protected my life. I know it was a miracle because he sunk all four fangs into me, and when I got home and took off my pants, there were no holes in the clothing where the teeth went through. Not even a thread was spread apart. They were made of closely woven fabric. I thank God for saving my life. The most important thing I got out of it was more faith in Him. I had been having trouble understanding how faith works, and God boosted my faith. Nothing teaches better than show and tell. He also showed me that God allows bad things to happen to his children if He sees that it will help them grow spiritually. Only time will expose all of the answers. God always has a good reason for what He allows.

When we do not choose to obey Him, we choose to obey the devil. He is a substitute lover. That's not love at all. No one likes to be substituted; even the substitute doesn't. Very few Christians worship carved idols of wood, stone, etc. Being a Christian means you love Jesus! You can't love Him and worship someone or something else at the same time. It's as simple as that! Obeying Him tells Him how much we love Him. He is patiently waiting for us to say, "I love You," through our actions of obedience. Look what God did for the people He chose for spreading the knowledge of His love to others. What a privilege it was!

And the LORD descended in the cloud, and stood with him" [Moses] there, and proclaimed the name of the LORD. And the LORD passed by before him, and proclaimed, The LORD, The LORD God, merciful and

gracious, longsuffering, and abundant in goodness and truth, Keeping
mercy for thousands, forgiving iniquity and transgression and sin, and
that will by no means clear the guilty; visiting the iniquity of the fathers
upon the children, and upon the children's children, unto the third
and fourth generation. (Exod. 34:5–7)

Our God is jealous of our affections and our safety. The guarding that
God does is to protect us. He informs us that there is an enemy out to get
us. That is one way He protects our freedom of choice. He guards our
choices and makes sure we have sufficient opportunities to know how to
serve Him and to let us know we are free to choose to serve or not serve
Him. He only allows us to choose to serve those other gods. That's real
freedom. He will not control us.

When we choose to obey other gods, He definitely is jealous. All of the
beings in heaven get busy when we do that. The Father, Jesus, the Holy
Spirit, and all of the holy angels get busy. All of them love us. They want
to be sure that everything we need for our salvation is available to us so
that we can be saved. Allow me to repeat—They, the True God, will never
control us. We definitely need to guard our right to obey God. The other
type of guarding is defined as "resentfully suspicious of rivalry." That's
not love! God's children should never be resentful of others. Freedom of
choice is a two-way street. Freedom of choice is also given to those who
choose to reject God as their Savior. How can we love our enemies if we
even resent those who are supposed to be our friends? How can we love
God and hate those He died for. Of course, God does not want us to have
other gods.

Any god, other than our true God, is out to destroy us. God wants to
give us eternal life in heaven with Him. I am glad our God is jealous of our
love. Of course, He is jealous! He wants to rescue us. He does not want us
to be under the control of the devil. The devil is the one who controls all
of those other gods. It is dangerous to get curious about him. Curiosity is
one of his lures. Remember, on the end of a lure, there is a hook. Stay as
far away from it as you can. Often, it seems as though lures jump right out
at you and haul you in.

3 *Thou shalt not take the name of the LORD thy God in vain; for the LORD*
will not hold him guiltless that taketh His name in vain. (Exod. 20:7)

Can you imagine taking God's name in vain? God would never do that to us. That's because He loves us so much. True love, such as God has, never causes pain to the one they love. That's what love is all about. If we take His name in vain, we are tarnishing it. God's love causes us to not take someone's name in vain. God pities us for doing things like that. Yes, He has compassion for us often vile humans. That's what love is all about.

It can happen in an instant by getting angry and saying, "God damn." Have you ever thought those words? It is commonly said, and no one seems to even think much about it. It has become ho-hum, the normal thing to do. We need to step back and think about whose name we are slandering. When you stop and think about it, isn't it shocking that we would even consider using God's name like that? We need to stop and consider how we feel when someone uses our name inappropriately. Exclamations of disgust or anger against God are shocking—not just ho-hum. No one likes to be sworn at. It certainly is no way to treat our God, even if we're not saying it to His face. God will not take it lightly. It hurts Him. I am so glad He knows our hearts and will forgive us and help us change.

When we claim to be Christians and then misrepresent Christ, we are taking His name in vain. Our actions teach others to take those words lightly too. If people stopped and thought about it, they wouldn't like it. When we are tempted to do things like this, it is none other than the devil tricking us into dishonoring God. When we do this, we are honoring the devil. Just the act of obeying Satan is an act of dishonor and hatred of God. When we do this, we are disobeying God's rules of love—the Ten Commandments.

Deep down, we love God's rules. It is only when we, someone else, or something else, become a god to us that it becomes difficult for us to follow His commands. If we really think about it, it is hard to picture anyone intentionally wanting to call God an evil-doer. Isn't God amazingly compassionate that He would forgive us for such mistreatment? We need to run to Him and, in gratitude, throw ourselves into His arms, and with tears streaming down our face, ask Him to forgive us. If we really are sorry, He will forgive. If we aren't sorry, we need to ask Him to help us feel sorry. He will even do that. What a God! It's a very dangerous path to be on when we are rude to God. It's none other than "flirting with the devil." If we are honest with ourselves, all of us will admit that we've been there and done that in some shape or form.

4 Remember the sabbath day, to keep it holy. Six days shalt thou labour, and do all thy work: But the seventh day is the sabbath of the LORD thy God: in it thou shalt not do any work, thou, nor thy son, nor thy daughter, thy manservant, nor thy maidservant, nor thy cattle, nor thy stranger that is within thy gates: for in six days the LORD made heaven and earth, the sea, and all that in them is, and rested the seventh day: wherefore the LORD blessed the sabbath day, and hallowed it. (Exod. 20:8–11)

This is the commandment that specifically tells us how to love and worship God personally. We show Him we love Him by spending that specific twenty-four-hour period of time with Him. He loves us so much that He sets aside one day a week to spend with us. It certainly seems like we would want to pause in our busy lives and come apart with Him on that special day. It means a lot to Him. It shows Him we really do love Him. It is the only day of the week He blessed and set aside for the purpose of having a weekly date with us. Remember how it was when you first met your guy or gal. You wanted to spend as much time with them as you could. That's the way love is, and God's love is especially that way!

God tells us how He wants to be worshipped. He does not leave us in the dark on such an important issue. When you love someone, you want to please them. You want to know how you can love them and make them happy. Our worship and obedience are what show Him how much we love Him. We honor Him when we worship Him the way He asks us to worship Him. He made the seventh day of the week especially for us to worship Him on. It is **His** special day. He wants us to come apart and spend that particular day with Him every week. Worshipping Him on any other day will not honor Him or be accepted by Him. All other days a person decides to worship Him on are not holy. The seventh day of the week is the only day God

> **"**
> *The seventh day of the week is the only day God made holy.*
> **"**

made holy. That's right! God made it holy! It is the only day that was blessed by Him for the purpose of worship.

All six of the other days are for work and play. God only asks us to keep only one day holy—one-seventh of the week. Also, note thatHe says, "Remember"! Don't forget! That it is His day—so it is special to Him—it is His day, and His alone. It does not belong to any other god. He is the One who made it holy, and He is the only One who really could make it holy. Any other god saying it is holy will not make it holy. Anyone else who claims to be God is not telling the truth. They are not God, even if they claim to be God. The same with the seventh day of the week. No other day is holy, even though someone calls it holy by calling it the "Sabbath."

There is someone who claims to be God. That someone is Lucifer, and he has tricked many people into believing Sunday is God's holy day of worship. But you can read your Bible from cover to cover, and you will not find God telling you Sunday has been sanctified by God. Instead, the opposite is true. Remember, Lucifer likes to be the big "IT." He is the one who instituted sun worship. It is a counterfeit day of worship. Sunday is the holy day of the pagans. They worship the sun on that day. When they worship the sun, they are actually worshiping the devil. Ouch! Most people just don't realize that truth.

The people back in Nimrod's day were sun-worshippers. Satan has the bigs, you know. The sun is the biggest star in our solar system. It suits his fancy. He likes to be the biggest and best. He desires to be better than Jesus. He can't stand to see Jesus being worshipped. So he instituted the day of the sun. Also note that Sunday is the first day of the week. Satan always wants to be number one—the best, the mightiest, the "FIRST." It fits his desires to a tee.

His greatest want is to be worshipped like Jesus is. He is jealous of Jesus—the wrong kind of jealousy. The selfish kind. He tried to destroy Jesus when He was here on earth. Jealousy is a deadly sin. It leads to all kinds of sin. Jesus did not do anything to him to cause Lucifer's jealousy. It came from the evil in his own heart. Remember! God never creates anything imperfect. Lucifer was perfect when he came from the hand of God. God says so! *"Thou wast perfect in thy ways … till iniquity wast found in thee"* (Ezek. 28:15).

"And on the seventh day God ended His work which He had made; and He rested on the seventh day from all His work which He had made. And God blessed the seventh day, and sanctified it: because that in it He had rested from all His work which God created and made" (Gen. 2:2–3). God sanctified the seventh day of the week by setting it aside for a special use. It was set aside for people to worship Him and spend time with Him. Obviously, God is a social Being. He likes spending time with us. And He is thrilled when we love Him back. When you love someone, you enjoy spending time with them. He loves us, so He wants to spend time with us. He wants us to worship with Him on His holy day. Now go back and read the fourth commandment again. It says, *"the seventh day is the sabbath of*

the L<small>ORD</small>." Did you hear that? God says the seventh day of the week is the Lord's day.

These four commands are the ones that teach us how to love and specifically honor God. The next six commands tell us both how to please God and how to honor and love our fellowmen. I believe those commands explain themselves. See if you agree.

5 *Honour thy father and thy mother: that thy days may be long upon the land which the* L<small>ORD</small> *thy God giveth thee. (Ex. 20:12)*

6 *Thou shalt not kill. (Exod. 20:13)*

7 *Thou shalt not commit adultery. (Exod. 20:14)*

8 *Thou shalt not steal. (Exod. 20:15)*

9 *Thou shalt not bear false witness against thy neighbour. (Exod.20:16)*

10 *Thou shalt not cover thy neighbour's house, thou shalt not covet thy neighbour's wife, nor his manservant, nor his maidservant, nor his ox, nor his ass, nor any thing that is thy neighbour's. (Exod. 20:17)*

God is jealous of our affection, our loyalty, and our safety. So He guards us! He does this to protect us. Oh, how He loves us. The freedom He gives us by allowing us to choose to serve Him or not serve Him is truly an immense expression of His love. It's not easy to choose to serve God. Satan makes sure of that; it certainly wasn't easy for Jesus to die to save us. But He did it anyway. He has promised to be with us through thick and thin.

When we disobey God, we choose to obey some other god, and it's no bed of roses. In fact, it's terrible. Talk about work. It's hard work when you do what the devil wants you to do. Just think! He gets you to lie, steal, drink, smoke, etc., etc., etc.— you name it—he gets you to do it. That leads to fights, accidents, sickness, fear, jealousy, etc.—the list goes on. Is that fun? And at the very end—a horrible death. Our God is definitely disappointed and jealous. I can just picture all of the holy beings in heaven getting busy when we do that—the Father, Jesus, the Holy Spirit, and all of the holy angels. All of them love us. They want to do everything They can to save us. But They will never try to control us. They willingly protect us. That's real love! This includes protecting Their law of love. They will help us love and understand Their law. God says, *"Blessed are they that do his commandments, that they may* have right to the tree of life, and may enter in through the gates into the city" (Rev. 22:14).

What a beautiful promise this is! God cautions, *"If any man shall take away from the words of the book of this prophecy, God shall take away his part out of the book of life, and out of the holy city, and from the things which are written in this book" (Rev. 22:19).* God wants us to know how very serious it is to break His law of love. When we obey God's law, we are loving Him, and we are loving each other too.

It's paramount to our salvation that we obey His law of love.

God has never changed any part of it.

No, not even one word of His law has ever been altered.

And He never will change it!

Remember!

Don't forget!

ALL

HAVE SINNED!!!

Every last one of us!

4

The Unpardonable Sin—What Is It?

We just looked at God's ten basic laws He rules the universe with and found that together they are called the Ten Commandments. They tell us how to love God and how to love each other. We found that even when we only disobey one command, we are sinning. In fact, James tells us, *"Whosoever shall keep the whole law, and yet offend in one point, he is guilty of all (James 2:10).* But God tells us He is willing to pardon any and all sin. So what does a person mean when they talk about the unpardonable sin? How can there be an unpardonable sin since God is willing to pardon all of them? The word "unpardonable" is not in the Bible. Truly, there is no specific sin that is unpardonable.

For instance; *"Surely at the commandment of the LORD came this upon Judah, to remove them out of His sight, for the sins of Manasseh, according to all that he did; and also for the innocent blood that he shed: for he filled Jerusalem with innocent blood; which the LORD would not pardon"* (2 Kings 24:3–4). But why wouldn't God pardon him? If you kill an innocent person, is that the unpardonable sin?

The answer is "NO"! The unpardonable sin is simply any sin we will not stop committing. And it is the one we will not ask God to pardon. Why won't we ask Him to pardon it? Because we love and cherish it. We want to keep committing it because we are so angry at the person that we are unwilling to forgive them. Our anger gets in our way. We allow Satan to keep us riled up toward the one we feel is offending or hurting us. Thus it is a sin we refuse to stop committing. It is a dangerous mindset to be in. It can rapidly lead to murder.

Naturally, God will not forgive a person who wants to keep harming someone. Anyone who does that is not sorry for their sin and keeps repeating it. That is why it is unpardonable. But if we allow him to give us real sorrow for sin, God is more than willing to help us stop repeating all sins if we ask Him for forgiveness. But we have to recognize we are sinning and want to quit sinning. Satan lies to us and makes us feel that it is more important to get even with whoever is harming or offending us than it is for us to obey God. The real problem is the built-up hatred in our hearts. What a shame that we cannot find it in our hearts to forgive whoever we are angry with. God cannot and will not forgive us if we will not forgive others.

We can ask God to open our eyes and give us sorrow for our sins. God always answers an honest prayer. But when we are in such a heat of anger, often we rebel violently at such an idea. Look at what Jesus told his disciples. *"For if ye forgive men their trespasses, your heavenly Father will also forgive you: But if ye forgive not men their trespasses, neither will your Father forgive your trespasses (Matt. 6:14–15)*. This tells me God cannot and will not forgive me if I will not forgive others. Satan purposely tries to keep us wrapped up in anger. I am sure everyone has gone through that type of experience. He is just leading us around by the nose and gloating about his power over us. So when we are in a situation like that, we direly need to ask God for a forgiving heart. It's a life-and-death matter.

When I am in a situation like that, it means the sin I am committing is more important to me than life itself. It means I would rather die than quit doing what the devil is telling me to do. It means I am not sorry for my sin. If I were sorry, I would quit doing it. Thus, it is unpardonable because I won't stop committing it over and over and over again. My sin becomes unpardonable when I refuse to stop committing it, keep hanging onto it, and am unwilling to ask for pardon. It takes faith to believe God.

Luke cements the fact that Jesus and his Father are both God. Listen to Him! Jesus had just healed a man. Notice also their faith played an important role in their forgiveness. We can't believe God and trust Him without having faith in Him. Trust is evidence of our faith. If you don't trust, you don't have faith. The two go hand in hand. Oh, how thankful we should be that God gives each one of us a special measure of faith. Notice also that the church leaders lacked faith. *"And when he saw their faith, he said unto him, Man, thy sins are forgiven thee. And the scribes and the Pharisees began to reason, saying, Who is this that speaketh blasphemies?" (Luke 5:20–21)*. How painful these false accusations must have been for Jesus. Can you feel His pain? God help us feel it!

They continued to condemn him. *"Who can forgive sins, but God alone?" (Luke 5:21)*. Unwittingly, they were condemning themselves. For they refused to admit Jesus was God. This should cause great joy in our hearts, for it gave Jesus the opportunity to tell the people back then and us still today that He was and still is God. *"But when Jesus perceived their thoughts, he answering said unto them, What reason ye in your hearts? Whether is easier, to say, Thy sins be forgiven thee; or say, Rise up and walk? But that ye may know th*at *the Son of man hath power upon earth to forgive sins" (Luke 5:22–24).*

Whew! Many of them may have been committing the unpardonable sin that day. For some of them never did believe Jesus was the Son of God. How sad for them, and how awful the rejection was for Jesus. Truly, I've been that stubborn about things before, too, and held onto a sin for a very long time. I dare say all of us have been that upset toward someone. When we are in a situation like that, we need to step back and contemplate what an extremely dangerous position we are in. It is Satan who pushes us to pout and feel sorry for ourselves like that. We truly underestimate the power of the devil when we refuse to listen to God's pleading voice. Oh, how it hurts God. But He will not force us to repent, for then there would be no love. Then the whole cosmos would be obliterated. But we do not need to worry.

> **"**
> *No parent wants to see their child suffer—especially God.*
> **"**

We have a God who truly is love. That is why He is allowing Satan to show all of us what the world would be like with Satan in charge. Unbelief in God is a dangerous path to tread. It's too bad. But there is no other way to take care of a situation like that. If there was, God would be doing it. For no parent wants to see their child suffer—especially God. What a wonderful, brilliant God we serve. We just need to hang onto Him and ask Him to help us with our hatred and angry feelings. We, too, need Him to give us a desire to repent for our sins. It will be well worth it. I yearn for a place where there will never be any more anger, jealousy, and death. Just the lack of those emotions alone will be worth everything we will ever have to go through.

The unpardonable sin can be any sin. For each person, a different sin causes them to be stubborn and ornery. Therefore, no one can know, except himself or herself, which sin is the unpardonable one for them. Actually, more than one type of sin becomes that way for every one of us. In times when we are so upset or determined and can't even see one blessing, we need to get down on our knees and ask God to help us see the blessings He is already giving us. Praise God. One blessing will remind us of another. That's just how God works. Always caring and good! Always with us, even when we can't feel His presence. It is Satan, our enemy, who sends us those wrong feelings, like desertion. He wants us to feel that God is unfair. But God is always present if we want Him to be. All we have to do is ask. And if we continue to feel that way after our prayer, then it is Satan making us feel that way. Give him the boot!

Down through the ages, God has said He would not forsake His people. He told Joshua, *"I will not fail thee, nor forsake thee" (Josh. 1:5).* Paul assured the people in his day, *"He hath said, I will never leave thee nor forsake thee" (Heb. 13:5).* How very blessed we are. Isn't it something how our enemy can get us to hang onto a sin even though we know it will separate us from God, the life-giver? That just shows us how determined Satan is to destroy us and how fickle we are. He likes to strike us at our weakest hour. That's just who he is. But he can never steal our freedom of choice. It is always available until we fritter it away.

So you see, any sin can become unpardonable. It becomes unpardonable because we choose to make it unpardonable. Simply put, we love it so much we will not ask God to help us stop committing it. Actually, we turn our back on God's will for our lives and choose to go our own selfish way. Since God is love, and love is all about freedom of choice, He will not have anything to do with force or control. Praise God! We are free to make our own choices in life. Unfortunately, we are our own worst enemy. Each one of us, if we do not really love God, will hang onto our own pet sin or sins. That hanging onto a sin is what makes it unpardonable. We won't allow God to pardon us.

When the devil was heckling Job, he felt that God wouldn't pardon him. But it wasn't God who was choosing to harm Job. It was Satan accusing God of being unfair. Job thought for sure he had done something wrong and had caused God to be angry with him. But it was not Job or God who was angry. It was the devil accusing God of giving Job unfair favors. Yes, Satan was heckling God. Just listen to what Satan had the audacity to say to God. *"Hast not thou made an hedge about him, and about his house, and about all that he hath on every side? thou hast blessed the work of his hands, and his substance is increased in the land. But put forth thine hand now, and touch all that he hath, and he will curse thee to thy face" (Job 1:10–11).* But God knew Job's heart. God knew Job would love and honor Him no matter what Satan did to him.

Just look what happened. *"And the LORD said unto Satan, behold all that he hath is any thy power; only upon himself put not thine hand. So Satan went forth from the presence of the LORD" (Job. 1:12).* Read the rest of the story to find out how cruel the devil was. We, too, when we are hurting, tend to think perhaps God is upset with us. But God is never unkind. He does allow Satan to do his dirty work, though! This allows us freedom of choice, and it allows the devil freedom of choice too. God allows every created being to have freedom of choice. We can either choose to serve God or Satan.

Here is what Job said to God. *"And why dost thou not pardon my transgressions, and take away my iniquity? For now shall I sleep in the dust; and thou shalt seek in the morning, but I shall not be" (Job 7:21).* Just as Job did not know it was the devil heckling him, many times, we don't realize the devil is battling with us and accusing God of being partial with us. God is doing battle with Satan over us. Thus it is crucial we trust God no matter what happens. Read Job chapter 41, which is a description of the devil, and chapter 42 tells what the end of Job's life was like after the harassment Satan put him through. God will be dealing with this harassment with the devil until He comes in the clouds of heaven to take us home with them. Just think what God is putting up with for us all these years.

The sin we stick to is the devil's tool for getting us hooked on something that will destroy our relationship with Him and with humankind. Remember, it only takes refusing to give up just one sin to cause us eternal death. God yearns to pardon us. Won't you get on your knees right now and ask Him to help you. Even if we don't have a sin we are hanging onto, we need to ask the Holy Spirit to help us. If we don't feel like we want His help, it is probably the devil lying to us and bossing us around. We need to ask God to change the desires of our heart because we know this sin will destroy us in the end if we do not overcome it. Quite often, I begin feeling picked on by people. Satan often uses the tools that worked when other people mistreated us.

The reason a person bucks against God's will is because all of us want to be in control of our lives. It's human nature. But we can't see what Satan is doing behind the scenes. Our only help is to trust God. We must turn our will over to Him, trust Him, and ask Him to guide us and forgive us. Ask Him to help you love Him. I did when I felt that everything was going wrong. But it took a long time before I realized it was the devil hassling me through other people. Yes, they were being used too. But God can open your eyes. He wants to show us where our sin will take us. The Holy Spirit can replace it with joy and love for God. But this gets Satan busy. So just be prepared. I promise you will never be sorry you obeyed God.

It won't be easy! But the love you will have for God will far outweigh the love you think you have for your sins. I will be praying for you. I've been there and done that! He has even erased the particulars of things that happened to me. Praise God! They are gone from my memory. And if they do come back, it will be the devil bringing them back. Then I will have to say, as Jesus did, *"Get thee hence, Satan: for it is written, Thou shalt worship the Lord thy God, and him only shalt thou serve" (Matt. 4:10).* Read the whole chapter for yourself. The Holy Spirit will help us just as He helped Job.

Read all of Job chapter 23. It will encourage you. Job said, after his harassment with Satan, *"But he knoweth the way that I take:"* (God, that is) *"when he hath tried me, I shall come forth as gold" (Job 23:10).* Also read James 1:2–8. It tells you how trying your faith gets you wisdom. The devil punctuates certain sins, the sins that tend to be the ones we think we do not want to give up. One of them is substance abuse—alcoholic beverages, tobacco, and other drugs that are habit-forming. How dare I call substance abuse a sin? It destroys our body, soul, and mind. That is very serious. If Satan can get us to damage ourselves with these substances, he knows he has a much better chance of totally destroying us. We need to flee from him when he tempts us with such things, so he can tell us what to do. God says, *"Know ye not that you are the temple of God, and that the Spirit of God dwelleth in you?" (1 Cor. 3:16).* God will not live in you if you do not want Him to. We are so blessed that He does not control us as the devil does.

Just take in how God looks at us. It blows my mind that God would look at us this way. *"If any man defile the temple of God, him shall God destroy; for the temple of God is holy, which temple ye are" (1 Cor. 3:17).* That's right! God sees us as His holy dwelling place. He wants to live in our hearts and minds. Why does God call us His temple? Because He wants to be with us and in us. God won't live in our heart if we refuse to clean it up. He wants to help us clean it up. But if we won't clean it up or allow Him to clean it up, He won't live there. He won't live in a dirty place.

Sexual immorality is also a sin against the body, just as drug abuse is. The devil knows these sins will control us. *Read 1 Cor. 6:15–20.* Sexual and drug addictions are pushed on us by Satan, the slave driver. But he can't be in us if we don't allow him. His tools take away our freedom of choice, while all the time, the devil tells us, "that's a hoax," and whispers in our ear, saying, "you can quit any time!" But that's a lie! **You can't quit on your own. You have to have God's help.** Ask Him to give you the desire to put Him first in your life. Decide not to do anything which will displease Him. Remember! You have to ask because God won't force you.

And also remember! It will be a battle. Just don't give up. Just when you think you can't stand it another minute, choose to think about Jesus on the cross. He went through all that agony to make forgiveness of sins possible for us. Remember how He cried to His Father. He had been on the cross for many hours. *"And when the sixth hour was come, there was darkness over the whole land until the ninth hour."* This was during daylight hours. The darkness occurred because they were crucifying the Son of God. *"And at the ninth hour Jesus cried out in a loud voice, saying, Eloi, Eloi, lama sabachthani? which is, being interpreted, My God, my God, why hast thou forsaken me?" (Mark 15:33-34)*. And then He died. He paid for your sins and mine.

It was the devil who made Jesus feel that His Father had forsaken Him. Jesus went through those feelings because they are what Satan will put us through. He will make us feel like God doesn't care. Jesus had to experience every emotion we will ever have to experience. And Satan will handpick what would be the hardest for us.

What a precious gift. Jesus promises to be with us. Don't believe Satan's lies. Even though we feel forsaken, even though we feel we can't do it, even though he belittles us and says God doesn't care, God will still be there. Isn't that a beautiful promise? He will never leave us. He will never forsake us. We are the ones who forsake Him. We need to chuck these promises in our memory, so we won't believe the feelings Satan is making us have. Our life depends on it.

The Bible does not say Jesus had confirmation from His Father that all was well. That He had successfully paid for our sins. We may not feel we have pleased God. Satan will whisper all kinds of lies in our ears. Don't believe him! Jesus' life and death is our example. Jesus showed us how we might be treated if we walk in His footsteps. It would be well worth it, even if all we did were please God and then received no more reward. But God has all kinds of rewards for us. Just listen to this! *"Eye hath not seen, nor ear heard, neither have entered into the heart of man, the things which God hath prepared for them that love Him" (1 Cor. 2:9)*. Pleasing God is well worth the pain Satan heaps on us.

God certainly deserves our love. His love is reward enough. Read Ephesians1:1–2:10 for more about faith. It is the same with sexual immorality. It is a sin against the body, too, just as substance abuse is, and it can be habit-forming too, just like substance abuse is. Many believe the devil's lie and crave it. But don't panic! When we say yes to Satan, we are saying we love him more than we love God. We are placing our desires ahead of God's desires for us. God desires nothing but good for us. He says, *"Trust in the L*ORD *with all thine heart; and lean not unto thine own understanding. In all thy ways acknowl-edge him, and he shall direct thy paths. Be not wise in thine own eyes: fear the L*ORD*, and depart from evil. It shall be health to thy navel, and marrow to thy bones" (Prov. 3:5–8).* He can get you out of either situation.

> **Just think! You can't even imagine how wonderful heaven is going to be**

Just think! You can't even imagine how wonderful heaven is going to be. For me, I feel any pain I go through will be well worth it. Like the icing on a cake, so to speak. He offers us heaven. The best will be His warm hug. Especially since God has promised to be with us at all times as He was with Jesus. He is even going to erase all bad memories of the earth from our minds. If our loved ones are not there, we will not remember them. I treasure that. It certainly would not be a happy place if I continued to miss them. Look at this beautiful promise. John, under the inspiration of God, wrote:

> *And I heard a great voice out of heaven saying, Behold, the tabernacle of God is with men, and he will dwell with them, and they shall be his people, and God himself shall be with them, and be their God. And God shall wipe away all tears from their eyes; and there shall be no more death, neither sorrow, nor crying, neither shall there be any more pain: for the former things are passed away. (Rev. 21:3–4)*

Now that's heaven. We certainly could not be happy if those memories followed us. Thank You, God.

Just get to know God's will for your life. Listen to these beautiful words from God. I've used this verse before, but it can't be repeated too often. It is so comforting. *"If we confess our sins, He is faithful and just to forgive us our sins, and to cleanse us from all unrighteousness" (1 John 1:9).*

God is anxiously waiting for every last one of us to come to Him. Don't be afraid to be bold! Tell the devil you belong to God. Turn your back on him. He has ulterior motives—selfish ones. He only loves himself. He wants to turn you away from God! He hates God. He knows when he hurts you, it hurts God very much. Satan is bent on hurting God. Picture him in your mind with nasty, angry scowls on his face and his surly lip out a mile. Satan is bent on hurting God.

Just as there are many types of substance abuse, there are many types of sexual abuse. All of those sins are ones Satan makes us feel we can't get along without. He makes us feel they are so pleasurable we can't give them up. That's a lie! Is it pleasant to have to hide what you are doing? Is it pleasant to fear you will get caught? God knows! And others know what we are doing! We cannot trust our feelings. Satan plays with them and feeds us lie after lie. The truth is, people suffer greatly from sexual sins. Consider all of the sexually transmitted diseases. They are not worth displeasing God for. The devil has an ulterior motive. He is going to be burned up in a lake of fire someday for his selfish hatred toward God. When every single person who has ever been born has made a firm decision, which they will not turn from, and when there is no one left who needs to repent of any sin they have committed, then Jesus will come and take those who love Him home to heaven with Him. Isn't that glorious? The most precious part about it is love; He pours His love on us now, and He will pour it on us in heaven. I can hardly wait for the bear hug I know He has for me—how about you? Why has He waited so long? Because there are still people who do not realize they are disobeying Him. Almost all the Bible prophecies have been fulfilled. It won't be long. So I encourage you, right now, this very moment, go to Him with whatever sin you have dogging your footsteps and ask Him to forgive you. You will be bringing the second coming of Jesus closer. When you read this, Satan may whisper in your ear something to side-track you so that you will put it off. No matter what Satan brings your way, never forget—God is never more than a prayer away. What a God! What a lover! He is the best God you will ever have. Stick to him! He will never tamper with your freedom of choice. So, if the devil is whispering these words to you right now, saying, "Not now! You need to wait and — first." Don't listen to him! Renounce him—he is a self-made god. The DEVIL! Yes, he is a devil, in every sense of the word. God is not a pusher! We have to ask him to forgive us, and He will.

So!

What is the unpardonable sin?

It is the sin you cling to,

And will not ask

God

to forgive!

Always remember!

Faith

Is the Victory

that

Overcomes the World.

(1 John 5:4)

5

God's Other Amazing Characteristics Which Belong Only to Them

Characteristic #1

Holiness: Only Our God Is Holy

God—all three of Them—are the only Beings who are holy to the degree God is talking about when He tells us about Himself. The Bible upholds this statement. God wants us to know no man is holy like our God is holy. God says so! Often we talk about men being holy, but it is a totally different holiness than the holiness of God. The men of God who wrote the books of the Bible were called holy. There have been many of them. God tells us through His prophets there will be a time when every mouth will tell God He is the only One who is holy. That will be the most glorious day ever. Men are only holy through Jesus' shed blood for them as they accept His gracious gift of loving forgiveness. It is Jesus' shed blood that washes away our sins. We are only holy as we ask Him to forgive our sins, and then through the power of God, we are able to forsake them. Jesus' death on the cross is the most precious gift that was ever given to any created being. Just look what John saw and heard in vision concerning those who will be made holy through their faith and trust in God. That holiness comes to us through His amazing gift of love. It is totally different than the holiness of God. We can only be called holy by accepting his shed blood for our sins.

How do we show Him we have accepted His gift of forgiveness and want to be holy? It is by obeying God. Yes, by loving Him. He says we tell Him we love Him when we obey Him. And how do we do that? God tells us how. He says, *"If ye love me, keep my commandments" (John 14:15);* *"Let us hear the conclusion of the whole matter: Fear God, and keep his commandments: for this is the whole duty of man" (Eccl. 12:13).*

Yes! We have to do our part. God will not and cannot save anyone who does not love Him. If He saved those who refuse to love Him, He would have to face this mess all over again. Nobody, and I mean NOBODY, would want that. We have to totally accept him as our Master, King, Lord, and Savior. He will **not** wash away our sins if we don't want Him to. We have to want Him to wash them away. And then we must go one step further. We must choose to allow Him to be the Lord of our life. He dearly wants to have a loving relationship with us. Love cannot be forced. God will never try to force us to love Him. If we do not love Him, He will not wash our sins away. When we fail to obey His Ten-Commandment law, we are sinning. Each law describes a different type of love, as we learned in the last chapter via James.

> **God tells us through His prophets there will be a time when every mouth will tell God He is the only One who is holy. That will be the most glorious day ever.**

It sounds as if James is living in our day when he talks about the problems between some of the rich and the poor. Of course, always keep in mind, there are loving and unloving people among both rich and poor. He says,

> *Hearken, my beloved brethren, Hath not God chosen the poor of this world rich in faith, and heirs of the kingdom which he hath promised to them that love him? But ye have despised the poor. Do not rich men oppress you, and draw you before the judgment seats? Do not they blaspheme that worthy name by the which ye are called? If ye fulfill the royal law according to the scripture, Thou shalt love thy neighbor as thyself, ye do well: But if ye have respect to persons, ye commit sin, and are convicted of the law as transgressors. For whosoever shall keep the whole law, and yet offend in one point, he is guilty of all. For he that said, Do not commit adultery, said also, Do not kill. Now if thou commit no adultery, yet if thou kill, thou art become a transgressor of the law. So speak ye, and so do, as they that shall be judged by the law of liberty. (James 2:5–12)*

The choice is up to each of us personally. I ask—how can we help but love a God like that? It should be an easy choice! All He asks us to do is give up things that will kill us. Sin kills! Satan is often referred to as the beast. By the end of this book, you will know why. You would think learning to love God would be easy, but it's not. That's because we have a fierce enemy. Originally, his name was Lucifer, but now it is Satan. He made a very bad choice. That's what this whole story is all about. We need to know what caused sin and how it came about so we can know how to deal with it and how to make a wise choice concerning our salvation. God shares that story with us. As we learn the truth about the battle between good and evil and between Christ and Satan, we will be able to choose whether we want to accept Jesus as our Lord and Savior.

We will choose to be saved or choose to die the second death and be lost. It's all about God's wonderful gift of salvation. Most importantly, we will choose to love God or choose to follow Satan's footsteps to our death. It's the fiercest battle there will ever be. Satan, God's enemy, will make sure of that. It is taking place right now—this very moment. Jesus has already died for your sins. So why not accept His fabulous gift of love today, at this moment. God bless you as you make your choice. And yes again! It is going on in every house on earth. And in every church on earth. Moment by moment, we are making our choice to love God or follow Satan to his death. The choice is ours. I hope you daily, actually minute by minute and hour by hour, make your choice to love and trust God. That's my choice! God help me because I can't do it on my own.

God really is LOVE, and He really does love us. Our enemy only loves himself. Actually, he really doesn't even love himself. Do you know why I say that? It is because no one destroys someone they really love. And the devil is destroying himself. Our relationship with God is changing all of the time as we accept or reject His love. Look at this beautiful word picture of those who will choose to become holy through the blood of the Lamb. Please notice that it tells us that only God is holy. That is a very important truth. Our enemy denies this statement every step of the way. But God will help us plug our ears and keep us from listening to Satan's lies if we ask Him to. I invite you to bow your head and say with me at this very moment, "Please, Lord, teach me the truth about You and our enemy Satan. Help me to know when to plug my ears because Satan is in disguise, trying to deceive me all of the time. Thank You, Lord, for answering my prayer."

Now let's learn about God's battle and ours with our fiercest enemy. Here is a beautiful picture of those who will win that battle.

And I saw as it were a sea of glass mingled with fire: and them that had gotten the victory over the beast, and over his image, and over his mark, and over the number of his name, stand on the sea of glass, having the harps of God. And they sing the song of Moses the servant of God, and the song of the Lamb, saying, Great and marvellous are Thy works, Lord God Almighty; just and true are thy ways, thou King of saints. Who shall not fear thee, O Lord, and glorify thy name? **for thou only art holy:** *for all nations shall come and worship before thee; for thy judgments are made manifest. (Rev. 15:2–4, emphasis supplied)*

When it says "made manifest," it is saying it will be made clear to us; we will understand what it is saying. Isn't that blessed? God never does anything in the dark. He is always open and honest.

That is a victorious rally cry. What faith this cry gives us. It's a cry from God to rally us to accept the victory Jesus makes possible. Isn't that beautiful? Jesus already won that victory for us. He died on the cross to pay for our sins. Now we must choose who we want as our God, King, and Lord. Nothing can take the place of God's love. We must keep our eyes on our glorious Lover as we learn how to defend ourselves from His and our enemy, Satan.

One of the distinguishing marks of our enemy is his love for high places. He wants to take God's place. Yes, he wants to wrest the throne from Jesus. God's throne is in His temple in heaven. That's right. Satan is fighting to take God's throne from Him. That is why he is striving to destroy God's church. In fact, he wants to take the power and the glory and the honor away from all three of the Beings who are our One God. He wants to steal the worship that belongs to Them alone.

Are you aware of the fact that the devil goes to church? Yes, he does! He is there to keep us from honoring God. He loves to cause confusion, fighting, and bickering among the members. Remember when he took Jesus up on a pinnacle of the temple? It was his aim to both destroy God's church and the God of the universe who resides in that temple. Nothing makes him happier than seeing a temple of God destroyed.

He has lied to himself so much that he believes he will win the battle he is having with God. He has tricked himself into believing he will destroy God and His people. But praise God! He has already lost that battle. He just won't accept the truth. That's been his problem all along. Now, all God is waiting for is for each person on earth to make their choice. God bless you as you make yours. It's a choice we need to make every moment because Satan hassles us every moment of our life.

There have always been those who claim to be God on earth. That is what Lucifer was trying to do when he tempted Eve in the Garden of Eden. He was dishonest when he called God a liar. He has been lying about God ever since. They say practice makes perfect. He had already had plenty of practice in heaven. Just look what a mess our world is in. We see untruth taking place on every hand as people allow their greed to take over. Yes! In high places. Even in God's church! And it has gone wild in governmental affairs. It's everywhere! And obviously, the devil isn't the only one who claims to be Christ on earth. When his followers claim to take Jesus' place, they are not being truthful. They may have been taught that from their childhood and do not know the truth. That is why people need to be careful they are not calling a person evil who may innocently be doing wrong. Satan hates Jesus. He thinks he should have been able to create things just like Jesus did. He has his lip out a mile. He vehemently hates Jesus and His Father. That's why he is causing all the trouble he is right now. He likes to have followers. He doesn't care whether they know the truth or not. He doesn't care what happens to them. He doesn't believe he will burn up in a lake of fire prepared by God.

Any man who claims to be Christ on earth is not telling the truth. Satan has many followers who are doing this all over the world. It's as simple as that! They are stealing God's honor, whether they know it or not. And they need to know the truth. Yes, some of them may be doing it innocently. We need to pray for them. They need to know that absolutely no one can take Jesus' place. We need to pray that the Holy Spirit will convict them that they are disobeying God. Also, God says we are not to call any man on earth "Father." God is not talking about our earthly father; rather, He is talking about calling our minister or pastor or priest "Father." Neither are they to be called "Master." If we address them by those titles, we are putting them instead of and in place of God. That is a sin. They are not to be called "Father" or Rabbi. **God says so!** Just listen to Him!

When Jesus was here on earth, He told the people, *"But be not ye called Rabbi: for one is your Master, even Christ; and all ye are brethren. And call no man your father upon the earth: for one is your Father, which is in heaven. Neither be ye called masters: for one is your Master, even Christ"* (Matt. 23:8–10). A master is someone in the spiritual realm people bow down to, worship, confess their sins to, and obey. God alone is worthy of this title. No man can forgive sins. When they do, they are claiming to be God.

Look at this verse about the rabbis in Jesus' day. They were exalting themselves. They liked to be praised and held in high esteem. Their God-given work was to point people to Jesus. But the rabbis rejected Jesus, the One who truly was their Master and Lord. They were causing people to be lost and to believe a lie. *"Then spake Jesus to the multitude, and to His disciples, Saying The scribes and the Pharisees sit in Moses' seat: All therefore whatsoever they bid you observe, that observe and do; but do not ye after their works: for they say, and do not" (Matt. 23:1–3).* They were teaching the right thing, but they were not doing what they told the congregation at the synagogue to do.

Does that sound familiar? It is happening today too!

For they bind heavy burdens and grievous to be borne, and lay them on men's shoulders; but they themselves will not move them with one of their fingers. But all of their works they do to be seen of men: they make broad their phylacteries, and enlarge the borders of their garments, And love the uppermost rooms at feasts, and the chief seats in the synagogues, and greetings in the markets, and to be called of men, Rabbi, Rabbi. (Matt. 23:4–7)

God makes it very clear that He alone is our Lord, Master, and Father. He alone is our spiritual Father. This is serious business! Neither are we to bow to a statue of someone or something. They are idols. Just read the second commandment in God's law. It, too, tells us not to bow down to images, let alone bow to a man. God says, *"I change not" (Mal. 3:6).* Look at Hebrews 13:8. It makes this statement! *"Jesus Christ the same yesterday, and to day, and for ever."* Absolutely no earthly spiritual leader is to be called father, priest, or master, or rabbi. If they ask men to do this or allow men to call them by that title, they are disobeying God and gaining self-praise. Neither can they be called God; only the Father, Jesus, the Son of God, and the Holy Spirit, are GOD! They alone are holy!

Characteristic #2

Omnipotence: God Alone Is Omnipotent—He Has Unlimited Authority

According to *Merriam-Webster's Collegiate Dictionary*, the word "omnipotent" is described thus: "1: Almighty; 2: having virtually unlimited authority or influence." This is a characteristic that also tells us about God's superiority. The fact that They are omnipotent means They, God, are the mightiest Beings in existence. They have unlimited authority and influence. Just look at the godly character trait of omnipotence, which is inherent to all three of Them. The very definition of the word omnipotent tells us God has unlimited authority. No one is above Them. They answer to no one, and no one can usurp influence over Them. They are in control, but They are not controllers. Dictators—if you please!

Talk about authority! That's real authority! The unlimited kind! Yes! Jesus definitely is omnipotent. He acts like His Father. Quite often we say of a child - he's the spitting image of his dad. Well! These words from God the Father tell us Jesus is the spitting image of His heavenly Father. This image includes the Father's righteousness. Jesus is just as righteous as His Father. Praise God! And He will be that way forever.

The type of control we think of is not even on God's mind. God does not want to control us. He loves us. Yes, love is what's on God's mind. God hates unloving actions, but They love sinners. This is why we can be assured the battle over evil will be won by God, and we can look forward to a time when no sin exists forever. Isn't that exciting? I sure think so! Here is a partial biblical word picture of what will happen after we have been in heaven with God for one thousand years. It concerns God's omnipotence. Just think how beautiful and true this praise is! *"And after these things I heard a great voice of much people in heaven, saying, Alleluia; Salvation and glory, and honour, and power, unto the Lord our God: For true and righteous are His judgments" (Rev. 19:1–2).* Now that's real praise!

Absolutely everyone will proclaim how wonderful God is and admit He was the One who saved them. And it's true. He is the only One who should receive honor, for He is the One who has all power. But most importantly, He is the only One who loves us enough to make salvation possible. In the final end, all people will know that He and His law are right about all things. And truly, all who love God are anxiously looking forward to the day when They, God, will come and take us on that glorious trip to heaven. Just look how the heavenly Father glorifies His Son, Jesus. He says, *Thy throne, O God, is for ever and ever: a sceptre of righteousness is the sceptre of Thy kingdom" (Heb.1:8).* The Father makes sure we know it is Jesus He is talking about. For He says,

> But unto the Son he saith, Thy throne, O God, is for ever and ever: a sceptre of righteousness is the sceptre of thy kingdom. Thou hast loved righteousness, and hated iniquity; therefore God, even thy God, hath anointed thee with the oil of gladness above thy fellows. And, Thou, Lord, in the beginning hast laid the foundation of the earth; and the heavens are the works of thine hands: They shall perish; but thou remainest; and they shall wax old as doth a garment; And as a vesture shalt thou fold them up, and they shall be changed: but thou art the same, and thy years shall not fail. (Heb. 1:8–12)

Did you notice the Father calls Himself Jesus' God? That's right! When Jesus was born down here in human flesh, the Father was His God just as He is the God of all of us.

A scepter is something that shows us a being has royal authority. Jesus was, and is, and will always be royalty of the highest degree. His scepter is not just a baton that signifies His royalty; His scepter is His righteousness.

> **"**
> *Anyone who chooses to love God can claim the Ruler of the universe as their Father.*
> **"**

There is nothing, absolutely nothing, better than that. And there can be no more sure proof that Jesus is God than this: *"The kingdoms of this world are become the kingdoms of our Lord, and of his Christ; and he shall reign for ever and ever" (Rev. 11:15).* Yes! The Father and Son will rule together. Both of Them are called Lord.

But when Jesus came to this earth in human flesh, He said, *"My Father is greater than I" (John 14:28).* He told Pilate, *"Thou couldest have no power at all against me, except it were given thee from above: therefore he that delivered me unto thee hath the greater sin" (John 19:11).* Jesus was telling Pilate that all of the authority He had was coming from God the Father. Jesus had given up His authority for the time being to come down here and give His life to save us. What a gift of love that was that He would give up His authority for any period of time, so He could show us He really was God and that the Father had chosen Him to be co-ruler with Him. We must be able to see that Jesus will keep His Word! Only then can Jesus rescue us from sin. Only then will Satan's accusations be seen for what they really are—lies about God.

In Jesus' human state, the heavenly Father was His God. For He said to Mary after He had been raised from the dead, *"Touch me not; for I am not yet ascended to my Father: but go to my brethren, and say unto them, I ascend unto my Father, and your Father; and to my God, and your God"* *(John 20:17)*. And truly, even in this world, the children of a king are subject to their father's rule all their life because he is their father. I liked the ring of those words when I read them. Yes! It means I can have Him as my Father, too! And so can you. But He is so loving that He leaves it up to us whether we want Him as our Father. What a priceless gift. What a blessed privilege. I am awed that anyone who chooses to love God can claim the Ruler of the universe as their Father. How truly blessed we are.

Characteristic #3

Omnipresence: Only God Is Omnipresent—Present in All Places, at All Times

Again, let's check the dictionary! The word is "omnipresent." The only definition the dictionary gives is the one I already gave above. God is the only One who is present in all places, at all times. God is Omnipresent—the Holy Spirit is the One who uses this gift to lead us to God and save us. So let's look at the work of the Holy Spirit concerning this special quality. Omnipresence is more than my mind can comprehend. Omnipresence holds hands with faith and love—that's how God lives in and with us. The word "omnipresence" means God can be with all of us at the same time. That's huge! It means God can be with me and clear across the world with you at the same time. Isn't that marvelous? I find it very comforting that I can have God with me at all times. In fact, it's even better than that. He is with every single person, no matter where they live, no matter who they are, at this very moment if they want Him and have invited Him to be with them. Wow! Only God could do that!

Isn't it wonderful that the Holy Spirit is willing to do this for all of us—no matter who or where we are? But! Remember! Don't forget! God doesn't just barge into our life if we don't want Him there. He only comes if we invite Him. All we have to do is ask and believe God does what He says He will do. He says He is omnipresent. All we have to do is have faith to believe Them. This means all I need to do is combine His omnipotence with my faith. It is true that we can only believe God is omnipresent through faith. It is a necessary ingredient, so we will talk about it in this description of omnipresence.

Omnipresence and faith must hold each other's hand. I believe that. How about you? But! Let's go to the Bible for clarification concerning which person of the Godhead has this characteristic. Are you ready for this? The truth is, Jesus said to His disciples, *"And I will pray the Father, and he shall give you another Comforter, that he may abide with you for ever; Even the Spirit of Truth; whom the world cannot receive, because it seeth Him not, neither knoweth Him: but ye know Him; for He dwelleth with you, and shall be in you"* (John 14:16–17). God still says that to us today. We need to thank Him every moment of our lives for His indispensable gifts.

Remember! It is to the Father we are told to direct our prayers. He is the One who gives the Holy Spirit to us. He oversees all things. He is the One in charge of all things. He is the One who keeps things running smoothly. For everything we humans do, too, there is usually one person who is over all the rest, one who has his finger in every pie, one person who keeps things running smoothly. But Jesus made another observation. He told His disciples to *"Watch and pray."* For what reason? *"That ye enter not into temptation."* Why did He say this to them? Matthew was given the answer. Listen! *"The spirit indeed is willing, but the flesh is weak" (Matt. 26:41). Jesus* had concern for His disciples. He still has that concern and care for His followers today.

Whenever we ask the Father to do something for us, we need to say, *"Thy will be done" (Matt. 6:10).* Why? Because They, the Father, Jesus the Son, and the Holy Spirit work together to save us. All of Them know what is best for us. Can't you just see Them, putting Their heads together, conferring with one another? I can! It's a thrilling scene. Together, They know what is best for each one of us. And the Father is the one we are supposed to talk with about everything. He coordinates what Jesus and the Holy Spirit do for us. What a wonderful team They are. Do you realize we are part of their team when we cooperate with Them? This knowledge gives me a warm, comfortable feeling. Just what we need, for everything that happens to us in our l down here. Isn't that precious? The disciples had a lot going for them, and so do we. All three of the Beings who are God, were looking out for each other. God gives us that same care. Isn't that beautiful?

Just think! Since the Holy Spirit is meeting with every single person who invites Him to come into their hearts, then the Holy Spirit is meeting with a mega amount of people, **all at the same time**. That definitely is amazing. Truly it is something only God, all three of Them together can provide for us! It is impossible for any of us to understand how the Spirit can be with all of us at the same time—but He can! That is one of the qualities which make Them God. Yes! This is more than my mind can comprehend, so I must accept it by faith. That is how each of us can come to understand it. And yes, it definitely takes faith to believe these special traits of our God. Faith is extremely necessary. It is one of the most valuable gifts God gives us. He gives us so many gifts. Isn't He marvelous?

Omnipresence is the characteristic that allows the Holy Spirit to guide us. It makes it possible for Him to be right at our fingertips!

Johnny-on-the-spot or whatever thought the Spirit brings to our minds. But, don't forget! Our thoughts must agree with the Bible. That proves who the thoughts came from. God says, *"If they speak not according to this word, it is because there is no light in them" (Isa. 8:20).* We talked about the Holy Spirit very briefly in the introduction, but now, let's look at Him more closely. When we look at His duties, realize more and more about His authority and influence upon mankind. He is also called *"The Spirit of truth" (John 14:17).* Truly, They rule together as One God and have complete authority over everything in existence. But They do not lord it over each other, and neither do They lord it over us. They give us total freedom to decide who we want to worship. They are love. Remember! Don't Forget! Love does not control! How thankful we can be that They are our one true God of love. I find this characteristic utterly amazing that I can have God with me at all times. Isn't it wonderful that the Holy Spirit is willing to do this for all of us no matter who we are? And He doesn't just barge into our lives if we don't want Him to.

Being present in all places all at the same time is a big order! For us, that is! But not for God. Remember, nothing is too hard for God. He said so when He promised to give Abraham and Sarah a child. It was many, many years after God gave them that promise before it was fulfilled. A lot happened during that waiting period. And Sarah got tired of waiting. Then she listened to the wrong spirit and obeyed him. What a shame. And her husband followed in her footsteps. They both submitted to unbelief in God. How sad. Then, *"Now Abraham and Sarah were old and well stricken in age; and it ceased to be with Sarah after the manner of women. ... the* LORD *said unto Abraham, Wherefore did Sarah laugh, saying, Shall I of a surety bear a child, which am old? Is any thing too hard for the* LORD*?" (Gen. 18:14).*

It was Jesus who was speaking face to face with Abraham. Did you notice the hints from God that tell us God had been omnipresent with them? He was still with them, but they didn't even realize it. He knew everything about them. But Sarah didn't trust Him. She trusted herself instead. Even when God came to them years later, she still wasn't really trusting God. She laughed. She thought she was too old to have a baby.

We are not any different. It blows my mind how we can be so blind and distrust God. Distrust is truly the work of our enemy, the devil. I find that truth downright scary! Actually, it's horrifying! It blows my mind that Sarah would distrust God like that. But I'm sure I have distrusted Him much more than she did. We all have! The sad part is—it hasn't always been just distrust. Too many times, it was my own selfish desires—wanting to have things my way—not God's way.

Let's take a moment and compare the devil's earlier actions. Adam and Eve walked and talked with God just like Sarah and Abraham did. It seems to me their experiences with the devil are just alike in content. The devil lied to Eve, and he lied to Sarah. It looks like Eve wanted to believe the fruit would make her wise—make her like God. But that fruit wouldn't do anything of the kind. She was already like God—made in His image. She knew the truth. It was the same for Sarah. She, too, walked and talked face to face with Jesus. Yes! God's omnipresence surrounded her. They both thought God had lied to them. They both lacked faith. But! God still sent the Holy Spirit to them.

He still does this for us today. What do you say we give all three of Them a great big bear hug right now and say thank You, Lord, for loving me that much? Thank You for showing me my selfishness, and please draw me closer to You. Thank You for this promise, Lord! You say to us, *"Submit yourselves therefore to God. Resist the devil, and he will flee from you. Draw nigh to God, and He will draw nigh to you" (James 4:7–8).*

That's good news! Omnipresence is HUGE! **It is good news! In fact—IT'S HUMONGOUS NEWS!** I am so glad our God is omnipresent and is here with us every moment of every day. And that the Holy Spirit is willing to be with us and help us. It makes constant protection available to each of us at all times. But again, only if we want and ask for it. God always honors our freedom of choice. That truth puts me in awe.

What a God! Just think how He hurts when we don't want Him in our life. Think about how we feel when our children get angry for a time and do not spend time with us. It really hurts! We need to ask the Holy Spirit to come and abide with us and not just take Him for granted. He is our Teacher and guide and our safety belt. When we are lax and not on our guard, Satan waggles his finger at God and says, "See, they like me better." That hurts God. He alone knows our minds. God will never barge into our lives as Satan does. That's a pet lie of his. God will also come into our hearts when someone who loves us prays and asks Him to. That is why we need to pray to God and ask the Holy Spirit to help all of us. It's called intercessory prayer.

What else does the Holy Spirit do for us? God says, *"Likewise the Spirit also helpeth our infirmities: for we know not what we should pray for as we ought: but the Spirit itself maketh intercession for us with groanings which cannot be uttered" (Rom. 8:26).* That is truly mind-boggling. It fills my heart with grateful appreciation. It tells me that when I don't know what to do and am all upset and perhaps pouting and thinking God isn't giving me what I want, He is still with me. Many times we don't even think about God when things are going bad. We're too scared! We don't need to be scared. Satan is a defeated foe. It's then that the Spirit yearns for someone else to ask Him to speak to our heart. Praise God for friends and family, who will ask God to come and tell us how much He loves us. Knowing this truth thrills me. God doesn't ever want to leave us destitute when we are ignorant of what is going on behind the scenes because of Satan's anger and selfishness. What a God! That He is always only a thought or a prayer away. I call that **AMAZING GRACE!** Thank You, Father. Thank You, Jesus. Thank You, Holy Spirit, for Your love. I am so glad You are omnipresent.

For me, the verse that really clinches this characteristic as far as the Holy Spirit is concerned is this one: *"And He that searcheth the hearts knoweth what is the mind of the Spirit, because He maketh intercession for the saints according to the will of God" (Rom. 8:27).* But just who is it that searches our hearts? Why it's Jesus. He is the one who intercedes between Satan and us. He's the One who died to pay for our sins. I'm so thrilled that all three of Them work together to save us and that the Holy Spirit is always only a prayer away, and that others can intercede for me when I won't come to God for myself.

Since God knows everything, He knows every thought and intent of my heart. He knows that sometimes I unknowingly disobey Him, either by believing a lie or by deliberately choosing to reject Him. Yes! He knows it all, but He still loves me. Truly He is our safety belt. It is through the Holy Spirit that He gives us a true picture of ourselves. He is still by my side and yours, too. And He convicts us of sin. He never leaves us in the dark concerning our spiritual condition. Isn't that wonderful? And are you convinced that Jesus can forgive all of your sins? Mark tells us Jesus can even forgive our sins.

Do you remember the story of the man Jesus healed when his friends let him down into a house from the roof? The religious leaders were there, and one of them said, *"Why doth this man thus speak blasphemies? who can forgive sins but God only?"* (Mark 2:7). Matthew answers his question. He quotes Jesus saying to another man, *"For whether is easier, to say, Thy sins be forgiven thee; or to say, Arise, and walk? But that ye may know that the Son of man hath power on earth to forgive sins, (then saith he to the sick of the palsy,) Arise, take up thy bed, and go unto thine house" (Matt.9:6).* What comfort this gives us just as it did this man.

It's so comforting to know the Spirit doesn't just leave us alone for the devil to destroy. When He speaks to our heart, we say it is our conscience speaking to us because then the Holy Spirit brings to our mind all the things we have learned concerning God's love for us. The Spirit shows us where we are wrong. God does not want us to be lost. He wants us to rule over the evil in our life. For when this happens, Satan is arguing with us. He wants us to be selfish like him.

> **66**
> *It's so comforting to know the Spirit doesn't just leave us alone for the devil to destroy.*
> **99**

We, every last one of us, must remember that we are all alike. This knowledge will give us compassion for one another. God gives us this beautiful verse to fall back on when we find ourselves being tempted. God says via Paul,

> *Therefore seeing we have this ministry, as we have received mercy, we faint not; But have renounced the hidden things of dishonesty, not walking in craftiness, nor handling the word of God deceitfully; but by manifestation of the truth commending ourselves to every man's conscience in the sight of God. But if our gospel be hid, it is hid to them that are lost: In whom the god of this world hath blinded the minds of them which believe not, lest the light of the glorious gospel of Christ, who is the image of God, should shine unto them. (2 Cor. 4:1–4)*

They have chosen to disbelieve the truth. How sad! There is a time when we can no longer come to God because we have said "no" so many times it has become habitual for us to obey the lies of the devil. We do it to ourselves. God doesn't leave us in darkness, but He will not take away our freedom to go our own selfish way. I think that is the worst possible reality to face—that we have rejected the love of God and chosen the devil as our god. But also know that Satan will tell us we are so bad we can't be forgiven. Remember, he is a liar. Jesus said so!

Jesus was probably talking with someone who had already committed the unpardonable sin. He told them if God were their Father, they would love Him and be able to understand what he was telling them. Then He said something astounding and very damning. He said,

> *Ye are of your father the devil, and the lusts of your father ye will do. He was a murderer from the beginning, and abode not in the truth, because there is no truth in him. When he speaketh a lie, he speaketh of his own: for he is a liar, and the father of it. And because I tell you the truth, ye believe me not. Which of you convinceth me of sin? And if I say the truth, why do ye not believe me? He that is of God heareth God's words: ye therefore hear them not, because ye are not of God. (John 8:44-47)*
>
> *There were certain of the scribes sitting there, and reasoning in their hearts, Why doth this man thus speak blasphemies? who can forgive sins but God only? And immediately when Jesus perceived in his spirit that they so reasoned within themselves, he said unto them, Why reason ye these things in your hearts? Whether is it easier to say to the sick of the palsy, Thy sins be forgiven thee; or to say, Arise, and take up thy bed, and walk? But that ye may know that the Son of man hath power on earth to forgive sins, (he saith to the sick of the palsy,) I say unto thee, Arise, and take up thy bed, and go thy way into thine house. (Mark 2:6-11)*

God never gives up! Isn't that thrilling news? He gives us time and time and more time to repent. What love! Sometimes we get scared and become afraid that we have gone too far and that God will **not** forgive us. But! You know what! If we are thinking that way, it is probable that the devil is placing those thoughts in our minds. Just know this! God never gives up on us. We are the ones who believe Satan's lies, and then we give up. Just look at these verses.

> *For the Word of God"* [that's Jesus and the Holy Bible—they are both called the Word of God], *"is quick, and powerful, and sharper than any twoedged sword, piercing even to the dividing asunder of soul and spirit, and of the joints and marrow, and is a discerner of the thoughts and intents of the heart. Neither is there any creature that is not manifest in His sight: but all things are naked and opened unto the eyes of him with whom we have to do. Seeing then that we have a great high priest,* [that's Jesus] *that is passed into the heavens, Jesus the Son of God, let us hold fast our profession. For we have not an high priest which cannot be touched with the feeling of our infirmities; but was in*

all points tempted like as we are, yet without sin. Let us therefore come boldly unto the throne of grace, that we may obtain mercy, and find grace to help in time of need. (Heb. 4:12–16)

We are so blessed. Just think what Jesus went through for us. He knows just how we feel. He knows just how mean, deceitful, and convincing the devil can be when he puts us down.

It doesn't feel good when we are wrestling with our conscience, but God is only a prayer away, and I am so glad God speaks to us when we are wanting to go our own selfish way. That's true love. What do you say we give all three of Them another one of those great big bear hugs right now if we can recall instances when They came through for us. No matter how we feel, God tells us to commit ourselves to Him and resist the devil. And when we strive to get closer to Him, He reciprocates. That's good news! How's your faith? God can heal it and make it well and healthy. Let's look at faith a little more. Omnipresence, faith, and love need to be our constant companions.

Here is how we can change and give our hearts a total turn-around. Listen to these words God gave Paul. *"But without faith it is impossible to please him: for he that cometh to God must believe that he is,"* most of us believe that, *"and that he is a rewarder of them that diligently seek him" (Heb. 11:6).* Most of us believe that, too. God also says, *"Seek ye first the kingdom of God, and his righteousness; and all these things shall be added unto you" (Matt. 6:33).* So! Faith only comes to us through hearing about God's love for us. That means it is extremely necessary for us to read or listen to someone else read the Bible. We need to hear about God's grace. It is the special kind of love God gives sinners. It is undeserved love. That's why it has to be a gift. I want to share an example with you. I know it is a flimsy one. But I think it gives us a good description of grace anyway. It used to be that when a person was late paying a bill, they would give you a ten-day grace period. In other words, they wouldn't charge you late fees until after you had exceeded that period of time. You didn't deserve the grace period, but you got it anyway. We don't deserve God's grace; nevertheless, He gives it to us anyway because He loves us so much.

The Bible also says we are to trust and obey. Trust is none other than the faith we have been talking about. Paul said, *"I am not ashamed of the gospel of Christ:"* Quite often when we are being uppity and feel we don't want to stand up for the gospel of Christ, it is really because we don't want to be made fun of or ridiculed, but often this is because our faith is waning. That's when we need to switch gears and remember the rest of what Paul said: *"For it is the power of God unto salvation to every one that believeth; to the Jew first, and also to the Greek. For therein is the righteousness of God revealed from faith to faith: as it is written, the just shall live by faith"* (Rom. 1:16–17).

But there is a cost for failing to love Him back. *"For the wrath of God is revealed from heaven against all ungodliness and unrighteousness of men, who hold the truth in unrighteousness"* (Rom. 1:18). God accepts us with all of our sins. But! Once we understand what sin is all about and how ugly it is, then we must strive to obey Him. It's so good of God to show us our sins and let us know how ugly sin is and how ugly we are when we are sinning and refusing to obey Him. Here is another verse that tells us what God is like. It says, *"Because that which may be known of God is manifest in them; for God hath shewed it unto them. For the invisible things of Him … are clearly seen, even His eternal power and Godhead; so that they are without excuse: because that, when they knew God, they glorified Him not as God, neither were thankful; … and their foolish heart was darkened"* (Rom. 1:19–21). How sad that we would choose to hang onto our sins. But! Every one of us has sinned and failed to honor God.

> **"**
> *God reads our hearts and knows our thoughts.*
> **"**

God is so patient and kind, always ready to forgive our sins when we ask Him to. He knows our frame (see Ps. 103:14). He is always willing to forgive us and cleanse us from all unrighteousness. So, I want to thank Him and, in thought, grab His hand. You are invited to join me if you so desire.

Dear Father, please help me to stop sinning and knowingly doing wrong. Please forgive me for the sins I have committed and don't know I have and also the ones I know about. Thank You, Lord, for forgiving me. Amen.

A trick Satan uses to get people to steer away from learning what God wants them to do is he whispers, "God can't hold you accountable for something you don't know about." That doesn't work! God reads our hearts and knows our thoughts. He knows if we want to evade an issue. He knows it if we do not want to learn His will. If we choose to put our fingers in our ears, God will hold us accountable. But He will allow us to have just what we want. That's where intercessory prayer from a family member or friend goes a long way. The Holy Spirit will continue to speak to their hearts. Our prayers for someone in that condition are very important.

God's grace gives us time to clean up our act. That is true for all of us, no matter where we are in our relationship with God. God's love is called grace because He accepts us just the way we are—sins and all. But if we don't love Him back or accept His grace, He can't save us. Faith helps us believe He really does love us. *"For by grace are ye saved through faith; and that not of yourselves: it is the gift of God: Not of works, lest any man should boast" (Eph. 2:8–9).* Grace has to be a gift because of our pride. When we begin to feel we are doing good, and we begin boasting and claiming we are obedient because of what WE are doing, our attitude shows others how much danger we are in. Amazing! Even when we think we are good, God says, *"all our righteousnesses are as filthy rags" (Isa. 64:6).* I am awed that God can love someone like me. Faith truly is my safety net. How about you?

Characteristic #4

Omniscience: Only God is Omniscient—Knows All Things

Notice what qualities explain what the word "omniscient" means. According to Merriam-Webster's Collegiate Dictionary 10th Ed., the word "Omniscient" is defined thus: 1: Having infinite awareness, understanding, and insight 2: possessed of universal or complete knowledge." And the word "infinite" is described as 1: extending indefinitely, endless 2: immeasurably or inconceivably great or extensive 3: subject to no limitation or determination 4 a: extending beyond, lying beyond, or being greater than any pre-assigned finite value however large b: extending to infinity c. Characterized by an infinite number of elements."

All three of the Beings who are our God are infinite. They have no limitations or boundaries. They have infinite awareness, understanding, knowledge, and insight. David said, *"Great is our Lord, and of great power: his understanding is infinite" (Ps. 147:5).* They have absolutely no limitations. Their existence is without a beginning, and They will never cease to exist. They are endless, extending into infinity. They are immeasurable in knowledge and understanding; both qualities are complete. They are all-knowing. David lets us know this in such a beautiful way. He tells us some of the wonderful things our omniscient God does. Listen to him! *"The Lord doth build up Jerusalem: He gathereth together the outcasts of Israel" (Ps. 147:2)*

That's God's people—Jew and Gentile—both from Jerusalem and the Gentile areas. *"He healeth the broken in heart, and bindeth up their wounds. He telleth the number of the stars; He calleth them all by their names" (Ps. 147:3-4).* Did you know that? I didn't. Until I read it just now. Isn't that something? Just picture in your mind how many stars there are. And realize God knows each one by its name. Just knowing each one has a name is unbelievable. Yet it's true. But even more astounding is His ability to comfort all of the outcasts of society and bring them to Himself. That's a real miracle. He knows each one's mental pain. Thus, He can heal all of the broken hearts. I'm so glad He knows just how to take care of it at precisely the right time—without force—when we are ready for Him, too.

Micah, the prophet, also tells us Jesus is from everlasting. *"But thou, Bethlehem Ephratah, though thou be little among the thousands of Judah, yet out of thee shall he come forth unto me that is to be ruler in Israel; whose goings forth have been from of old, from everlasting" (Micah 5:2).* Jesus witnessed to the Jewish people and told them He was from everlasting. To them, this meant He was claiming to be God because God alone is everlasting. Jesus said unto them, *"Verily, verily, I say unto you, Before Abraham was, I am" (John 8:58).*

They understood what Jesus was saying. This Bible passage lets us know they were refusing to believe Jesus was God, for when He said to them, *"I am He: before me there was no God formed, neither shall there be after me. I, even I, am the LORD; and beside me there is no saviour" (Isa. 43:10-11)* they reacted adversely. They did not, and a majority of them still do not recognize Jesus as the Messiah. But praise God, there are more and more Jewish people who are believing Jesus is the Messiah.

God is still working with them, just as He is working with us, the Gentiles. He dearly loves all of us. They were misled by the devil, just like all of us are. Notice what they did next. *"Then took they up stones to cast at him: but Jesus hid himself, and went out of the temple, going through the midst of them, and so passed by" (John 8:59).* There is lots more proof that Jesus and His Father are omniscient. I hope you have a happy learning session all by yourself as you locate more proof texts on this subject. For starters, look in the Bible where God told Jeremiah and Isaiah about it: see Jeremiah 1:5 and Isaiah 44:2. There are many instances where the Bible writers show us Jesus is all-knowing. Here is one more for your list. Jesus was talking to the Jews. He knew which of them believed what He told them and which ones did not (See John 6:49–64). Then He said to them, *"But there are some of you that believe not. For Jesus knew from the beginning who they were that believed not, and who should betray him. And He said, Therefore said I unto you, that no man can come to me, except it were given unto him of my Father" (John 6:64–65).* Yes! Jesus definitely was omniscient. He knew their very thoughts.

Characteristic #5

Immortality: Only God is Immortal—Has No Beginning or End

The dictionary says the word "immortal" is described thus: 1. Exempt from death < the gods > 2. Exempt from oblivion: imperishable < fame >. 3. Connected with or relating to immortality. Immortality: the quality or state of being immortal. a. unending existence b. lasting fame." Eternal life, such as God has, is very puzzling to us. It is something we can't understand. Perhaps when we get to heaven, God will give us understanding of it. Wouldn't that be super! He has many wonders in store for us. The unknown just gives us things to think about and contemplate. He says, *"But as it is written, Eye hath not seen, nor ear heard, neither have entered into the heart of man, the things which God hath prepared for them that love him" (1 Cor. 2:9).*

When you love someone, you want to give them things they like. God loves us. He has magnificent gifts prepared for us. But as for me, I will be extremely happy just not having the negative things of this world, such as hatred, killing, sickness, and the list goes on. That will be heaven for me, and seeing God will top them all!

The prophet Isaiah said concerning Jesus, *"Of the increase of His government and peace there shall be no end, upon the throne of David, and upon his kingdom, to order it, and establish with judgment and with justice from henceforth even for ever" (Isa. 9:7).* Jesus was immortal, but He became mortal and subject to death while He was down here. Why? So He could pay for our sins! He chose to be mortal for the suffering of death. That is the type of death He died for us! What a gift. It is the gift of gifts! And when the battle with Satan is over, and everyone has made their choice, we will experience these eternal things. Look how Paul described Jesus' most expensive gift. It's the blessed hope. And all who love God are looking forward to it. He says, *"Behold, I shew you a mystery; we shall not all sleep, but we shall all be changed, In a moment, in the twinkling of an eye."* When? Why? It is when Jesus comes to earth to raise those who are dead to life so that He can take them to heaven with Him. *"At the last trump: for the trumpet shall sound, and the dead shall be raised incorruptible, and we shall be changed (1 Cor. 15:51–52). God says, "This mortal must put on immortality" (1 Cor. 15:54).*

We will become immortal quickly, like the blink of an eye, when Jesus comes to earth the second time. The first time He came as a baby in a manger. The second time He will come as our glorious king. Isn't that exciting? If we love Him, He will raise us to life and take us on that exciting trip He has promised us. It can't get better than that! Then, we, too, will be immortal. Hoo-ray!

Timothy tells us,

But thou, O man of God, flee these things; and follow after righteousness, godliness, faith, love, patience, meekness. Fight the good fight of faith, lay hold on eternal life, whereunto thou art also called, and hast professed a good profession before many witnesses. I give thee charge in the sight of God, who quickeneth all things, and before Christ Jesus, who before Pontius Pilate witnessed a good confession; That thou keep this commandment without spot, unrebukeable, until the appearing of our Lord Jesus Christ: Which in His times He shall shew who is the blessed and only Potentate, the King of kings, and Lord of lords; Who only hath immortality, dwelling in the light which no man can approach unto; whom no man hath seen, nor can see: to whom be honour and power everlasting. Amen. (1 Tim. 6:11–16)

This is talking about all three of Them.

He tells us to have faith in Him, and He lets us know that even though we belong to Him, we will continue to have affliction until He comes to take us home with Him. We won't have an easy road, but we will win in the end and stay true to Him **if** we trust Him. Here are His words. He tells us our suffering helps perfect us.

After Saul was blinded by the brightness of Jesus' glory, Jesus told Ananias to go talk with him. Then Saul *"heard a voice saying unto him, Saul, Saul, why persecutest thou me? And he said, Who art thou, Lord? And the Lord said, I am Jesus whom thou persecutest: it is hard for thee to kick against the pricks" (Acts 9:4–5).* Then Jesus gave Ananias a vision and told him to go and talk to Paul. Jesus said to Ananias, *"I will shew him how great things he must suffer for my name's sake" (Acts 9:16).*

And here is Paul's testimony when he appeared before King Agrippa.

I said, Who art thou, Lord? And he said, I am Jesus whom thou persecutest. But rise, and stand upon thy feet: for I have appeared unto thee for this purpose, to make thee a minister and a witness both of these things which thou hast seen, and of those things in the which I will appear unto thee; Delivering thee from the people, and from the Gentiles, unto whom now I send thee, To open their eyes, and to turn them from darkness to light, and from the power of Satan unto God, that they may receive forgiveness of sins, and inheritance among them which are sanctified by faith that is in Me. (Acts 26:15–18)

What a beautiful mission. What a closeness Paul had with Jesus. He will be with us, too, when we go through trials because we are witnessing for Him, just as Jesus' Father was with Him. What we will go through is like cat's play compared to what Jesus went through to make our salvation possible. The Bible says we are to walk in Jesus' footsteps. Just look at what He went through to make salvation possible for us. There is no way anything I do for Him could ever be even a faint shadow of what He has done for me. He gives each one of us a measure of faith *"according as God hath dealt to every man the measure of faith" (Rom. 12:3)*. Since it says "the measure," I believe every person receives the same amount. That certainly sounds like our fair, honest God. What love God has for all created beings. It's not His choice to destroy any of them.

> **"**
> **The Bible says we are to walk in Jesus' footsteps.**
> **"**

6

Our Faith Tells God We Love Him—People Who Had Great Faith

Two more words for love are grace and faith. What is faith? It is total trust in God. We really can't truly know Him without understanding what grace and faith are all about. My Bible tells me God's love is—

Indescribably Wonderful and Marvelous!

Are you aware, do you know, that *"the very hairs of your head are all numbered" (Matt. 10:30)*? And do you know He says to us to each one of us, *"Behold, I have graven thee upon the palms of my hands; thy walls are continually before me" (Isa. 49:16)*. Now, that's amazing love. So, what is faith? It is total trust in God and in His Word—the Bible. God wrote the Bible, so we would have a guidebook to follow. We are free to accept it or reject it. But, if we love Jesus and want to be in heaven with Him someday, it is imperative that we accept and use it. Below is a list of the most important parts of some verses about faith and God's grace. These two gifts are what produce love in the human heart, and studying the Bible plays a huge role in helping us learn about God's grace and faith. What gifts they are! We cannot be a child of God without loving Them and trusting Them. These two gifts, grace and faith, work together and uphold each other. So! It is my prayer, dear brother and sister, that each of us, myself included, will totally do what this Bible verse guides us to do. *"Trust in the LORD with all thine heart; And lean not unto thine own understanding. In all thy ways acknowledge him, and he shall direct thy paths. Be not wise in thine own eyes: Fear the LORD, and depart from evil. It shall be health to thy navel, and marrow to thy bones (Prov. 3:5-8).* When we talk about fearing God, it is about being afraid we will hurt Him by not loving Him. He loves us so much. Just consider how much They love us as you read the next verse.

Grace is an example of perfect love—the kind of love only God can give. And faith is total belief and trust in God, the One who loves us so much. *"God saw that the wickedness of man was great in the earth, and that every imagination of the thoughts of his heart were only evil continually. And it repented the LORD that He had made man on the earth, and it grieved Him at His heart" (Gen. 6:5–6).* Why wouldn't it grieve Him? He is a lover. It is His nature to love. He knew the future that lay ahead. He knew everything. And God created mankind anyway. Just look what He has done and is still doing for people even though the majority of them spurn His love.

The Bible exposes all the hatred and jealousy that has gone into why God had to come to that decision. So let's look at God's solution to the sin problem at that time in history! *"And the LORD said, I will destroy man whom I have created from the face of the earth; both man, and beast, and creeping thing, and the fowls of the air; for it repenteth Me that I have made them" (Gen. 6:7).* Yes! Just look how grieved God was that He had made mankind, and all because it hurt Him so much to see people being hurt. God cannot stand grief, sorrow, and anger, fear, greed, and the get-even spirit of sin. The very next verse shows us the extreme love God had for those wicked people. He never stopped loving them! But! You might say sin made God sick at heart! Then the one who wrote the Bible said, *"But Noah found grace in the eyes of the LORD" (Gen. 6:8).* WOW! This makes me think He was sick at heart because of what would happen as a result of sin clear down to the end of time. Yes, He could see it all.

God was sick because of all the evil the devil was going to cause. I'm sure He was more sick than any human would or could ever be. But He loved the evil-doers just the same. Doesn't that blow your mind? It does mine. But, He knew it had to be that way! God didn't like doing what He had to do, but He knew if He refused to create Lucifer and others so they could not sin, there would be no freedom of choice, ever. Humanly speaking, it truly was a heartbreaking road for the Lover of all mankind. God always does the right thing, no matter how painful it is. What a lover He is! How blessed we are because, in the end, all who choose to love God will be glad God did things the way He did. We will see and understand God's love better than we ever could have had He not done so. Come! Let's look at God's character of love.

Why is love another word for grace? Because real love is a love we don't deserve. It was the kind Noah saw in God's eyes. It's called grace. There is only one thing we can do that causes God to pull away from us. And that is, "choose." Yes! That's the action! We can choose to reject

God's love. How awful that we would do such a thing. Have you ever really loved someone and they refused to love you back. Remember how much it hurt! God experiences it all of the time. Oh, how He hurts. And just think! He still loves them, even though they have rejected Him. He never stops loving them. But He can't still love them and also accept their evil ways. God knows their rejection will lead them away from Him. Spending no time with Him severs the relation.

Noah knew God very intimately, or he wouldn't have perceived His grace. That love in God's eyes gave Noah the faith he needed to do what God asked him to do. Yes, faith that God would see him through and accept him gave Noah the strength to go through those one hundred and twenty years of dealing with the taunting and persecution those people dished out. In that one look, Noah saw that God wanted to save humanity, even though mankind was rotten to the core. Noah was God's man. He truly was the only man available for God to use in helping Him save the human race. And I just know within my heart that God was thrilled. All of us like to be loved, especially our God does. The kind of love called grace is for wicked people who need a grace period. It's a kind of love that will accept any wicked person who is willing to change their evil ways and turn around and run into the arms of God for help. Oh, that each of us would do that when we are heckled by someone who needs a closer walk with God. Each one of us has walked in the heckler's shoes. God help us!

So, that's where faith comes in. To make that kind of love grow, it must be bolstered by faith. The Bible says faith is total trust in God. When someone really does believe God loves them that much and that God will do what He says He will do, that's called faith. We don't have that kind of trust on our own. It has to be given to us. And God freely gives faith to all who will accept it. That's right! All we have to do is accept it. It only comes through God's great love for the human family. Every last one of us can have that kind of trust, that faith. When we accept it, we are telling God we love Him. Then He says, *"Freely ye have received, freely give"* *(Matt.10:8)*. In other words, He tells us to pass the faith on. We are so blessed that He willingly accepts our loving trust.

If the grace hadn't been there, Noah wouldn't have seen it! I'm so glad it was there for Noah to see. It tells us volumes about our God. What God did next verifies that grace is love. He gave those people mega time to change their ways. But they did not believe what Noah told them about God. They refused to change their ways! God didn't really want to destroy them. He was doing something very difficult for Him to do. It was God's love (grace) that saved those eight people who believed Him. Here are a few examples of people who have had total faith in Him.

The woman with an issue of blood

> *And, behold, a woman with an issue of blood twelve years, came behind Him, and touched the hem of his garment; for she said within herself, If I may but touch His garment, I shall be made whole. Jesus turned him about, and when he saw her, he said, Daughter, be of good comfort; Thy faith hath made thee whole. And the woman was made whole from that hour. (Matt. 9:20–22)* That trust is the reason Jesus could make her whole.

The centurion who had a sick servant with palsy

(In this story it was not the faith of the person who was sick, it was the faith of the one who had a sick servant) The centurion said:

> *"Lord, I am not worthy that thou shouldest come under my roof: but speak the word only, and my servant shall be healed." (Matt. 8:8)*
>
> *When Jesus heard it, he marvelled, and said to them that followed, Verily I say unto you, I have not found so great faith, no, not in Israel. (Matt. 8:10)*
>
> *And Jesus said unto the centurion, Go thy way; and as thou hast believed, so be it unto thee. And his servant was healed in the selfsame hour. (Matt. 8:13)*

Noah is another person who totally trusted God.

Let's briefly go back to Noah again. He built the ark God told him to build in a place far away from any water. See how many people you can add to this list! There are many—happy hunting! Faith is our part—grace is God's part—what a lover He is! There is one nasty being who is here on planet earth, who causes us trouble just like he caused Jesus. He is the one who really needs to be exposed. Yes, this book is about exposing Satan's real self. That's a subject the Bible makes very open and clear. We don't want to dwell on his life, but we need to know who he is and how he is impacting our lives today. He will never be in heaven again. Hooray for that! But the bad news is, he is very much here on earth right now. He certainly is alive and well.

Satan is here on Planet Earth. And he is being his old self. But I don't think he will be around much longer. I think his jail sentence will be taking place very soon. All because of selfishness—love of self. Let's talk about how all of the evil in this world came about. It's all about a misuse of a person's freedom of choice. If God had not given Lucifer freedom of choice, He could not have given it to other created beings either. What a wonderful gift God passed on to us. That freedom is the key to everyone's choices. God could have decided not to give freedom of choice to anyone except Himself. But what would it be like if He had decided to do that?

> **" Faith is our part— grace is God's part— what a lover He is! "**

The closest similarity I can come up with is a dictatorship. And no one wants that except the dictator himself. Then there was Lucifer. Yes! Lucifer became the devil—a dictator, if you please. He is the worst dictator there will ever be! Come and see how all of his wickedness came about. But first, we need to look at the background that guided God's decision.

7

The Most Terrible Dilemma ... God's Dilemma That Is!—The High Cost Jesus Paid Is What Provided Us with Freedom of Choice

To answer the question, "Why did God create Lucifer since God knew he would sin and become the devil," is to describe what love is. First of all, love is a choice. Without choice there is no love, as we have already learned. If God had decided to only create beings who could only act exactly as He allowed them to act, then there would not be any freedom of choice. All mankind would have been locked into strict obedience to God's will. They would be nothing but robots with programmed feelings, performing rote obedience. Our loving God would not think of placing all of creation under such a debt of blind control.

All, and I mean ALL of us, have to make choices. But we will never have to make a choice on the same level as God had to make. They, yes, I said They had to choose whether They would create Lucifer and give him freedom of choice. Whenever you give beings that freedom, there is a possibility that they may sin. God says all of us on this earth have sinned. What is sin? God says, "Sin is the transgression of the law" (1 John 3:4). Another word we could use for it is rebellion, the act of refusing to obey God's law. His law is perfect! Yes! His law of love. It is impossible to perfect something which is already perfect. To change it would be to mar it.

Since God knows everything even before it happens, They knew if They created Lucifer with freedom of choice, he would sin and become the devil. But to refrain from creating him would be even worse. Why? If God had refused to create beings without this freedom, He would have become a controlling God. A dictator, if you please! He would have created only those who would totally obey Him. That's total control! That's just not who our God is. His character is love! Love does not control.

He could not and would not fail to be the lover He is. So He created Lucifer. The Bible is a history of the traumatic result of Lucifer's sins. Adam and all of his descendants are paying a high cost for Lucifer's freedom of choice. I am glad I was not the one who had to make that decision. How heart-wrenching it must be for God as He watches Lucifer continue to make his awful choices. The Father knew His Son, Jesus would come up with the right solution. One that would pay the high price of allowing all mankind to choose who they want to obey. What a pair They are! The Father would never have ever forced His Son to die for sinful man. No! He would never have removed Jesus' freedom of choice. The freedom the Father gave His Son was the most awesome gift ever given to anyone. Jesus' payment of dying on the cross for our sins was the only payment that could save us from the second death. Both gifts were awesome, and without the Father's gift, the Son would not have been able to give us His gift of salvation. The best way for us to tell Them thank you is to give Them our loving obedience.

Most people who refuse to accept Jesus' death for their sins will die two times. All of us die when we get old. But those who love Jesus and are still alive when He comes to take us home with Him will never have to die even one time. That's right! And those who are righteous and die before He comes back to earth will be raised to life at His coming. They will come out of their graves and go to heaven that very day along with the living righteous. Thus that group of people will only die one time.

Here is God's glorious picture of that day. He tells us through His prophet Paul: *"But I would not have you to be ignorant, brethren, concerning them which are asleep"* (notice God is talking about them being asleep in death and in the grave), *"that ye sorrow not, even as others who have no hope. For if we believe that Jesus died and rose again, even so them also which sleep in Jesus will God bring with him."* (This is talking about God bringing them back to heaven with Him, not bringing them down from heaven.) Remember! In this verse God has just come down from heaven to wake up the dead who love Jesus.

Then He says, concerning the people who are alive when He comes and watching the righteous dead come up out of their graves, the Bible tells us what they will do too. Here it is!

For this we say unto you by the word of the Lord, that we which are alive and remain unto the coming of the Lord shall not prevent them which are asleep. For the Lord himself shall descend from heaven with a shout, with the voice of the archangel, and with the trump of God: and the dead in Christ shall rise first. (1 Thess. 4:13–16)

In other words, they will rise into the air to meet Jesus in the air when they come out of their graves. That's right! The righteous people who are raised from the dead will be caught up to meet Jesus in the air along with the righteous who are alive. They will be together in the clouds, where Jesus, His Father, and all of the holy angels are.Now, let's think more about what will happen to those people who are alive when He comes. If they are near a cemetery when it takes place, they will see the righteous dead come out of their graves. Won't that be exciting? Paul says, *"Then we which are alive and remain"* [and are standing there near the cemetery] *shall be caught up together with them in the clouds, to meet the Lord in the air: and so shall we ever be with the Lord. Wherefore comfort one another with these words" (1 Thess. 4:17–18).*

I sure like God's take on what happens to our dead loved ones. It is much better than what most people are taught. Now here is what will happen to the wicked who are alive when Jesus comes to take the righteous home to heaven. They are those who have refused to repent of their sins. They refused to change their ways when the Holy Spirit convicted them; they kept disobeying God. They continued to obey the devil. That is why God can't take them home with Him. He would love to take everyone home with Him, but He can't take the disobedient ones home with Him because then we would have to go through these thousands of years of battling sin again. No one wants that, probably not even the sinners *"And then shall that Wicked be revealed, whom the Lord shall consume with the spirit of his mouth, and shall destroy with the brightness of his coming" (2 Thess. 2:8).* This is the first death.

God is always fair. Jesus' payment for our sins exceeds the fairness list. What love Jesus had for all mankind. God gave John a picture of what will happen to the devil and his angels too. John tells us about it.

And I saw an angel come down from heaven, having the key to the bottomless pit and a great chain in his hand. And he laid hold on the dragon, that old serpent, which is the Devil, and Satan, and bound him a thousand years, And cast him into the bottomless pit, and shut him up, and set a seal upon him, that he should deceive the nations no more, till the thousand years should be fulfilled: and after that he must be loosed a little season. (Rev. 20:1–3)

He and his angels will be awaiting their sentence. They will be in jail down here for a thousand years. The reason I call it jail is because they will have no one to tempt. In my mind's eye, I can just see them bickering, fighting, and playing the blame game. But each really one has no one to blame except himself. I am sure there will be many pity parties and blaming sessions.

The people who have chosen to spurn God's love are *"that Wicked"* who are destroyed *"with the brightness of His coming: Even him, whose coming is after the working of Satan with all power and signs and lying wonders. And with all deceivableness of unrighteousness in them that perish; because they received not the love of the truth, that they might be saved. And for this cause God shall send them strong delusion, that they should believe a lie"* (2 Thess. 2:8–11). Why will God do this? *"That they all might be damned who believed not the truth, but had pleasure in unrighteousness"* (2 Thess. 2:12). They will be dead during this one-thousand-year time. That fact is what makes this earth like a prison for the devil and his angels. They will be all by themselves. No one to tempt!

A beast in the Bible represents a political power. There are many beasts. Satan is the ruler of this world. Not because God gave it to him, but because mankind obeyed him and forfeited their home to him. Eve gave her allegiance to him in the Garden of Eden. Thus he holds the worship and political power of this world to a degree. Of course, he could have nothing if God did not allow it. But God values true love, not control. Jesus backs this claim up through a conversation the devil had with Him.

> **66**
>
> *Satan is the ruler of this world. Not because God gave it to him, but because mankind obeyed him and forfeited their home to him.*
>
> **99**

Do you remember how severely the devil tempted Him in the wilderness to turn a stone into bread? What the devil was trying to do was get Jesus to worship him. Jesus was there for forty days before the devil did this. That's a very long time to go without food. Jesus was very compromised. We could say He was starving to death. That's most likely how He felt. But notice what the devil was really doing. *"The devil said unto him, If thou be the Son of God, command this stone that it be made bread"* (Luke 4:3, emphasis supplied). That's right; he was egging Jesus to prove He was the Son of God. He knew who Jesus was. He was just taking advantage of His weakness from lack of food. He does that to us too. He has a lot of tricks up his sleeve.

What did the devil really want? Watch and listen! Next, he took Jesus up into a high mountain and *"shewed unto him all the kingdoms of the world in a moment of time" (Luke 4:5)*. Also note! He did not give Jesus time to think! He was pushing Him to make a quick decision. He didn't want Him to think things through. He does that to us, too. What did he do next? Just listen to his bragging and lying. Jesus cut the devil's remarks to the core. He knew what Satan was really after. Listen to what Jesus said to him. *"Get thee behind me, Satan: for it is written, Thou shalt worship the Lord thy God, and him only shalt thou serve" (Luke 4:8)*. Yes, Jesus knew what Satan was demanding. He wanted Jesus to worship him.

But the devil didn't stop his heckling of Him even then! What he really wanted was to get rid of Jesus. And he could see that his tricks were not working. He must have been getting very desperate; because *"he brought him to Jerusalem,"* (Notice that he kept repeating the word "if." It is a tiny word with huge ramifications. Its main function is to spread doubt.)*"and set him [Jesus] on a pinnacle of the temple."* If that had been me, I would have been scared to death. Just listen to what he told Jesus to do. *"And said unto him,* **If** *thou be the Son of God, cast thyself down from hence: For it is written, He shall give his angels charge over thee, to keep thee: And in their hands they shall bear thee up, lest at any time thou dash thy foot against a stone" (Luke 4:9–12, emphasis supplied)*. He often tempts us to destroy ourselves too. God does not protect us from being killed when we deliberately disobey Him. In that case it would have been presumptuous for Jesus to cast himself down. Look up Psalm 19:12–13 and 2 Peter 2:10–22. Those verses tell very well what that word means.

And yes! It is Satan at the helm when people have suicidal thoughts. If Jesus had cast Himself down, He would have died as any human being does. That's what the devil was banking on. The devil knew Jesus had come to earth in human flesh so that He could feel our hurts and frailties. God sent Jesus to earth this way so Satan couldn't point his finger at God and say, "The test wasn't fair! Jesus could not have any help that we don't have." Otherwise, Satan could claim we had an advantage he didn't have. He is the one who causes all of the problems in this world. He is the one who makes us sick. All sickness is ultimately caused by him.

Remember! It began in the Garden of Eden when he enticed Eve to disobey God. His first lie to her was about food and slandering God, calling Him a liar. Do you realize that it was Jesus who created our world?

Look up Ephesians 3:9. The devil's first lie on earth was also about food, slandering God, and calling Him a liar. He appeared to Eve in the form of a serpent and contradicted Jesus and told her she would not die.

The devil even taunted Jesus when he was on the cross. He used one of the other men who was crucified that day to cause Jesus mental pain. Listen to him. Read Luke 23:32–33. Just look what Jesus did, even in His agonizing pain! He said, *"Father, forgive them; for they know not what they do" (Luke* 23:34). It makes me feel like crying when I read it, and at the same time, my heart bursts with love for Jesus who died for me.

Look what else they did, along with what the religious leaders did to Him. *"they parted his raiment,"* (Luke 23:34, last part). *"The rulers also with them derided him, saying, He saved others; let him save himself, if he be Christ, the chosen of God" (Luke 23:35, emphasis supplied).* Oh, how their taunting must have hurt Him. Especially the "if." I am sure the devil tried to make Jesus feel like no one believed or loved Him. I am so glad He had such a good relationship with His heavenly Father. *"And at the ninth hour Jesus cried with a loud voice, saying, Eloi, Eloi, lama sabachthani? which is, being interpreted, My God, my God, why hast thou forsaken me?" (Mark 15:34). "And Jesus cried with a loud voice, and gave up the ghost" (Mark 15:37).* Oh, how my heart agonizes for the pain He willingly went through for you and me. What a lover He was and still is. What a high cost He paid for our freedom to choose Him as our Lord, Master, and wonderful friend.

We, too, may be taunted and persecuted for our faith in Jesus. The knowledge of our God's presence may be shrouded from us in our hour of temptation. We do well to remember what Jesus went through for us. Who knows but that our allegiance to God may help someone break from their infatuation with sin at a last moment in their life. Jesus' Father did not desert Him, and He won't desert us in our hour of trial either. But the devil may be screaming his lies into our ears just as he screamed them into Jesus' ears. God will be with us. It is then that we need to say to Satan, as Jesus did to Peter when Satan was tempting Peter. Jesus knew Peter's fear was getting in his way and causing him to rebuke Jesus. He knew Peter loved him. So Jesus said to him, *"Get thee behind me, Satan: thou art an offence unto me: for thou savourest not the things that be of God, but those that be of men" (Matt.16:23).* Jesus will know our heart too, and that we love Him. The Bible also gives us these encouraging words. They show us why Jesus had to be tempted so terribly and what the Holy Spirit did for those who were watching His crucifixion that day. *"And when the centurion, which stood over against him, saw that he so cried out, and gave up the ghost, he said,* **Truly this man was the Son of God***" (Mark 15:39, emphasis supplied).* Doesn't that make your heart well up with gratitude and love for what Jesus did for us? It tells us Jesus felt forsaken, just as we may feel in the time of trouble that will come on the earth just before Jesus and His Father come to take us home with them.

Jesus had to experience what we will experience from the devil. Oh, how wonderful it is that Jesus was willing to do this for us. We can never say thank you enough. What wonderful gifts of love He gave us. Those who love God will go to heaven with Them when They come to get us. God tells us what it will be like when They come to take us home with Them. The Bible says, *"Behold, he cometh with clouds;* [I believe those clouds are clouds of angels] *and every eye shall see him, and they also which pierced him"* (Rev. 1:7). I would sure hate to be one of those men who crucified Jesus.

You see, when Jesus went back to heaven, while His disciples watched, an angel said these words to them: *"And when he had spoken these things, while they beheld, he was taken up; and a cloud received him out of their sight. And while they looked steadfastly toward heaven as he went up, behold, two men stood by them in white apparel; Which also said, Ye men Galilee, why stand ye gazing up into heaven? This same Jesus, … shall so come in like manner as ye have seen him go into heaven"* (Acts 1:9–11). And Matthew says, *"When the Son of man shall come in his glory, and all the holy angels with him, then shall he sit upon the throne of his glory"* (Matt. 25:31). We can't even imagine how glorious it will be. Its beauty will be breathtaking. But! The scene will be so brilliant the wicked will be *"destroyed at the brightness of his coming"* (2 Thess. 2:8).

Do you remember what just one angel did to the guards at Jesus' tomb? An angel came from heaven to Jesus' tomb that Sunday morning. This story shows us the brightness of just one angel. Listen to Matthew's report.

> *In the end of the sabbath, as it began to dawn toward the first day of the week, came Mary Magdalene and the other Mary to see the sepulcher. And, behold, there was a great earthquake: for the angel of the Lord descended from heaven, and came and rolled back the stone from the door, and sat upon it. His countenance was like lightning, and his raiment white as snow: And for fear of him the keepers did shake, and became as dead men. (Matt. 28:1–4)*

Now, that's mighty power! That is the brightest light any of us has ever seen. Lightning is a piercing white light. And this was only one angel. Jesus is coming to earth with all the holy angels with Him. WOW!

Do you realize there will be people who will be raised to life just to see Him come? In fact, there will be more than one, but I believe looking at just one will suffice us. When you read it, notice who else failed to stay near Jesus when He was being tormented by His enemies. That, too, must have greatly hurt him.

> *In that same hour said Jesus to the multitudes, Are ye come out as against a thief with swords and staves for to take me? I sat daily with you teaching in the temple, and ye laid no hold on me. But all this was done, that the scriptures of the prophets might be fulfilled. Then **all** the disciples forsook him, and fled. And they that had laid hold on Je'-sus led him away to Caiaphas the high priest, where the scribes and the elders were assembled. But Peter followed him afar off unto the high priest's palace, and went in, and sat with the servants, to see the end. Now the chief priests, and elders, and all the council, sought false witness against Jesus, to put him to death; But found none: yea, though many false witnesses came, yet found they none. At the last came two false witnesses, And said, This fellow said, I am able to destroy the temple of God, and to build it in three days. [Jesus was* talking about His body temple; but they did not understand] *And the high priest arose, and said unto him, Answereth thou nothing? What is it which these witness against thee? But Jesus held his peace, And the high priest answered and said unto him, I adjure thee by the living God, that thou tell us whether thou be the Christ, the Son of God. Jesus saith unto him, Thou hast said: nevertheless I say unto you, **Hereafter shall ye see the Son of man sitting on the right hand of power, and coming in the clouds of heaven.** (Matt. 26:55–64, emphasis supplied)* Clouds of angels!

This is confirmation from Jesus that Caiaphas will be raised from the dead to see Jesus come in the clouds of heaven and all the holy angels of heaven with Jesus. Certainly, it will be very frightening for him. Then God gave John a picture of what will be taking place for those who will go home to heaven with God when He comes to wake up the righteous—those who love Him! When we are in heaven for those one thousand years, God will be showing us why friends and loved ones were destroyed at His coming. Yes! God will show us all of the things that will help dry up our tears for them. He will be showing us that it was their choice. God wanted to save them. But they wanted to go their own way. We need to search our own hearts today and ask ourselves whether we are ready. The one we really need to ask is the Holy Spirit. We need to give our all to Jesus, who gave everything to save us. What love it is that Jesus came up with that unique solution.

The Father knew His Son would offer to die for those who would sin. There's that tiny word with huge possibilities. "If" they would follow in Jesus' footsteps, His death would save them! Now it is our turn to choose to love God back or go the easy route. What a choice it is. But it is a choice we must make it. I said "easy," but the path mankind chose is the farthest from the truth, and Satan's path is anything but easy. He will make that choice be the hardest thing we will ever have to do. But! Never forget! The Holy Spirit will be with us every inch of the way. Remember! He says, *"I will **never** leave thee" (Heb. 13:5, emphasis supplied).* Sin is so awful! It materialized extremely fast. Just think how very few generations there are from Adam to Noah. The sixth chapter in the Bible talks about the greatness of man's sin. But just look at the beautiful picture of God Noah gives us. Noah looked into God's eyes, and what did he see? *"Noah found grace in the eyes of the LORD" (Gen. 6:8).* How thrilling it must have been for Noah when he saw that love in God's eyes.

❝

Someday, if we truly love Him, all of us will have the privilege of seeing that love in His eyes.

❞

Someday, if we truly love Him, all of us will have the privilege of seeing that love in His eyes for ourselves. I can just envision the smile He will have on His face and the one we will have on ours, too. We will be ecstatically happy and thankful. Can you imagine yourself sympathizing with the Father and Jesus? I'm looking forward to sitting down with them and asking each one about the agony They went through for mankind. Our hearts will swell with gratitude when we look at the nail prints in Jesus' hands. That will definitely call for another big bear hug. Just knowing that God wouldn't have thought of doing it any other way fills my heart with gratitude. Isn't God's love wonderful? Real love is never pushy, neither is it controlling. No, not ever! Everything God does is done out of pure love. It is so heart-wrenching for Them as They witness the depth of suffering all of us are going through right now! But it's nothing compared to what They went through for us. But for Them, any other choice was unthinkable.

I am grateful that God is willing to put up with Lucifer until he has filled his evil cup to the brim. It's almost full. I'm having a hard time waiting, but I wouldn't have it any other way. I, too, want to wait until every single person has made his or her choice. Don't you? It's worth waiting for! We, too, don't want even one friend or family member to be destroyed if they will come to Jesus when they realize He is waiting for them. Then the final end of all of this evil will come to its permanent end. I can almost hear those trumpets blowing (see Matt. 24:31) and see in my mind's eye our wonderful, compassionate God coming with the glorious clouds of obedient angels. Now that's worth waiting for! The Bible gives us enough information so we can make our own educated choice through faith.

Faith is so wonderfully comforting. You can't totally trust someone until you find out whether they do what they say they will do and always keep their promises! We need that kind of trust in God right now. We can learn to trust Him as we see Him keeping His promises and never making a mistake. He is always truthful. Remember! God never lies. If He did, He would not be a God of love. So what do you say we trust Him and realize why They made the choice They did. It was the best choice possible under the terrible circumstances which They had to choose from. The devil is still very much alive. He shows up around every curve and bend in our road of life. His number of attacks is quickly ramping up. There is more and more cruelty and vengeance each succeeding day. The nightly news is astonishing, as we witness the rights of peaceful, law-abiding people being removed from them. The lying and fraud of all mankind, from the preacher to the president, is unbelievable. Everywhere you turn, there is someone scamming an innocent person. Or aren't they as innocent as it appears? Perhaps those who are scammed are just reaping the consequences of a desire to get rich themselves? Only God knows! People are at their wit's end. They have nothing and get scammed even of their bread and butter. My heart cries out for them. That is why I am writing this book. I want everyone to be aware of the eminence of Jesus' coming to rescue us so they can get ready.

The devil is anxiously waiting for all of the violence to come to an end too, but for very different reasons. He is determined to win in the end. Our Bible tells us he will not win. Praise the Lord! I'm sure Satan is the mastermind behind those fires in California as he destroys people. I can hear God's cries of pain as He allows Satan to fill his cup of sin to overflowing. I know our God is grieved beyond compare as He witnesses the destruction of innocent people. My prayer is that each one has placed him or herself under God's saving grace. If they have, the next thing they will see is Jesus and His Father coming in the clouds of heaven to take them home with Him and end sin forever. What a shout of praise that will bring.

A person's guilt or innocence is something we cannot know—only God can read each heart and mind. Just think how surprised Stephen (see Acts 6:8–15) will be when he sees Saul in heaven, the one who stood by and watched him be stoned for telling the truth. Read Stephen's answer to the high priest as he relates the history of their sins and what they did to him after his honest reply (see Acts 7:1–60). Saul stood by, watching all of this (see Acts 8:1). I sure would like to see that meeting. How about you? It brings a smile to my face, along with a happy giggle right now.

If we place total trust in God and choose to do His will, the Holy Spirit will guide us every step of the way just as He guided Stephen. God gives us this assurance: *"I will never leave thee, nor forsake thee (Heb. 13:5).* Sorry! I couldn't resist using it again. It fits the occasion so well. When Jesus was on the cross, He felt deserted by His Father, but He wasn't. Satan placed those fears in Jesus' heart to cause Him to fail. Someday, we, too, may go through like experiences. God will be there for us, too, as Satan lies to us. All down through the ages, God has been with His people as they made those hard choices. Steven, Paul, and the list goes on. Jesus and His Father are our examples. When Jesus was on earth, His heavenly Father was with Him, even when Jesus didn't feel like He was. We know this because when He was on the cross at the ninth hour, He cried out, *"My God, my God, why hast thou forsaken Me" (Mark 15:34).* And then He died. His Father hadn't forsaken Him! Satan was heckling Jesus and trying to tempt Him to distrust His Father. How sad! Satan wanted Jesus to recant so he could usurp God's kingdom from Him. Praise God, Jesus came through victoriously. Jesus had to experience the pain because Satan will try to make us feel forsaken by God, too. He must feel everything mankind will feel. Otherwise, Satan would scream, "Unfair, unfair, You didn't pay the price." We, too, will have to choose to put God first, under the severest attacks of Satan and unbelieving people.

The Father will be there for us just as He was for His Son. Jesus had to experience every human feeling we will ever feel when Satan tries to cause us to stumble. Just think what the Father must have gone through when Jesus spoke those words! This record of what Jesus went through is designed to give us faith. And look at this. *"Jesus Christ the same yesterday, and to day, and for ever."* God knows our minds. I am so thankful for that. God knows the devil will place doubts in them. I am glad God knows that too. It sets my mind at ease, knowing He is savvy to everything I am going through. Paul, the writer of the book of Hebrews, verifies that Jesus never changes His mind. Jesus is always the same. *"Jesus Christ the same yesterday, and to day, and for ever" (Heb. 13:8).* I believe it! It is a wonderful promise—just what we need. Thank You, Lord.

God! Help us plug our ears and not listen to the devil when he tries to trick us into disobeying You. I ask this for each person who is reading this book. Father, the tests you will allow to come our way will be nothing compared to the choice You, your Son Jesus, and the Holy Spirit had to make. You know it is pure hell for a father to see their child suffer, especially when they have done nothing wrong. Thank You so much for choosing to keep freedom of choice intact. I am so thankful that You hold the life of all humanity in Your hands. Father, forgive me for the times I have accused others of doing the same thing I have done. I think we've all felt that rush of adrenalin we get from the get-even spirit that rushes over us because we think someone has been mean to us. Yes! I have certainly been there and done that. I've felt the lift of Satan's whispered suggestion in my ear, "serves you right," God help me! It is none other than me following Satan in his get-even mode. We've all succumbed to it. Yes, we are all sinners. Not one of us is better than another. I am so ashamed of the times I've willingly allowed Satan to lead me around by the nose. When we are in the throes of such an experience, please send the Holy Spirit to tell us to get down on our knees and thank Jesus for dying for our sins. God, help us all to do that.

What a responsibility Jesus had! But, after all, Jesus is the One who got down in the dust and formed us in His own image. Oh, how glad I am that He was the Creator of all things and that forming us in His image was His crowning act of love. Just think! He was willing to die on the cross to save us. And something just as important is the fact that the Father accepted Jesus' solution to the sin problem. All three of Them faced heartache and are still are facing it. Have you gained enough faith in God to really believe the Bible when it says Jesus formed us in Their image, out of plain, ordinary dirt? Have you really thought about what a miracle that was? It is amazing that God would allow His Son to create us in Their image, let alone from dirt. But stop and think what the result would have been if He hadn't. We would not be looking forward to that glorious trip to heaven. We would not be able to spend eternity with Them. Most of all, we would not have a future with God devoid of sin. What a fabulous gift They are offering us. Now, all who have ever been created know what the result of sin is. That should be enough to make everyone want to stay away from it. I am looking to that day in the near future when all sin and sinners will be destroyed. That's both sad and glad at the same time. That's why we need to pray for one another. And it's why we need to hold tightly onto God's hand. Each of us, in our own way, is striving to know and understand God's will for our life. Isn't it glorious that once this life on this earth is over, those who love God will never choose to sin again?

The only reason there is affliction is because there is freedom of choice. And each of us has chosen to sin. It's that simple. That's what causes affliction. There will be no sin, and thus, no affliction in the earth made new. What a promise! No wonder God was willing to go through all this mess for us. They knew Their gift would delete sin forever. Yeeeaaah! In the new earth, each person will not be vying for supremacy. There will be no more killing, stealing, or mental and physical abuse. No one will have selfish desires to rape or murder someone. These sins are booming right now. No one will want to sin and go back to the horrifying scene we have today. Our world is not the only world God created. We know this is true because of something God said. Listen to Him: *"God, who at sundry times and in divers manners spake in time past unto the fathers by the prophets, Hath in these last days spoken unto us by His Son, whom He hath appointed heir of all things, by whom also He made the worlds" (Heb. 1:1–2)*. We do not know how many worlds God has created. But we do know the beings on those other worlds are watching this dramatic gift of God's love unfold. They know it is Satan who is the troublemaker. The leaders of those other worlds witnessed how ruthless Lucifer was when he met with God at their councils in heaven (see Job 1:6). They, too have freedom to love. I say love because God is displaying to the universe what happens when some love and others refuse to love. The beings on those other worlds will be thoroughly convinced that God truly is love. They will not want to be disloyal to Him. They will know without a trace of doubt that God is love and that freedom of choice is the only safe route. Look what else is perfect. *"The law of the Lord is perfect" (Ps. 19:7)*.

It is freedom of choice that allowed Jesus to pay for the sins of every created being who will ever exist. Can you place yourself in the Father's sandals? Or in Jesus' sandals? What if it were your son who was having this dilemma. Would you be willing to let your son go through what Jesus decided to go through just to create another angel? Jesus told His Father

He was willing to die to pay for our sins. The Father knew what His Son was going to say even before Jesus told Him what He was willing to do. Together They decided Jesus could do this! We are like Them. We were made in Their image. It hasn't been easy for us. And it wasn't easy for Them. Satan is making sure of that! We need to place the blame where it belongs. The devil is to blame for the problem. We are, too, for our part in it.

We are a theatre for all of the unfallen worlds. They are watching what is taking place. They see how damaging sin is. We are their lesson book. This is so everyone can make his or her own choice. God wants them to know just what lack of freedom of choice does and causes. God does this, so nothing like this will ever take place again. What a gift freedom of choice is. Let's look at that wonderful promise. Nahum says to us through the inspiration of God, *"The Lord is good, a strong hold in the day of trouble; and he knoweth them that trust in him. But with an overrunning flood He will make an utter end of the place thereof, and darkness shall pursue His enemies. What do ye imagine against the LORD? He will make an utter end: affliction shall not rise up the second time"* (Nah. 1:7–9).

We are free to love God and live eternally like the other created beings and the holy angels, or we can rebel as Lucifer and Adam and Eve did. The choice is ours. We can go our own selfish way, or we can accept the forever gift of love and peace God is offering us. If we don't make a choice, Satan will choose for us. The devil is always pushing and shoving us to choose his way. We must not give up. He won't! When we feel exhausted from the strain Satan places on us, a good thing to do is read our Bible, pray, and help someone else who needs help. Singing always cheers and comforts me. These measures will take our minds off our own problems. I like to leaf through a songbook. Find a song with words that fit my need, and then ding it out on the piano if it is new to me and then sing it. It lifts my spirits; maybe it will yours, too. If you don't sing, involve someone who likes to sing and knows a lot of songs. You could be a tremendous help to each other. Just tell them why you want to do it. I pray that they will help you. God bless you.

Why in the world would anyone choose to die as a sinner? This life is rough, but when we choose to suffer with Jesus, the end of the battle is wonderful peace and happiness. With the other fearful choice, we will be burned up and face the final judgment for our sins. There's no comparison. We must keep our eyes on the final end, the time when Jesus takes us home with Him. I choose to put God first! God help me! Giving God that bear hug of love is something all who choose to walk in Jesus' footsteps look forward to. Actually, we do that every moment of our life by giving Him first place as each trial comes along. All we have to do is say, "Yes, I will obey Your Law of love." Isn't it wonderful that God's law teaches us how to love? He will be with us every step of the way if we ask Him to. He says, *"Let your conversation be without covetousness; and be content with such things as ye have: . . . So that we may boldly say, the Lord is my helper, and I will not fear what man shall do unto me." (Heb. 13:5-6).* God help us! God is **always** just a prayer away. And what does He tell us? *"Whoso keepeth His Word, in him verily is the love of God perfected: hereby know we that we are in Him" (1 John 2:5).* And Timothy says, *"Study to shew thyself approved unto God, a workman that needeth not to be ashamed, rightly dividing the word of truth" (2 Tim. 2:15).*

When we hold God's hand, we bring the coming of Jesus closer and quicker. He promises us the same thing Jesus promised His disciples the day He left earth to go back to heaven with His Father: *"But ye shall receive power, after that the Holy Ghost is come upon you: and ye shall be witnesses unto Me both in Jerusalem, and in all Judaea, and in Samaria, and unto the uttermost part of the earth" (Acts 1:8).*

Yes, Jesus has paid the debt! It's a done deal. All praise goes to our God. So, now we are telling everyone we can all about His wonderful gift of salvation He offers to each one of us. But He never says it will be easy. It wasn't easy for Jesus, and it won't be easy for us either. But! Never forget—God is always only a prayer away. If God asks us to do something great for Him to help others see His will for them, the Holy Spirit will be with us, just as He was with Daniel in the lion den and Stephen, who was stoned for his faith. That is the Holy Spirit's part of the gift. Yes! Love requires freedom. Love can't exist without it. That's the biggie. And it's huge! Yes, God is free! Free to do whatever He pleases. I am so glad He gave us that marvelous gift through freedom of choice. What a God! What a gift! The freedom He gives us is another way we are like Him, and He wouldn't have it any other way. It is imperative we have it! It is **not** possible for love to exist without it.

If God hadn't given this freedom to all of the beings He created, there wouldn't be a devil. But neither would there be love. I'm sure you have heard the saying: to have friends one must show themselves friendly. Well! For humans to receive love, they must show love. How blessed we are that it's not that way with God's love. Yes, God's love is different. It's abundant and lavish. God's love is the model for all love. It's the kind of love God has for all of His created beings. God is the only Being who is love. That makes Him the originator of it. Yes, love is original with God. Just think what freedom of choice makes possible. It allows a person to be totally devoid of love—a very dangerous situation. Yes, that's what God allows. Why? Because without it, there would be no love at all. When beings do not have freedom, they clamor for it. That produces chaos and resentment.

It takes only one word to describe a total lack of love. It's called **"selfishness."** The Bible tells us who that selfish being is. His name was *"Lucifer, son of the morning" (Isa. 14:12)*. We need to stop right there. When I first looked at this verse, I thought Lucifer couldn't possibly be a son of God. But you know what! I ran into this verse, which says, *"That the sons of God saw the daughters of men that they were fair; and they took them wives of all which they chose. And the LORD said, My spirit shall not always strive with man" (Gen. 6:2–3).*

> **"**
> *God's Word alone should be our guide.*
> **"**

Did you notice that these sons of God, and also Lucifer, were recorded in the Bible with a lower case "s"? Denoting that none of them were like God's true Son—Jesus. There's a huge difference. Lucifer, just like us— is only a created being. There are at least two denominations that claim that Lucifer is a true son of God. I am not even going to print the word "son" with a capital "s" because I consider that to be blasphemy when it is speaking of the devil. They think of him as a true son of God spelled with a capital S. How sad! We need to pray for them and love them. The Holy Spirit can reach them. Perhaps our love can help them, too. But we must not get involved with the lies they believe. It is easy to get sucked into the workings of Satan. Rather, we must not do as they do but do what God does. The difference is, they do not know the truth. They are not taught to use the King James and other unpolluted Bibles. I believe the book they read is different. The majority of them may be innocent of their sin. They may not have grasped the truth yet. I am writing this book to help people's eyes to be opened, and God alone is able to open the eyes of their understanding. The truth is in God's Word, the Bible.

That truth is the only thing that can free people from the lies of Satan. God's Word alone should be our guide. They need to get a version that has not been tampered with by some church. The King James Version is one of the good ones, for it has not been changed. There are many good people being led astray by the devil through the many antichrists. All of us have been led the wrong way at some time in our life. God loves all of us. We need to have the freedom to love Him back. Many people may be innocent and really believe the devil is God's son—spelled with a capital "S." In fact, probably most of the people in those churches sincerely believe this lie. The Holy Spirit can point them to the truth that is in the Bible—God's true Book. I encourage you, dear reader, to ask the Holy Spirit to speak to every person you know who is believing a lie. It was inspired by God via His holy prophets! I am hoping each of you will recognize who I am talking about and check out God's Word. The Word of God is our only true guide. You should check my words out, too. Please pray for me if I have unknowingly written something that is untrue. The Holy Bible truly is inspired by God and written by the prophets.

Lucifer committed blasphemy. In fact, he was the first created being to do that. God says, *"All manner of sin and blasphemy shall be forgiven unto men: but the blasphemy against the Holy Ghost shall not be forgiven unto men" (Matt. 12:31)*. Yes! God would have forgiven Lucifer, the angel, if he had asked to be forgiven and had acknowledged his wrong. Here is the proof that Lucifer was created and that he was an angel. This was Lucifer's sin. He claimed to be God. He was an angel, a created being, just like we are. When the high priest said to Jesus: *"I adjure thee by the living God, that thou tell us whether thou be the Christ, the Son of God" (Matt. 26:63)*. Then Jesus said:

> *"Thou hast said: nevertheless I say unto you, Hereafter shall ye see the San of man sitting on the right hand of power, and coming in the clouds of heaven" (Matt. 26: 64)*. Notice what the high priest did next. *"Then the high priest rent his clothes, saying, He* [Jesus] *hath spoken blasphemy; what further need have we of witnesses"? behold, now ye have heard his blasphemy" (Matt. 26:65)*.

Also, do you recall what Jesus said in Isaiah that before Him, there was no God formed, and there wouldn't be one formed after Him either? Lucifer was definitely not God and not in the same league as Jesus, God's true Son. Yes! Jesus truly is God. Jesus was not a created being. So let's take a closer look at our enemy, Satan. He is the one who causes us to go through such pain. We will talk about him in the next chapter—meet you there. God is being more than fair with him. Come and see why I say that!

8

When God Created Lucifer He "WAS" Perfect

His name was **"Lucifer,"** and that name is only mentioned one time in the Bible. It is the prophet Isaiah who shares it with us. When Isaiah was talking about him, God was already asking Lucifer how come he had fallen from heaven. Here are God's own words. *"How art thou fallen from heaven, O Lucifer, son of the morning! how art thou cut down to the ground, which didst weaken the nations!" (Isa. 14:12).* How sad! This means he had gone to the other worlds and tried to cause them to feel God was unfair. He had a big me and little you attitude! Can you imagine that? It's hard to understand how Lucifer could feel that way. He was comparing himself with the King of the universe! How amazing!

And what was the reason God gave for asking him that question? God knew what Lucifer was doing. Lucifer should have known the holy angels he was fussing to about God, would let God know what was going on. Lucifer was looking for brownie points, striving to rile up the other angels against God. So our God of love brought it out in the open so that it could be taken care of. God worked with Lucifer long and hard to get him to see his wrong. He needed to protect His other holy angels, too. So He let Lucifer know He knew what he was doing. And through Isaiah, God let us know what took place so that we could be protected from his anarchy, too. He was striving to wrest the kingdom from God. It is utterly amazing how God took care of it. Here is what God said to Lucifer. *"For thou hast said in thine heart, I will ascend into heaven, I will exalt my throne above the stars of God: I will sit also upon the mount of the congregation, in the sides of the north: I will ascend above the heights of the clouds; I will be like the most High" (Isa. 14:13–14).*

Lucifer's words were very damning. His ambition was to be like God. But it was not in a good way. He was not seeking to idolize God; he was striving to steal His throne from Him. Lucifer bragged to the other angels that he would be better than God. In fact, his ambitious desire was not just to be like God. Oh, no! His desire was to be God! Then God told him what would happen to him because of his refusal to repent. *"Thou shalt be brought down to hell, to the sides of the pit" (Isa. 14:15).* I'm sure he understood what hell was, for God always makes things plain. And then we hear God mourning. Can you hear the hurt in God's voice as He says to Lucifer, *"Thou wast perfect in thy ways from the day that thou wast created, till iniquity was found in thee" (Ezek. 28:15).* God is saying, I did everything I could to give you what you want. What more could I have given you and still be a loving God? The answer is—nothing. The only thing Lucifer wanted was to be God.

He became a god, all right. And what a god he is. A god of his own making—straight from hell. Yes, Lucifer was a created being. He was only an angel, a created being. And, of course, he was perfect when God created him. Everything God creates is perfect. Adam and Eve were perfect, too! But there is a huge difference between them and Lucifer. They asked God to forgive them. They were sorry for their sins. Not only that! God gave Lucifer a highly honored position. One where he could see God's character whenever he was at his post of duty. Remember, the Ten Commandments are a transcript of God's character. He made Lucifer one of two angels who guarded His ten-commandment law. The ten-commandment law is the law of all kingdoms except this one. It is supposed to be our law, but many do not obey all of it. That's because people do not realize they are disobeying it. Lucifer was different. He knew he was disobeying the law of God. Our God is so fair. He wanted Lucifer to have every possible opportunity to do what was right. God bent over backward, so to speak, to be sure Lucifer knew He loved him. And God also wanted to be sure Lucifer knew what love was. God did not want there to be any way Lucifer could say he did not know what God expected of him.

Even though God knew Lucifer would **not** obey Him, He showed him mercy. That's just who God is. He's the fairest, most honest Being who has ever lived! Lucifer knew God said that He showed *"mercy unto thousands of them that love me and keep my commandments" (Deut. 5:10).* God wanted to be merciful to Lucifer, too. So that is what God did—He literally showered Lucifer with mercy. Do you know where God's law is kept and displayed for all to see? It resides in His throne room in heaven. The throne of God sits on top of the *"ark of the covenant."* The Ark is the box that holds and protects God's law. It resides in the part of the tabernacle that is called the *"Holiest of all" (Heb. 9:3).* And God calls His Throne, *"the mercy seat" (Exod. 25:21).* Isn't He some God? He did not want Lucifer to be lost. Oh, how it must have hurt Him since He knew what Lucifer would do. God gave the children of Israel instructions, too, telling them just how He wanted them to build His sanctuary on earth. It was a copy of the one in heaven. This word picture of God's throne room gives us the privilege of knowing how fair God was to Lucifer. He had the privilege of knowing what God's law said, backward and forward.

God instructed the Israelites to make a replica of His tabernacle down here. It was to look just like the one in heaven. He wants us to know all about His law, where it resides, and how important it is. Here are the instructions God gave his people. God said, *"And thou shalt put the mercy seat above upon the ark; and in the ark thou shalt put the testimony that I shall give thee" (Exod. 25:21).* Testimony is another name for God's ten-commandment law. Those are the laws of God's government. Just think how understandable God makes things for all beings. We have thousands of laws, but God only had ten. All of our laws fit under the category of the Ten Commandments. There were two cherubim who guarded the ten-commandment law of God. Lucifer was one of those cherubs. The Lord says so! It was Jesus who placed Lucifer in that position. He did it with the agreement of the Father, of course. Listen as Jesus talks to Lucifer! He says, *"Thou art the anointed cherub that covereth; and I have set thee so" (Ezek. 28:14).*

> **When God created Lucifer, he was perfect.**

What did the cherubs who guarded God's law do? The Bible says, *"And the cherubim shall stretch forth their wings on high, covering the mercy seat with their wings, and their faces shall look one to another; toward the mercy seat ... above upon the ark; and in the ark thou shalt put the testimony that I shall give thee" (Exod. 25:20–21).* Hear the grieving voice of Jesus saying, *"Thou wast upon the mountain of God; thou hast walked up and down in the midst of the stones of fire" (Ezek. 28:14).* Let's see what took place at the throne of God! Moses met with God at the throne God had them build down here. In looking at the throne room down here, we can more easily visualize what took place at God's throne in heaven. God told Moses down here, *"And there I will meet with thee, and I will commune with thee from above the mercy seat, from between the two cherubim which are upon the ark of the testimony, of all things which I will give thee in commandment unto the children of Israel" (Exod. 25:22).*

God verifies that Lucifer was given that prized position in God's throne room in heaven. Here are God's own words to him. *"Thou art the anointed cherub that covereth; and I have set thee so: thou wast upon the holy mountain of God; thou hast walked up and down in the midst of the stones of fire"* *(Ezek. 28:14).* And yes again! When God created Lucifer, he was perfect. You can read about it in Ezekiel chapter twenty-eight. Enjoy! It is very eye-opening! I guarantee you will enjoy reading it. When Ezekiel talked about Lucifer's perfect beauty, he was talking both about the beauty of his covering and his brightness. He was fabulously beautiful. But he allowed his beauty to go to his head and make him proud. We know this because God said to him: *"Thine heart was lifted up because of thy beauty, thou hast corrupted thy wisdom by reason of thy brightness"* *(Ezek. 28:17).* Finally, God said to him, "Thou hast sinned: therefore I will cast thee as profane out of the mountain of God: and I will destroy thee, O covering cherub, from the midst of the stones of fire" (Ezek. 28:16). But this did not happen overnight. Now, are you ready to hear what happened next?

9

Lucifer's Attacks on God

Attack #1 The Devil Called Jesus a Liar (Lucifer—The First Antichrist)

The words antichrist and antichrists are only mentioned in the Bible five times. Here they are: 1 John 2:18; 1 John 2:22; 1 John 4:3; and 2 John 1:7. (it is mentioned two times in 1 John 2:18). John tells us there are many antichrists. He said, *"it is the last time."* He was talking partly about his own day because he said, *"even now are there are many antichrists; whereby we know that it is the last time" (1 John 2:18).* John began that same verse by saying, *"It is the last time: and as ye have heard that antichrist shall come."* That's not so long after Jesus was here on earth. John was the one who often said, "that disciple Jesus loved." He was talking about himself. They had a very close relationship. They thought antichrist was alive and well in their day. And truly, he was. They called anyone who was against Christ—antichrist. It's true to a different degree. But as we continue, we will realize how specific the real antichrists are.

Here is another clue about who antichrist is and what he is like. *"And every spirit that confesseth not that Jesus Christ is come in the flesh is not of God: and this is that spirit of antichrist, whereof ye have heard that it should come; and even now already is in the world" (1 John 4:3).* Then John repeats it, probably for emphasis. *"For many deceivers are entered into the world, who confess not that Jesus Christ is come in the flesh. This is a deceiver and an antichrist" (2 John 1:7).* All antichrists walk in the devil's footprints. He is their master.

Remember, Jesus told the devil he was a liar. In fact, Jesus called the devil the father of lies. And truly, he was the first liar on earth. He is the one who made all this mess. He lied to Eve about God way back in the garden of Eden. Yes! He was the first antichrist. In fact, he was becoming antichrist when he was causing trouble in heaven and when he had a fit

119

because he couldn't be the one to create our world. He is the great, true, blue antichrist. What a title. He should be shaking in his boots about now.

Lucifer was in heaven for a long, long time, doing his dirty work. The Father allowed him to thoroughly show the whole universe his true colors. His jealousy of Jesus steadily grew. Lucifer thought he should be honored just as much as Jesus was. But he was not God's holy Son. He was not "God"—the Son of God, who ruled everywhere and everything with His Father. He thought he should be able to do everything Jesus did. So when Jesus began creating our world, Lucifer pouted and got angry. He thought he should be able to create things, too. He was angry about the injustice he thought the Father was heaping on him. He thought God was being unfair, and it made him angry. Do you notice his thoughts were all me, me, me? I this and I that! He came from heaven to this earth and watched as the Father, His Son, and the Holy Spirit worked as a team to create our world. Yes, right here! Where we live! All three of the Beings, who are our One God, were present and took part in its creation. Since God knows everything, They knew Lucifer was sneaking around and watching Them. Nothing can be hidden from God. He says, *"Mine eyes are upon all their ways: they are not hid from my face, neither is their iniquity hid from mine eyes" (Jer. 16:17).*

Thus! Earth became Lucifer's proving ground. Because of him, no one is safe, especially today. He has had gobs of experience. Can't you just see him, going around tempting all the other angels in heaven who would listen to him—lying about God and telling them God was unfair? A whispering campaign in heaven—if you please. How would you have liked to be the other cherub who guarded God's holy law in heaven? That certainly must have been an uneasy place to work. And just think! Lucifer knew God's law backward and forward. It was right in front of him every single day. He heard God counsel those who came to Him from all of the other worlds.

Jesus tells us Lucifer was the very first liar. That's right! He was the one who fathered the first lie that makes him the father of lies. Listen, as years later, God's Son, Jesus, tells us that! He said to the Jews who were giving Him trouble, *"Ye are of your father the devil, and the lusts of your father ye will do. He was a murderer from the beginning, and abode not in the truth, because there is no truth in him. When he speaketh a lie, he speaketh of His own: for he is a liar, and the father of it" (John 8:44).* Jesus was not against those Jews. He was trying to open their eyes. And lest we, the

Gentiles, get proud, we need to realize we, too, are liars. We are all guilty, every last one of us, of being untruthful.

Many of the Jewish leaders were believing the lies of the devil. We are often victimized by the devil, too. God tells us we all have one Savior and one Father. We are all descendants of Adam and Eve. The whole earth is of one family. But the devil wants us to think God is a liar and that we should follow him—not God. Listen to Malachi as he expounds on this issue. I will include the background for it to help us understand why Malachi said what he did. Remember! He is a prophet of God. What God said, Malachi repeated to the priests. Just as God wanted them to do. Malachi began by saying, *"O ye priests, this commandment is for you"* *(Mal. 2:1)*.

Who gave it to Malachi? It was Jesus, for it says: *"saith the LORD of hosts" (Mal. 2:4)*. That's Jesus, and He was talking to the priests and correcting them through Malachi. He told them: *"But ye are departed out of the way; ye have caused many to stumble at the law; ye have corrupted the covenant of Levi, saith the LORD of hosts. Therefore have I also made you contemptible and base before all the people, according as ye have not kept my ways, but have been partial in the law" (Mal. 2:8–9)*. Then, He, the Lord, asked them, *"Have we not all one father? hath not one God created us?" (Mal: 2:10)*.

We all have one Father. Our Father is God the Father if we accept Him and honor Him by obeying Him. That's why God took Abraham under His wing and coached him. He was a good man. He listened to God and loved Him. God is willing to do that for each of us, too. That is what He wants us to do—obey His Laws. But! It has to be our choice! He will not encroach on our freedom to choose. Thus, the Father chose to have His Son come through Abraham's family line. So Jesus was a little Jewish boy. God loves all of us. Jesus was trying to wake up the Jewish leaders.

The first lie God tells us about in the Bible is when the serpent lied to Eve about God. It was an astonishing lie. God called him a "serpent." In Revelation 12:9, the Bible gives us a whole string of names for the devil. Let's look at them: *"And the great dragon was cast out, that old serpent, called the Devil, and Satan."* That's right! Remember! God considered Lucifer to already be a serpent. Jesus had just finished creating our world and its first inhabitants. Eve was honest and innocent. When the serpent talked to her, she told him the truth. He asked her, "Didn't God say you could not eat from every tree in the garden?" She corrected the serpent and told him there was one tree in the garden that they could not eat from.

And that God said if they ate from it, they would die. *(see Gen. 2:16–17; 3:1–3)*. Yes! He was already the devil before our world was created.

Now notice what the devil did next! He told her God had lied to her. Isn't that amazing? He slandered Jesus and called Him a liar! The liar called the one he was lying about—a liar. May I ask, who would know what a liar was like better than the devil himself? They say, "It takes one to know one." Since he was the one who was lying, that shows us what was uppermost in his mind. It was his purpose to blacken Jesus' name just because he was jealous. The truth is, the serpent was privileged! God had pampered him and done everything He could to honor him and make him feel loved and accepted. And isn't it interesting that he could make himself appear as a serpent? Not very smart, though! He stupidly played right into God's hands. That's what happens to us, too, when we choose to disobey God.

People still believe that same lie today. Yes, the devil is still telling people they won't ever die—that they go to heaven when they die if they are good. That they don't really die. But Jesus didn't go to heaven the day He died. For He said to Mary on the day He rose from the tomb, *"Touch me not; for I am not yet ascended to My Father" (John 20:17)*. He had been in the grave dead for three days. He is our example. We go to the grave when we die, too. We will sleep in death until He comes and wakes us up to take us home with Him at His second coming. We will all go to heaven together. What a joyous trip that will be!

The devil was still telling that same lie to the Jewish people after all those years, and Jesus lets us know it is still a lie. I am so glad to see quite a few Jews seeing the light and understanding that Jesus truly is the promised Redeemer. It is so thrilling to see them accept Him as their Savior. Mentally, I can see all of heaven rejoicing when each person accepts Jesus as their Savior. But Jesus must rejoice exceedingly when His own earthly family accepts Him as their Savior. He must be counting the days when He will see them face to face. He is anxious to throw His arms around them. I'm wondering if His mom will be the first one to meet Him in the clouds. Won't that meeting be exciting to see? Jesus rejoices when the Gentiles come to Him, too. What a wonderful day to look forward to!

The devil never changes. It is his habit to lie. He is stuck in a rut! We must be careful that we do not fall into the ruts he creates. We might not get out, just as Lucifer himself didn't. Now that's scary—but true. He is still contradicting God, telling people God is a liar! So, watch out! Read your Bible for yourself. God is the only One you can trust. He never has and never will lie. He puts up with so much guff from us, just as He did from the deceived Jewish people. Yes, God loves all people. But He doesn't love their sins. He wants us to turn from them as soon as we realize we are sinning. Listen to what God said to Paul when He talked to him about how he was persecuting Him.

> *Saul, Saul, why persecutest thou Me?" (Acts 26:14).* And Paul replied, *"Who art thou, Lord? And he said, I am Jesus whom thou persecutest. But rise, and stand upon thy feet: for I have appeared unto thee for this purpose, to make thee a minister and a witness both of these things which thou hast seen, and of those things in the which I will appear unto thee; Delivering thee from the people, and from the Gentiles, unto whom now I send thee, To open their eyes, and to turn them from darkness to light, and from the power of Satan unto God, that they may receive forgiveness of sins, and inheritance among them which are sanctified by faith that is in Me. (Acts 26:15–18)*

Every last one of us has lied. I'm so glad Jesus paid for our sins at Calvary! I want to know the truth. It comes from God alone. That's why we need to be copycats and walk in Jesus' footsteps. We need to ask the Holy Spirit to guide us. We need to decide in our hearts that we will not do anything that is displeasing to God, and the Holy Spirit will help us. Oh, yes! We will make mistakes! We will fudge on our obedience. But God will forgive us if we are sincerely sorry and turn from our sin. *"If we confess our sins, He is faithful and just to forgive us our sins, and to cleanse us from all unrighteousness" (1 John 1:9).* What a precious gift.

> **" I'm so glad Jesus paid for our sins at Calvary! "**

Then He helps us grow more and more like Him as we strive to obey Him. God loves us and wants us to win the battle over sin.

Satan is always just around the corner with another lie to tell us. *"Then said Jesus to those Jews which believed on him, If ye continue in my word, then are ye my disciples indeed; And ye shall know the truth, and the truth shall make you free" (John 8:31-32).* What a beautiful promise. The Holy Spirit works with us, too, if we ask Him to. Satan certainly had turned a corner. His first lie on earth sank our world. It was a continuation of the lies he had already told in heaven. It has always been his goal to ruin God, slander His holy Name, and hate those who love Him. He wants to get us to follow in his footsteps. He will burn in hell for every sin he caused God's children to commit. Those who do not go to heaven will suffer for their own sins. So the more people he can trick into serving him, the less he will have to burn. That certainly does give him a reason to get us to follow him.

And just think! God still allowed him to go back and forth between heaven and earth till Jesus died on the cross. When He caused the death of Jesus, he cooked his goose; there was no way he could be redeemed. But this did not stop him from continuing his dirty work. His goal, still today, is to ruin God's name and cause God's people as much trouble as he can. You see! He knows when he hurts us, that hurts God terribly. It is mind-boggling that such cruelty would make him happy. Stay away from him and close to God. He gets more sinister every day. He's had lots of practice. God says that someday those who love God will watch God *"cre-ate new heavens and a new earth"* again *(Isa. 65:17).* Won't that be exciting? According to prophecy, it won't be long till Jesus comes to take us to heaven for a thousand years. The devil still has his lip out! His devilish work lets us know why God will soon destroy him. Hoo-ray!

But in the meantime, let's look at the time period when he could still go back and forth between heaven and earth! It will give us a clearer picture of what the devil wanted to gain by his attacks on God and his followers. He was angry with the Father for not making him a Son with equal privileges. But there is no comparison between him and Jesus. Jesus is God—always was and always will be. As we said earlier, Jesus was not created. He has been in existence forever. Lucifer is just a created being—like us. He was so angry with God that he determined in his heart to do everything he could to hurt Them. See you in his next escapade. Come and see how Lucifer hurt God by hurting all of us down through the ages.

10

The First Tragedy on Earth

Attack #2 The Serpent Tempted Eve to Sin (The Serpent Was None Other Than Lucifer in Disguise)

The first command of God recorded in the Bible was given to Adam right after God created him. God never leaves us in the dark about things. He warned and cautioned Adam that there was a sinister being prowling around. Then *"the LORD God* [that's Jesus— He is the Lord] *commanded the man, saying, Of every tree of the garden thou mayest freely eat: But of the tree of the knowledge of good and evil, thou shalt not eat of it: for in the day that thou eatest thereof thou shalt surely die" (Gen. 2:16–17).* Why did God tell Adam and Eve this? Because He knew Lucifer's mindset. He also knew the serpent was going to allow himself to be used by Lucifer. God knew that Lucifer was going to use the serpent to deceive Eve. He had truly become God's enemy—the devil. So God told them what they needed to do to be safe. God was upfront with them. God is never illusive! His words are always honest and upfront. I like that very much! He told Adam what he needed to do to be safe. That certainly was an act of love. It's a good thing because there was a serpent in the garden who would decide to let Lucifer use him. The Bible tells us God did not create a devil. Jesus, talking to this angel and bemoaning his choice to be evil, told Lucifer what would happen to him as a result of his wicked choices. What an amazingly loving God we serve.

God again expressed amazing love when He forbade Adam and Eve to eat from the tree in the center of the garden and told them something terrible would happen to them if they did. That command was given to them because God loved them and did not want them to die. I am so glad we serve a loving God. Just take a moment and stop and think where that love took Jesus our Lord. It took Him to the cross! Now, that is ultimate love. God tells us how we can say thank you for what Jesus did for us.

He says, if we want to say thank you and tell Him we love Him, we will keep His commandments. Lucifer did the opposite. I think now is a good time to take a closer look at what happened to him and study the anatomy of sin. What was sin? And how did it cause him to feel? It was pride and jealousy. For God says, *"For thou hast said in thine heart, I will ascend into heaven, I will exalt my throne above the stars of God: I will sit also upon the mount of the congregation, in the sides of the north: … I will be like the most High" (Isa. 14:13–14).* He wasn't happy about being just a very special angel. He was determined to steal the throne and be exactly like God. Yes, he was determined to be GOD! A thief, and dictator, if you please! But this privilege was not his to have.

Now let's look at how one gets to be the way the devil is. There was a snake in that garden. It obeyed Lucifer. It, too, was not honest! For the first thing God tells us in the Bible about the snake is that *"The serpent was more subtil than any beast of the field which the* Lord *God had made" (Gen. 3:1).* Now, we know that everything God created was good. He says so! *"And God saw every thing that He had made, and, behold, it was very good" (Gen. 1:31).* Notice it wasn't just "good." It was "very good." Also, remember all of them, from the minutest insect and up, all were given freedom of choice. That is the only way God will create other living creatures. Why? Because without freedom of choice, there is no love. We serve a God of love.

Everything living thing was created with this special freedom. The serpent had this special freedom. And it chose to do what Satan tempted it to do. Now, I believe it is time that we look at the anatomy of sin. As I just said, the serpent yielded to the temptation of this angel and followed in his footsteps. In other words, the serpent became a little antichrist. Any living creature who places itself instead of and in place of Christ becomes an antichrist. Wow! That's a tall order! A deceptive position. A lie, if you please, because no one, absolutely no one's feet can fit into God's shoes. They only think they can! They are living a lie! And most often, it probably happens so subtly it is difficult for them to detect when and how it took place. That's what lies are all about—trickery and deceit.

Sin is always deceptive! For notice, God says, *"the serpent was more subtil than any beast of the field which the* Lord *God had made" (Gen. 3:1).* That is why Lucifer could use him for doing his dirty work. Something or someone caused the serpent to be that way. Now notice what he did first. He insinuated that God was lying to her. That was the beginning of the blame game. He said, *"Hath God said, Ye shall not eat of every tree of the garden?" (Gen. 3:1).* By asking her this question, he placed her in jeopardy. What was his insinuation? That God had given her permission to eat of every tree in the garden.

Do you realize what he just did? He repeated a half-truth. But! It was still a bald-faced lie. If was only half of what God had said to her. You see! After saying that, God went on to tell her there was a specific tree in the garden she was not to eat from. If you only tell half of the truth, you have made room for deceit. You haven't given the whole truth. Half-truths are not informative enough. They only provide half of the information; in other words, half of the story. Thus, they are deceptive. Really, a half-truth is no truth at all—a lie is a lie; that's the plain unvarnished truth.

There's a saying I've heard people repeat—often the very ones who are deceitful. I had someone repeat this to me! And they knew about it from experience! It went like this: "Oh what a web we weave when we practice to deceive." Shocking, isn't it? They admitted they were deceitful, and they admitted they had experienced the trouble it gets the user into. This is what the serpent was doing. He was weaving a web of deceitful lies and walking in Lucifer's footsteps. When Satan whispered it in his ear, he probably craved being like the devil, but he probably didn't really know what Lucifer was like. He just looked up to him. Remember! Satan was beautiful. God is the only one we can safely look up to. Notice, Eve told the serpent the truth. This proves she knew what was right to do. She told *"the serpent, We may eat of the fruit of the tree of the garden: But of the fruit of the tree which is in the midst of the garden, God hath said, Ye shall not eat of it, neither shall ye touch it, lest ye die" (Gen. 3:2–3).* This proves she knew and understood what God asked her to do.

Now, watch the next turn of events. The devil never gives up. Her knowledge of the truth did not dampen his resolve to deceive her. But look what he did to get her to sin. We too often continue to hang around with the wrong person after we realize they are trying to get us to disobey God. It's dangerous! He's a slick liar and a persuasive talker. He wheedles people into doing his dirty work. They will either say, "Oh, just eat a little of it," or "just do it this once."

God says, *"Know ye not that the friendship of the world is enmity with God? whosoever therefore will be a friend of the world is the enemy of God"*

(James 4:4). But praise God, He doesn't stop there. He continues by saying,

> *But He giveth more grace. Wherefore he saith, God resisteth the proud, but giveth grace unto the humble. Submit yourselves therefore to God. Resist the devil, and he will flee from you. Draw nigh to God, and he will draw nigh to you. Cleanse your hands, ... ye double minded. Be afflicted, and mourn, and weep: let your laughter be turned to mourning, and your joy to heaviness. Humble yourselves in the sight of the Lord, and He shall lift you up. (James 4:6–10)*

Eve continued to talk with the serpent; he was feeding her the lies of the devil. We all know how dangerous it is to hang around with those who have been duped by him. He proceeded to feed her lies. Remember: a man convinced against his will (i.e., against his desires) is of the same opinion still. She chose to continue talking with him even though he was insinuating that God was not being honest with her. How dare he! He disagreed with God and said, *"Ye shall not surely die" (Gen. 3:4).* Do you realize what the serpent really did? He called God a liar. Isn't that ironic? The liar is calling his Creator a liar. Tell me! Did Adam and Eve die? They surely did, and it was because they disobeyed God. They failed the test.

And he didn't even stop there. He blackened God's name further. In fact, he came right to the crux of the matter. What the devil really wanted was to be GOD. He didn't just want to be like God. So watch what he did next. He placed a desire in her heart. What was that desire? Why! It was the very thing the devil wanted and still does desire for himself. In fact, he has tricked himself into believing he will overtake God's throne someday. He believes his own lie—that he will be the ruler of the universe and the "god" of all the beings in it. How wrong he is!

So, listen to his next words to her. *"For God doth know that in the day ye eat thereof, then your eyes shall be opened, and ye shall be as gods, knowing good and evil" (Gen. 3:5).* And notice, he was offering that privilege to Eve. Unfortunately, she did think it was a privilege. That was the devil's goal—to be like God—and know good and evil. It certainly wouldn't be my goal. The devil knew what it was like to be evil. Why in the world would he want to give it to others? Because he was evil. He chose to be evil. Therefore, I want to stay as far away from him as I can—how about you? God's great heart of love is mourning over us just as He was mourning over Eve when she fell into the hands of God's enemy—the devil.

Now, there are a couple of things we need to think about. Yes, Eve would know good and evil. But! Just like the beginning of their conversation, he was telling her a half-truth. She would only be like God in a very small way. Are we happy that we know evil? I can loudly exclaim **"No"**! I bet you agree with me. If it is only half-true, it is not true at all.

As soon as Adam and Eve sinned, they realized they were naked. Yes! They had lost their God-given covering. Before Adam and Eve sinned, they were *"clothed with a robe of righteousness" (Isa. 61:10)*. Isaiah talks about it. It is the robe we will be wearing when God raises us from the grave to take us to heaven. God will restore the robes Adam and Eve lost when they sinned, just as He will forgive all who admit they are wrong and ask Him to forgive them. What a precious gift that is! You see, God knew what had happened to Adam and Eve. He knew immediately what they had done. He even knew they were going to do it before they did it. But, by allowing them to make that awful choice, God was also protecting their God-given right to exercise their freedom of choice. When God honored their choice, He kept freedom of choice intact. He exercised His right, too. He chose to not become a dictator. He did that by letting them choose who they wanted to serve. God or themselves, which was really serving the serpent, called the Devil.

Jesus went walking in the garden just as He usually did to talk with them. They had just committed their sin! Also, take note that God did not let on He knew what they had done. He wanted to give them the privilege of 'fessing up. He wanted them to tell Him they had

> **66**
> *We must confess our sins to God alone, not to some pastor or priest*
> **99**

done wrong so that He could forgive them. God still says to us today, *"If we confess our sins, He is faithful and just to forgive us our sins, and cleanse us from all unrighteousness" (1 John 1:9)*. What a blessed gift that is! It comes to us through the wonderful gift of Jesus Christ, our Lord and Savior. Just consider all of the sins of every person, all of the people He has ever created. He died the most painful, cruel death possible on a cross—for each one. Yes! Jesus paid for every sin every child of God has committed if they are sorry for them and ask forgiveness and confess that they have sinned.

Without confession to God and forgiveness from God, they will be lost. I want to pause and say something really important. We must confess our sins to God alone, not to some pastor or priest. God is the only one who can wash our sins away and forgive them. Listen to Jesus. He is the Son of man. He was talking to Jewish people. He had just told a sick man his sins were forgiven. They knew it was only God who could forgive sins. They just didn't know Jesus was God. Nowhere in the Bible are we told we need a go-between. God wants us to go directly to Him with our sins. When we pray to the Father, the Holy Spirit takes our prayers to Him. That is one of His jobs.

Those Jewish priests knew they could not forgive anyone's sin in place of God. Priests are no holier than any other human, and they certainly cannot take God's place. When they do, they sin. They are not God on earth. If they claim to be Christ on earth, they are placing themselves instead of and in place of Christ. That is blasphemy against Jesus. God doesn't ask us to pay money to have our sins to be forgiven. Forgiveness is a gift; it can't be bought or paid for with money. *"Forasmuch as ye know that ye were not redeemed with corruptible things, as silver and gold, from your vain conversation received by tradition from your fathers; But with the precious blood of Christ, as a lamb without blemish and without spot"* (1 *Peter 1:18–19).* Jesus paid our debt for us on the cross. He paid for our sins with His shed blood. *"The blood of Jesus Christ his Son cleanseth us from **all** sin"* (1 John 1:7, emphasis supplied).

Isn't this special? The Holy Spirit helps us, too. *"the Spirit also helpeth our infirmities: for we know not what we should pray for as we ought: but the Spirit itself maketh intercession for us with groaning which cannot be uttered. And he that searcheth the hearts knoweth what is the mind of the Spirit, because he maketh intercession for the saints according to the will of God"* (Rom. 8:26–27). The three of Them work together for our salvation. Also, look at John 10:33: *"The Jews answered him, saying, For a good work we stone thee not; but for blasphemy; and because that thou, being a man, makest thyself God."* Jesus wasn't just a man. He was God.

The blessed truth is if a person sins, the Holy Spirit convicts them of their sins. It is a built-in blessing if we have invited Him into our hearts, and as long as we have **not** said "no" to the Holy Spirit. So many times, our conscience has been seared. The Holy Spirit keeps coming to us and guiding us into all truth if we want Him. If your conscience is troubled, God is pricking it, not some man. God loves you dearly. Run to Him in prayer. Don't believe the lies the devil whispers in your ear, either. It's just another lie to get you to think bad about God and cause you to disobey Him. That's what the devil is all about. He just loves to slap God in the face. His anger probably gets hotter and more worked up the closer the time comes to when he will be burned up. He just loves to get us to think God is the liar—not him.

If the devil can get you to distrust God or make you think God won't forgive you, then he has had the privilege to slap God in the face. Yup! That is the goal of Satan—to cause God and you misery. Don't let him do it. God is always willing to forgive and accept an honest confession. The devil's goal is to make you fearful because that hurts God. Don't help him out. There is no sin God can't forgive, except the one you won't confess or ask Him to forgive. He's so wonderful. So! After Eve's conversation with the serpent, God went to the garden and *"called unto Adam, and said unto him, Where art thou?" (Gen. 3:9). "And he said, I heard thy voice in the garden, and I was afraid, because I was naked" (Gen. 3:10).* That was a tip-off that they had sinned. They hadn't known fear, and they didn't know anything about nakedness. They had never experienced either one before.

Fear is a nasty thing. It is one of the tactics the devil uses to keep us from confessing our sins. It leads people to do all kinds of sinful things— even reject God because they are afraid of what will happen to them if they do not do what the devil tells them to do. They trusted God before they sinned. But now, they no longer trusted Him. If they had only known God was still trustworthy. He wasn't out to cause them trouble. He was there to help them.

Notice God's next words. They had told Him what they had been up to. *"And he said, Who told thee that thou wast naked?"* That's right! God came right to the crux of the matter. He didn't wait for them to lie to Him. God certainly would not want to give the devil an opportunity to lie to them more and worsen their problem. So, with His next breath, He faced them with a direct question concerning what they had done. How much better that was than what the serpent did. Now they could choose to tell the truth or lie to God. He said, *"Hast thou eaten of the tree, whereof I commanded thee that thou shouldest not eat?" (Gen. 3:11).*

Praise God, they chose to tell the truth. I can imagine God speaking those words in a calm, pleasant voice, not an accusing one, as a loving Father would do. Notice also that God's words showed them He knew who had led them into sin. Right then and there, the blame game was born. Now we know who created it—it was the devil himself. He's the one who pushed Adam to blame Eve! So, when we blame others, we, too, are obeying the devil. It's another one of his tactics for causing trouble between people today, too.

The next time God talked with them, He told them what would happen to them as a result of obeying the serpent. Yes, they chose to walk in
the devil's footsteps. They ate the fruit God had forbidden them to eat.
Right away, God had to drive them out of the garden, so they could not
eat from *"the tree of life" (Gen. 3:24).* God had to work fast before the
serpent got them to eat from the other special tree in the garden. *"And
the LORD God said, Behold, the man has become as one of us, to know good
and evil: and now, lest he put forth his hand, and take also of the tree of life,
and eat, and live for ever: therefore the LORD God sent him from the garden
of Eden" (Gen. 3: 22–23).*

Just think! If they had eaten from that other tree, they would have
never died. They would be just like the devil in temperament, forever!
God certainly had a lot at stake. That's a hard picture to look at. One God
would never allow. We think our life is bad now because of sin, but being
in hell forever would be unthinkable. It would be much, much worse. Even
the devil is not going to face hell forever. The forever, in that context,
means until they are all burned up. They will burn only as long as it takes
them to burn up.

The Bible teaches us God is good all the time. I am so glad God placed
this conversation in the Bible so that we could see how evil Satan is. It was
Jesus who talked with Adam and Eve in the garden. Oh, how I love Jesus.
How can we help but love Him? God does not tell us how long Adam and
Eve were in the garden before this happened. But I don't think the devil
ever lets the grass grow under his feet. He is always anxious to do evil.
What a sinister being he is. Lying and death are his specialties. He is still
getting even with God that way. He has been causing people to die ever
since. When the serpent said, *"Ye shall not surely die" (Gen. 3:4),* he was
telling his first lie on planet Earth. And he has been telling it ever since.

There are only two people I know of who never died. They were Enoch
and Elijah. *"By faith Enoch was translated that he should not see death; and
was not found, because God had translated him: for before his translation he
had this testimony, that he pleased God" (Heb. 11:5).* And the other one was
Elijah. He, too, was translated.

After Adam and Eve sinned and lost their robe of righteousness, God
told them what they would need to do to be saved. I am sure Jesus told
them the whole story of how He would die to pay for their sins. Just think
how that must have crushed them. And I'm sure the devil rubbed it in.
They say misery loves company. Who would know better than him! He

just loves to make us miserable. But our precious Jesus told them He was *"the Lamb of God that taketh away the sin of the world" (John 1:29)*. Then He instructed them to slay a lamb to show they believed He, Jesus, the Son of God, would come and die for their sins so that they could be saved. Wow! What a beautiful promise. Can you visualize the relief that must have washed over them? But just think of the grief that must have swept over them too. Now Jesus would have to die to pay for their sin. Right then, *"Unto Adam also and to his wife did the LORD God make coats of skins, and clothed them" (Gen. 3:21)*. Yes! It happened in rapid succession. We know it was a lamb that was slain that day because later when Abel slew a lamb to worship God, it was accepted.

It is interesting that the very next thing that happened was also about death. The devil works fast. Eve became pregnant and gave birth to her first child. She named him *"Cain" (Gen. 4:1)*. And it appears that very soon, she had another child and called him *"Abel" (Gen. 4:2)*. Both boys knew how to worship God, for God had instructed them to slay a lamb to show they believed Jesus, the Lamb of God, would die for their sins. Worship is what the devil craves. We must make a choice. If we love God, we will keep His commandments. That is one of the ways we worship Him. We have to choose who we will worship and obey. Nothing is more important than that. Absolutely nothing! The main question is, do we love God, or do we love ourselves more than we love Him? God answers that question. Here is His answer. *"He that saith, I know Him, and keepeth not his commandments, is a liar, and the truth is not in him. But whoso keepeth his word, in him verily is the love of God perfected: hereby know we that we are in Him" (1 John 2:4–5)*. Abel obeyed God! *"Abel was a keeper of sheep" (Gen. 4:2)*. *"Abel ... brought of the firstlings of his flock, and of the fat thereof. And the LORD had respect unto Abel and his offering" (Gen. 4:4)*. He brought the gift God told him to bring. His gift told God he understood the preciousness of the gift Jesus was offering him. It showed he believed Jesus would save him from his sins. It also shows he realized he was a sinner and in need of God's grace.

"Cain was a tiller of the ground" (Gen. 4:2). Both boys knew what offering they were to bring to God. Both knew the lamb represented Jesus' death on the cross to pay for their sins. But *"Cain brought of the fruit of the ground an offering unto the LORD" (Gen. 4:3)*. He defied God. He refused to obey Him. He brought the fruit he had grown in his garden instead of the required lamb. The produce from his garden did not represent anything

Jesus would do for them. Neither did it represent how Jesus would shed His blood to save them.

It was a counterfeit gift. One the devil concocted. It was instead of and in place of the true offering of love. It did not show Jesus that Cain was grateful for His promise of salvation. Cain did what he wanted to do rather than what God asked him to do. If he had sacrificed a lamb, he would have shown God his thankfulness for the promise of eternal life with Him someday. But Cain wasn't thankful. He went his own selfish way and did what the devil led him to do. Any time we disobey a command of God and do something else in its place, we are sinning. Read Exodus 20:3-17. As you review them, think about what people use for a replacement. That replacement becomes our god. I just read them and found:

Command #1 It is whatever you choose to take His place.

Command #2 It is choosing to pray to an image.

Command #3 It is swearing and taking God's name in vain.

Command #4 It is keeping some other day in place of the seventh-day Sabbath.

Command #5 It is either physically killing them or destroying them in other ways. There are many ways—calling them names and thus ruining their image, mistreating them, thus again destroying their mental image of themselves, and the list goes on.

Command #6 It is the same as # 5.

Command #7 It is committing adultery.

Command #8 It is stealing.

Command #9 It is lying,

Command #10 It is wishing to steal.

Truly, the wages of sin is death! Yes! Cain was stubborn and went his own selfish way. He offered God the fruit of his garden. Something he had produced by the work of his own hands. He refused to obey God. So the Lord could not respect his offering. (see Gen. 4:5). He had no faith in God. His faith was in himself. How sad that must have made Jesus feel. Thus, the Lord did not accept Cain's offering. *"But unto Cain and to his offering he had not respect. And Cain was very wroth, and his countenance fell. And the Lord said unto Cain, Why art thou wroth? and why is thy countenance fallen? If thou doest well, shalt thou not be accepted? and if thou doest not well, sin lieth at the door. And unto thee shall be his desire, and thou shalt rule over him" (Gen. 3:5–7).*

The very next verse tells us that *"Cain talked with Abel his brother: and it came to pass, when they were in the field, that Cain rose up against his brother, and slew him" (Gen. 4:8)*. The devil had won again. He had brought death to one of God's children. How quickly he made inroads. The first baby born on earth had gone the way of God's enemy. That's fast work. With lightning speed, Cain became the first murderer. He had walked in the footsteps of Lucifer and committed the first crime. The devil still craves power. He wants to control everyone and everything. He is the worst dictator and ruthless despot the universe has ever known.

Rapidly the devil damaged the whole earth. By the time we get to the seventh chapter of Genesis, the first book in the Bible, the devil has totally trashed the whole earth. God had to destroy all of the wicked, and He did it via a flood. God offered to save all who would believe in Him. But only eight people accepted God's invitation and went into the ark. God used desperate measures to clean up the earth from all the evil people. He opened up the windows of heaven and cleansed it with a flood. It was crucial, or God wouldn't have done it. Not even one of those who were lost would have ever honored and accepted Jesus as their Savior. It would have been fruitless to leave them on the earth. Now mankind could try again. Very few were saved during those years. And Jesus had not yet died to save sinners. So He could not nor would he let all who loved Him fall between the cracks. No! Not our God of love! That's something He would not do—not Jesus! Perhaps Satan thought he had bested God. But he hadn't. God will never allow Himself to be bested by the devil! The devil really wants to do that, but he can't. I'm sure he thought he had done a quick work. He had! But God will be the winner in the end. Praise the Lord! God won! Let's continue to worship Him. Of a truth, Satan will never slow down his process of hurting God. From here on out to the end of this book, we will be talking about what Satan is doing to punish God and overthrow His government of love. His constant desire is to harm God. He does this through any and every

> **God offered to save all who would believe in Him. But only eight people accepted God's invitation and went into the ark.**

means he can hatch up. Our God will continue to be the loving God He is. Yes! To the very end. He will come to get us when there is absolutely no one who can be saved. What a patient God He is. Thus, Lucifer, the most beautiful angel in heaven, became antichrist. He, in his mind, put himself in place of Christ.

11

The First Human Who Claimed to Be "God"

Attack #3: Nimrod: Mighty Hunter "Before the Lord" (A Copycat of Lucifer—The Second Antichrist)

If I have counted correctly, there were only four or five generations of people between the time when the flood ended until we got to the person who thought he was a mighty hunter before the Lord. His name was Nimrod! I am astounded at how rapidly Lucifer again polluted the world and used Nimrod's anger and determination to try to control God. The devil never gives up. He got Nimrod very worked up concerning the flood God brought on the earth. Nimrod was determined to make sure God would never bring a flood like that on the earth again. Imagine that! He thought he could control the actions of God. He thought he could be "God." Unfortunately, Nimrod was just like the people God had just destroyed. And he determined in his heart he was **not** going to allow God to ever destroy him with a flood. He didn't need to worry! God had no plans to destroy anyone by flood again. Nimrod was way off the beam, thinking he could outsmart God, actually thinking he could take over and be "God." There is something else we need to remember. Right after the flood,

> And Noah builded an altar unto the LORD; and took of every clean beast, and of every clean fowl, and offered burnt offerings on the altar. And the LORD smelled a sweet savour; and the LORD said in His heart, I will not again curse the ground any more for man's sake; for the imagination of man's heart is evil from his youth; neither will I again smite any more every thing living, as I have done. (Gen. 8:20–21)

Our compassionate God knows how much we can handle. He knows our frame (see Ps. 103:14). What a loving, compassionate, longsuffering God He is.

But! He also knew there was someone who was about to get the bigs. God was ready for him. God had another way to handle the situation, but it wasn't going to be another flood. Watch God work in an unusual way to take care of sin with an individual who would refuse to repent. Remember!

And Noah begat three sons, Shem, Ham, and Japheth. The earth also was corrupt before God, and the earth was filled with violence. And God looked upon the earth, and, behold, it was corrupt; for all flesh had corrupted his way upon the earth. And God said unto Noah, the end of all flesh is come before me; for the earth is filled with violence through them; and, behold, I will destroy them with the earth. (Gen. 6:10–13)

All three of Noah's boys had gone into the ark with their mom and dad and were saved from the flood. Likewise, pairs of the other living creatures were saved in the ark, too. And all of them also went forth out of the ark. Yes! They all survived. God took good care of them. God says so: *"And Noah went forth, and his sons, and his wife, and his sons' wives with him: every beast, and every creeping thing, and every fowl, and whatsoever creepeth upon the earth, after their kind, went forth out of the ark"* *(Gen. 8:18–19).* Not even one living creature became extinct during the whole time they were in the ark. Now, look what Noah did next.

He *builded an altar unto the* LORD; *and took of every clean beast, and every clean fowl, and offered burnt offerings on the altar. And the Lord smelled a sweet savor; and the* LORD *said in his heart, I will not again curse the ground any more for man's sake; for the imagination of man's heart is evil from his youth; neither will I again smite any more every thing living, as I have done. (Gen. 8:20–21)*

After the flood, Noah's youngest son, Ham, became the father of four sons. Here are their names. *"Cush, and Mizraim, Put, and Canaan" (1 Chron. 1:8). "And Cush begat Nimrod: he began to be a mighty one in the earth" (Gen. 10:8).* How sad! Nimrod began to think he could take over and be the "God" of this earth. And again, I say, what a God we serve. I never cease to be amazed at the freedom God gives everyone: both those who are trying to walk in Jesus' footsteps and those who are upset with God and deliberately following Satan. Notice! Nimrod wasn't being God;

rather, he had just switched bosses. He was following the devil instead of following God. He wasn't in control at all. The devil was in control of him, and he didn't even know it.

It grieves me at how much sadness Nimrod's rejection brought God. But God is happy every time a sinner comes to Him to be saved. We are all sinners. We will continue to be sinners unto our dying day. I say this because there isn't a day that goes by but that the devil whispers in our ear and makes us feel hurt, picked on, or causes us to have a high and mighty attitude. There is no one on this earth who is not a sinner. God has pled with every person who has ever been born on a daily basis. So I know He pled with Nimrod. But Nimrod would not listen. Nevertheless, God was fair with him; God is always fair and compassionate.

Every day, we too, either choose to admit our wrongs and ask God for forgiveness, or we choose to believe Satan's lies as Nimrod did and proudly gloat about how good we are. I know from experience. I wish it were not true, but it is true. Even the best of us cave in to unhealthy, unloving thoughts and actions. Sins if you please! That is why these Bible stories are so important. God waits and works with us to help us realize our need and bring us closer to Him. He will save us if we let Him. Those who are really mighty are the ones who give God all the glory. Like Adam, Noah, Enoch, and Abraham, to name a few. Each and every one of us can be one of those few. It is God's desire that all of us be in that group. We each add happiness to God's life when we obey Him.

God has taken the brunt of the actions of every person who has ever lived. It has been that way ever since Eve sinned. Of Adam and Eve's first three sons, Cain was the only one who hated God. Amazing, isn't it, that the very first child born on earth chose to hate God? How devastating it must have been to his parents. They were fresh from the hand of God. We must run to God and never underestimate the wicked control of Satan, and on the other hand—God's love for sinners. How blessed we are to have access to His saving love.

Nimrod placed himself on the losing side—on Satan's side. He was not a mighty man for God. Instead, Nimrod was a mighty man for himself, even though with his own eyes he had seen the just and personal way God took care of the sin problem. He thought he knew God forward and backward. He thought he had one last chance. Look what he did with it. He listened to Satan's lies. Unfortunately, he was like all of us are to a point. For every person, there comes a turning point. A time when we will make a deadly, selfish choice, or we choose to serve God. There are only two choices. Nimrod was at that turning point. He had nursed his selfish feelings far too long. So he chose to follow in Lucifer's footsteps. He proceeded to enter the point of no return. God would not forgive him because he would not ask to be forgiven.

Each of us will face that issue in our life if we tell God "no" so many times it becomes impossible for us to hear the pleading voice of the Holy Spirit. But if we think about God at all and worry that we might be lost, this is a signal that we have not committed the unpardonable sin. When one has crossed that line, they will not care whether they have crossed that line. I am so glad God is so longsuffering. He keeps sending the Holy Spirit our way as long as He can get us to listen even a little bit. It is very difficult to grieve the Holy Spirit that much. There are lots of people who think they have grieved the Spirit too much, but that is just one of the sneaky lies Satan deceives people with. He doesn't want us to know we can still come to God and be saved if we are still desiring salvation. I am so glad this is true. If we feel we have committed the unpardonable sin, we need to get down on our knees and talk to God about it. Very likely, we are dead wrong. Keep going to God about it. Never give up.

> **"There are lots of people who think they have grieved the Spirit too much, but that is just one of the sneaky lies Satan deceives people with."**

Believing that lie is a dangerous path to take. The devil does this to make us give up on God. We can't see what's around the bend in the road ahead of us. That is why we need to trust God no matter what Satan is screaming in our ear.

Nimrod needed God's help. There is nothing in God's Word that says Nimrod asked for help. I pray that each of you, dear reader, myself included, will not let another day go by where we fail to talk with God on this issue. Satan is causing these types of painful situations this very day, and he will continue to do so the next day, and the next, and the next. Yes! Until the very day Jesus comes to take us home with Him.

Come and look at Nimrod's rebelliousness. He simply determined in his heart to do his own thing. It can happen in a moment. We must be on guard against these brief lies from the father of lies when no matter what God says, we refuse to listen! Let the chips fall where they may. There was nothing God could do for him. God would not remove his freedom of choice, and he had made up his mind to defy Him all the way. How sad! We must not let this happen to us. God bless you.

> *And the whole earth was of … one speech. And it came to pass, as they journeyed from the east, that they found a plain in the land of Shinar; and they dwelt there. And they said one to another, Go to, let us make brick, and burn them thoroughly. And they had brick for stone, and slime had they for morter. And they said, Go to, … let us make us a name, lest we be scattered abroad upon the face of the whole earth. (Gen. 11:1–4)*

Just look what happened next. *"And the Lord came down to see the city and the tower, which the children of men builded" (Gen. 11:5).* Jesus, our Lord, was not happy with Nimrod. But He had a solution for helping out His people. That brings a smile to my face. How about you? What a loving God we serve. He said, "Behold, the people is one, and *they have all one language; and this they begin to do: and now nothing will be restrained from them, which they have imagined to do.…Let us go down, and there confound their language" (Gen.11:6–7).* It sounds like all three of Them, at least two of the Beings who are our One God, came down where Nimrod and his friends were working. I say this because the writer used the pronoun "us."

I am amazed at what a simple way God took care of the haughty, determined attitude of Nimrod and those who followed him. All He did was confound their language. God has such simple, down-to-earth ways of taking care of sin. And look what Paul noticed about God. He said,

> *Because the foolishness of God is wiser than men; and the weakness of God is stronger than men. For ye see your calling, brethren, how that not many wise men after the flesh, not many mighty, not many noble, are called: but God hath chosen the foolish things of the world to confound the wise; and God hath chosen the weak things of the world to confound the things which are mighty; and base things of the world, and things which are despised, hath God chosen, yea, and things which are not, to bring to nought things that are: that no flesh should glory in His presence. (1 Cor. 1:25–29)*

Nimrod surely was on a downward path. There was nothing more God could do for him, for he refused to listen. I am awed at how easy it was for God to take care of this serious situation. Man uses all kinds of complicated ways to take care of problems they feel are unsolvable. But God did it so simply and quickly. Almost before you could say a word, bingo,

God had the problem solved. Isn't He some God? His simple solutions are awesome! And I stand here exclaiming how great God is! So let's look at what God did about Nimrod's dictatorial attitude and how He handled those who were living in the city Nimrod founded.

When God came down and looked at what was happening, what was the result of that check-up? Moses says, *"So the LORD scattered them abroad from thence upon the face of all the earth: and they left off to build the city" (Gen. 11:8).* Now wasn't that simple? Thus, God lets us know how different nations came about and why there are so many different languages. Consequently, the ones who were building the tower could not understand each other. It must have been very confusing when the one who brought the bricks asked them how many he should bring, and the carrier just mumbled something he couldn't understand.

Thus, the nations were born. Sometimes a solution to a problem can be so profound. You wouldn't think it would take a rocket scientist to come up with that solution! I think we tend to make things difficult. Especially when we are stubbornly doing things our way. Nimrod was smart enough! He just didn't have his hand in God's hand. Again I say, how sad! What a God we have. His solution should bring praise for Him to all of our lips. So, the name of the city was *"called Babel; because the LORD did there confound the language of all the earth: and from thence did the LORD scatter them abroad upon the face of all the earth" (Gen. 11:9).* It truly shows us the harmlessness of our God. Compare, as you read further, the astonishing difference between Nimrod's attitude compared to God's attitude.

Many scholars believe Nebuchadnezzar built his temple years later on the base of Nimrod's broken-down tower. He, too, demanded worship but not for himself. He worshipped idols and demanded that everyone bow to the idol he worshipped. That's wrong but totally different from Nimrod. But in the end, Nebuchadnezzar gave his heart to Jesus. Isn't that beautiful? And it was all because Daniel and his three friends kept witnessing to him and refusing to bow to his idols. God knew Nebuchadnezzar's heart; God knew he would give his heart to Him. Nimrod would not. We are so blessed that our one true God is love. Nimrod did not have a spirit of love—only the spirit of control and selfishness.

No created being will ever be equal with God or rise above Him. If they were able to do that, then they would be God, and that cannot and will not ever happen. Just look how many warring groups have lived on Planet Earth since Lucifer was created. We see his control right now, as we witness the choices of various world leaders in the news. Look at the violent means by which they try to get their own way—from murder to intimidation.

Then consider the calm, non-harmful way God took care of Nimrod's desire to become the god of this world. Satan's way certainly does not attract me. I pray that God will speak to the hearts of the leaders of our world at this present time. God is giving each one of them a choice and what choices they are making. It seems to boil down to money. God points His finger at the problem, saying, *"No man can serve two masters: for either he will hate the one, and love the other; or else he will hold to the one, and despise the other. Ye cannot serve God and mammon" (Matt. 6:24).* He will help each one of us come to Him if we want to come. That's just who our God is!

Do we love Him enough to give up our sinful ways? And Yes, I said "WE." I yearn for the day when Jesus comes to take all those from every nation of earth home to heaven with Him. Again, I say, it won't be long. I can almost hear God's trumpet blowing. Listen! I invite you to say hooray with me! For one of these days, God will again step in and stop the impostors in their tracts! It's time for that to happen—the prophecies leading up to that time have been fulfilled. Are you ready to go home with Jesus? I am! He can't come too soon.

12

Some Good News Before We Face the Bad

Icringe at the very thought of writing this chapter because the subject is so sensitive. But the good news is God loves all sinners no matter what their sin is. He is more than willing to forgive all kinds of sins, but there is one sin He cannot forgive. It is the sin against the Holy Spirit. If we continue to resist His guidance, it will lead us to eternal death. We talked about it earlier, but I want to accentuate it before we delve into this touchy problem. It is a good thing this sin will be totally eradicated someday. Notice that it is not one of the sins listed in God's ten-commandment law. So the only name we can give it is the "unpardonable sin."

God can and will forgive all sin. In fact, there is no sin He refuses to forgive if we ask Him to forgive it. But here is the problem! It's not God who refuses to forgive us. The problem is, we will not ask Him to forgive us because we want to hang onto it. We don't even want to know about it. It concerns our relationship with God. If this is our attitude, it shows plainly that we do not want a relationship with Spirit. Rather, we want Him to bug out. That's where the problem lies. That is why we fail to ask to be forgiven. We selfishly want to go our own way. Our selfish stubbornness causes the problem. Yes, it lies within our own deceitful hearts. It's a heart problem. Now! Knowing that, let's take a closer look at God's marvelous promise. It gives us great hope. It says, *"If we confess our sins, He is faithful and just to forgive us our sins, and to cleanse us from all unrighteousness" (1 John 1:9).* Did you catch that? What did God say? He will forgive **ALL** sin. Every bit! So it is not God's fault if some of our sins are not forgiven. It's our fault.

What makes this so bad? It is because of a very special gift God gives us. It's called freedom of choice. God will never remove our freedom of choice or violate it. So, the reason He won't forgive this sin is because He will always honor our freedom to choose what we want to do. We have to go to Him and tell Him we want Him to change us and give us a heart of love. The problem comes when Satan whispers in our ear and tempts us with something he knows we want to do—something unloving. Something that will harm other people. Something selfish that he makes us think we can't get along without. I've been there! Done that! So I can vouch that it is a very dangerous road—one you would not want to go down if you could see the end from the beginning. God can see that end. Trust Him. I know you will be happy in the end if you do. That certainly is true for me. I have finally given Him my whole heart. Thank You, Lord, for Your gift of the Holy Spirit.

If we become so stubborn and so bound to do something our own way, a way which is contrary to God's law of love, and choose to turn our backs on His loving ways, placing our hands over our ears and refusing to listen to His pleas for us to come to Him, pretty soon His voice will become so faint we can't hear it when He tells us we are sinning. That is the sin against the Holy Spirit. He can't speak to us if we can't hear Him. It only happens from total rejection of Him. If He continued to speak to us and harassed us, He would no longer be a God of love. And it certainly would not cause us to turn to Him. He would be a dictator, pusher, control freak, and whatever other derogatory name you can come up with. God will never try to force us to forgive Him. We are the ones who determinedly choose to go our own selfish, sinful way.

It's scary! I've been very close to making that fatal choice. I've had the experience of asking God to forgive me and then screaming at God, "but I don't want to stop committing this sin." That is a very hard spot to be in. And extremely close to committing it. But God has good news. The sin against the Holy Spirit is extremely difficult to commit, for God does not give up on us easily. He knows, via Jesus' trials, how terrible the pressure is that Satan presses on us. The Holy Spirit watched Jesus go through it. Jesus was pressured more than any other human. It had to be that way for Jesus, or it would have been unfair. The Spirit invites and encourages our family and friends to pray for us when we won't come to Him in prayer. He whispers in their ears and asks the Father to send Him to intercede on our behalf.

God knows His enemy, the devil, will never give up. Satan has a plan for destroying us with every hateful breath he takes. Yes! With every thought and breath he takes, he has our destruction in mind. He is evil through and through. There is no one as evil as he is, and there never will be anyone else that evil ever again. You see, he knows if we go to God and give our heart to Him, he, the devil, will have to suffer for the sins he has caused us to commit. It comes right back around to that old blame game he taught Adam and Eve in the Garden of Eden.

Satan doesn't want to burn in hell. That is why he keeps adding lie upon lie and tries to keep us feeling responsible for our own sins. He wants us to burn for them—not him. But why should we do that, since Jesus has already paid for them? The devil is the one who caused all the trouble in the first place. He's going to burn up in hell no matter what we do. He is going to burn for enticing us to sin. You see if we love Jesus and have asked Him to forgive our sins, and if the devil will burn for his part in causing us to sin, that sounds fair to me. But he has never been sorry for his sins, and he never will feel sorry for them. My Bible tells me, *"The devil sinneth from the beginning"* (1 John 3:8).

> **" If we could know and see the end from the beginning, we would choose to go God's way. "**

We are so blessed that Jesus died for those sins. When we know the truth about our enemy, and know how he works, how much God loves us, and believe the Bible when it says, *"God is faithful and just to forgive us our sins and to cleanse us from all unrighteousness" (1John 1:9),* then we will choose to run into the protecting arms of Jesus. God will never remove freedom of choice from us. But if we have made our hearts wicked by choosing to do evil things, God still wants to cleanse us from those evil desires. He will do everything He can to turn our hearts toward Him—including me. We will never be sorry we did. Each time we choose to say "NO!" to the devil, we are saying "YES" to God. Each time we say it to Him, it will be easier for us to say yes the next time. Issue by issue, sin by sin, we draw closer to God or closer to going our own stubborn way. But if we could know and see the end from the beginning, we would choose to go God's way. So, my prayer is, dear reader, if you have a sin you unswervingly hang onto, please take a moment right now, and ask God for the power to resist the sin Satan is tempting you to commit. It is a situation we face daily, but we can still have God's presence with us all the time while we are battling with Satan. Just ask Him. And know that if it feels like God is not with you, and you feel like you cannot get along without committing this sin, it is Satan lying to you again. God bless you.

Yes! God is always willing to forgive our sins. We are the ones who refuse to ask to be forgiven because we love and cherish the sin we are harboring. How wrong we are! Sin is never nice. It always leads to death. Yes! It's as simple as that; God does not pardon us because we do not want Him to. Since we don't want him to pardon us, we do not ask Him to. But all other sins can be forgiven if we have not already committed the unpardonable one. Think about it! Why would God keep speaking to us if we have kept refusing to listen to His pleading voice? But let me stress again—it is difficult to reach this level of sin. The thing that makes it a sin is our refusal to listen to Him as He coaches us to obey Him. If you are afraid you have committed this sin—rest assured you have not, for if you had committed it, you wouldn't be worried about it. Your worry indicates that God is still pleading with you to come to Him. And you may be very close to committing it. God always wants to be your friend and guide. You are the only one who can cut yourself off from Him. No one else is to blame.

There is a sin I am really concerned about today. It is the sin of sodomy. This sin is increasing at lightning speed. In fact, the devil specializes in getting us involved with all manner of illicit sex. Even young kids are becoming involved. This definitely needs to be discussed. But I am fearful if I write about it, those it affects will not continue to read this book, and everyone needs to know what God has written about it because that knowledge is paramount to a good relationship with God. What is most important is that everyone has the opportunity to know how much God loves them. You see, God loves the person, but He doesn't love their sin. With God, sin is sin. He does not grade any certain sin differently from another, except the unpardonable sin. There is nothing God can do about that sin because that sin is rejection of Him. We have total control over our choice to reject Him. It never pays to distance oneself from God. He is the One who gave us our life in the first place. And He still holds our life in His hands even when we are rejecting Him. Thank You, Lord, for still holding me in Your hand even when I am believing Satan's lies about You.

So, I ask! What are you afraid of? Are you afraid God will convict you and help you realize you are sinning? If so, why are you afraid? He allows you to choose what you want to do about it. If you are convicted that you are sinning, it will no longer be a problem. Why? Because once you are convicted, you will make a choice. You will either choose to obey Him or plug your ears. So I am praying that you will continue reading this book and give Him the privilege of showing you how you are mistreating yourself. I wish you would give every bit of your heart to Him. And so does He. So I am going to continue telling you about this sin because someone needs to give you an opportunity to know God loves you, even if you are committing this sin. How else can you make a choice? You have to know what your choices are before you can choose wisely. You see, if you don't investigate this subject, you will eventually commit the unpardonable sin and be rendered unable to come to God. Then it will be too late. You hold the key to your future in your hand. That key was given to you when God created you in your mother's womb. You will not be able to come to God once you have committed the unpardonable sin. But! God waits, and waits, and waits. He wants to spend eternity with you. And there is a lot more to sinning than illicit sex and the act of allowing the devil to lead you around by the nose. I hope you will give him the boot by loving Jesus.

My heart goes out to anyone who resists this knowledge. I love you, brother, sister! Hang in there. The information is not that bad. It only feels bad because Satan has all of us hog-tied on certain sins, and he doesn't want to let go of us. I can't think of anything worse than being under the control of Satan. We do not have to be under his control. It is we ourselves who give the devil that control. God created us with wonderful freedom. And when we allow God to be in control, then there is dual control. It won't be easy. But most worthwhile things are not easy. They are worth working for. Nothing can be better than that! He will never snatch our control from us, but He will partner with us. It is so nice to have someone who loves us that much. He is beside us every moment of our lives via the Holy Spirit, and He can answer all of our questions. God helps us all! God bless each of you, dear reader, as you make your choice on this issue. God offers us a key to the solution: He tells us if we *"confess our sins."* that means admitting we are sinning, *"He is faithful and just to forgive us our sins, and to cleanse us from all unrighteousness" (1 John 1:9).* He wants us to confess our sins directly to Him—not through a go-between, pastor, or priest. They are sinners like us—humans needing God's grace.

They, too, make mistakes. The devil just loves to cause them to sin because he can destroy so many more people by tricking them into thinking they are different. They need our prayers. They are in a hard spot. God confirms and protects all of us. We are His kids. That is if we choose to accept Him as our Father.

13

Satan's Next Strike to Hurt God

Attack #4: The Devil Led Lot to Sodom and Gomorrah! (He Was Following in Lucifer's Image)

So let's look at what God says about sodomy. It was the sin the devil was fostering in Sodom. It goes along with the sins of the city we are talking about. The people I have known who have committed this sin are very loving and kind. You would never guess they were practicing sodomy. So let's continue to learn about it. Please have an open mind and accept what God says to you as He speaks to your heart while you read the Bible verses God has given us on this subject. Whoever you are, if you do not know what God thinks about sodomy, you are in great danger of committing sin against Him.

My story begins with this background information! We just finished talking about that old serpent called the devil and Satan, and how he mistreated Adam and Eve. He thought getting them to sin was a big victory for him—at least he thought it was to him. He believed his own lie. It was part of what would cause him to be thrown into the lake of fire prepared for him. It is terrible how many people will have to be destroyed because of Satan's sin. But we know God will be the winner of that battle over in the end. It looks like that time is very close. But only God the Father knows. We know this because Jesus told His disciples what will take place just before He comes to get us. And He finished by saying to His disciples, *"But of that day and that hour knoweth no man, no, not the angels which are in heaven, neither the Son, but the Father. Take ye heed, watch and pray: for ye know not when the time is"* (Mark 13:32–33). *"Watch therefore: for ye know not what hour your Lord doth come"* (Matt. 24:42). You might enjoy reading all of Matthew 24.

Things went from worse to downright rotten in Ur at lightning speed shortly after Abraham was born. So his father took him and Lot, his nephew, to the land of Canaan. This all happened within a few hundred years. Amazing, isn't it? God knew just what to do. God is the originator of everything, of course, and one of His most prized possessions is family life.

> **" God is the originator of everything, and one of His most prized possessions is family life. "**

No wonder Satan's attacks were against families. He loves breaking up homes. It is his specialty. And, of course, when he got Eve to eat the forbidden fruit, that put stress on family relations. So, what's new? In the subject we are looking at now, sodomy, it was just another way the devil had for attacking the family from another direction.

From the first day of creation, it has been Lucifer's aim to harm God. And what better way than by destroying the things He created. When God created mankind in His image, that was His crowning act of creation. Just think how special that is! To be made just like God. So Adam and Eve looked like God and had the same characteristics as God. Yes! I said had! Let me repeat!

Adam and Eve had the
SAME CHARACTERISTICS
as God did, at the time
HE CREATED THEM!

But that didn't last long. It happened in the Garden of Eden. As we have seen, family life quickly deteriorated. And Satan's control of Sodom was a slap in the face aimed at Jesus, too. This is why Jesus told Abram to leave Ur of the Chaldees to get still farther away from Babylon. *"So Abram departed, as the LORD had spoken unto him: and Lot went with him"* (Gen. 12:4). Lot was his nephew (see Gen. 12:5). There was a famine in the land *(see Gen. 12:10)*. *"The famine was grievous" (Gen. 12:10)*. So they went back to Bethel. But both of them had large flocks and herds, *'And the land was not able to bear them, that they might dwell together: for their substance was great, so that they could not dwell together. And there was a strife between the herdmen" (Gen. 13:6–7)*. So, Satan optimized on this problem and began working on Lot's power of choice. Lot was delighted when *'Abram said unto Lot, Let there be no strife, I pray thee, between me and thee, and between my herdmen and thy herdmen; for we be brethren" (Gen.13:8)*. How gracious Abram was to his nephew. Lot did not complain. This was his uncle's solution. So Abram said, *"Is not the whole land before thee? separate thyself, I pray thee, from me: if thou wilt take the left hand, then I will go to the right" (Gen. 13:9).*

This was just what Lucifer had been waiting for. He went into action immediately. I believe what happened next was **not** just happenstance. I believe it was Satan using Lot's desires to destroy him. See what you think. *"And Lot lifted up his eyes, and beheld all the plain of Jordan, that it was well watered every where, before the LORD destroyed Sodom and Gomorrah,...Lot chose him all the plain of Jordan; and Lot journeyed east" (Gen. 13:10–11).* But! Not only did he choose to live on this lush plain, he *"dwelled in the cities of the plain, and pitched his tent toward Sodom" (Gen. 13:12).* Oh, what a poor choice it was. It offered Satan the privilege of tempting him to become entangled with the life of this wicked city. And this is exactly what happened. It never pays to mingle with those who are deliberately choosing to sin and then keep continuing to do so even after you know the truth. They may encourage you to sin, too. Especially if you find it tempting. Satan had Lot right where he wanted him. Remember! To be tempted, one must either chin-chin with those who like their sin or go where the sin is being committed.

But! Hallelujah! Satan would find Lot was rock solid when it came to his Lord. He was a godly man. But he made a very poor choice. It was not good for his family. It was not a good choice, for other reasons, too, for later he would lose part of his family because of that unwise choice. This must have grieved him terribly when it took place. What a victory it was for Satan when Lot moved to Sodom. That's the way the devil works. He gets us to go away from God to where sin resides. It happens little by little. Each time we choose to get a little closer to the thing Satan is tempting us with, the more dangerous our situation becomes. That's what happened to Lot's family. Oh, how God must have mourned. But Satan exulted! For hurting God was his main goal. He wanted to punish God. Remember! He wanted to be God!

On the other hand, Abram listened to God, just as Jesus did when He was on this earth. He listened both to his earthly father and his heavenly Father. Jesus chose to place His heavenly Father first in His life. Abraham obeyed God, too. He moved farther away from Sodom. He had no desire to be anywhere near that city. Abram wanted to be as far from temptation as possible. He was a smart, godly man. It was a very wise choice. One which eventually proved very valuable to Lot. When one of the kings of the area came and raided Sodom, they *"took all the goods of Sodom and*

Gomorrah, and all their victuals" (that's food), *"and went their way. And they took Lot, Abram's brother's son, who dwelt in Sodom, and his goods, and departed"* (Gen. 14:11).

Someone was nice enough to come and tell Abram that Lot had been captured. When Abram heard, he armed his trained servants and sent them to rescue him. Can you feel the gratitude Lot must have felt toward both God and his uncle? Acts of kindness like that are always fathered by God. The fact that Lot's uncle had not moved to that wicked area was a life-saver for both of them. If Abraham had moved to Sodom with Lot, perhaps no one would have been able to rescue Lot. Isn't God something? He provided Lot with a built-in rescuer. God is good all the time, even when things look bad. He never removed Lot's freedom of choice, and He is always available for all of us to talk with. We just have to ask, trust, and obey Him.

The story concerning Lot makes me just have to say WOW! God is so good. Then Lot's uncle Abram was blessed with a visit from Jesus. You can't beat that! Truly, that is a real WOW! Jesus had two reasons for His visit. First and foremost, God came to let Abram know his wife was going to give birth to a very special baby. One who would become the father of the kingdom of Israel. Jesus also came to tell Abraham about something else He was going to do. *"And the LORD said, Shall I hide from Abraham that thing which I do; Seeing that Abraham shall surely become a great and mighty nation, and all the nations of the earth shall be blessed in him?"* (Gen. 18:17–18).

Just listen to what Jesus said about Abraham. *"For I know him, that he will command his children and his household after him, and they shall keep the way of the LORD, to do justice and judgment; that the LORD may bring upon Abraham that which he hath spoken of him. And the Lord said, Because the cry of Sodom and Gomorrah is great, and because their sin is very grievous; I will go down now, and see whether they have done altogether according to the cry of it, which is come unto Me; and if not, I will know"* (Gen. 18:19–21).

Then we have those famous verses where Abraham tried to persuade God not to destroy the city. I am awed at how casual Abraham was with the Mighty God of the universe. I am sure Lot and his family were huge on Jesus's mind, for our longsuffering Savior was very lenient with them. He told Abraham He would save that wicked city even if there were only ten righteous people in it who could be saved. I cringe, just thinking about it. I am amazed Abraham dared to push God that much. What a fabulous relationship there was between them.

14

The Destruction of Sodom and the Saving of Lot and His Daughters

T he Bible tells us two angels came to Sodom that evening. Lot was sitting at the city gate, and he stood up and bowed to them, *"with his face toward the ground" (Gen. 19:1)*. Then he welcomed them warmly and *"pressed upon them greatly" (Gen. 19:3)* to come and spend the night at his house. You see, Lot knew how wicked the city was and that it was unsafe for them to lodge anywhere else. Do you understand what I just said? Lot's house was the only one in town where they would be safe.

Then what they said to Lot must have scared him to death. They said, *"Nay; but we will abide in the street all night" (Gen. 19:2)*. He thought they were ignorant of how bad the city was and that they were being foolish.

> **66**
> *Lot's house was the only one in town where they would be safe.*
> **99**

Lot did not know they were not mere men. In a way, they were because God called Adam and Eve *"man" (Gen 1:26)*. Remember that He also calls the angel man. The difference between God and man is that God is not created—He has always been in existence. God created man from the dust of the ground. So keep in mind that Lucifer was an angel. Just a created being just as we are! Now combine that knowledge with this story about Abraham. Go back to verse 1 when they met at the gate of the city. It actually says, *"There came two angels to Sodom at even" (Gen. 19:1)*. That's right. Lot was **not** just dealing with fallen mankind. He was dealing with unfallen, holy angels. Just think what we would see if we were able to see all the angels around us. Wouldn't that be exciting? But not good because we would be destroyed by their brightness unless God shielded us from their glory! God says, when He comes, the wicked will be destroyed by the brightness of His coming. (see 2 Thess. 2:8). I believe part of the destruction of the wicked will be from all of the shining angels. Of course, we also know God's glory will outshine all of them. We can't even imagine how glorious it will be.

A good example is what happened when Jesus was resurrected. *"In the end of the sabbath, as it began to dawn toward the first day of the week, came Mary Magdalene and the other Mary to see the sepulchre. And, behold, there was a great earthquake: for the angel of the Lord descended from heaven, and came and rolled back the stone from the door, and sat upon it. His countenance was like lightning, and his raiment white as snow: And for fear of him the keepers did shake, and became as dead men" (Matt. 28:1–4).* But Lot did not seem to recognize them as angels. Their brightness must have been disguised, or it would have blinded him. God does that sometimes today, too, with godly people who He wants to help just as He did with Lot. Doesn't that bring a big smile to your face! I have not seen angels that I know of. But I have experienced their protection.

Lot was so concerned for the angels' safety he invited them to come and eat with him. God says, *"and he made them a feast, and did bake unleavened bread, and they did eat" (Gen. 19:3).* Lot was a man of God living in a demon-possessed town. That's what we need to do, too. Stick our necks out for God if we believe He is telling us to do so. But! We must know who we are obeying. We must not take things into our own hands. Remember! Satan is devious. God tells us what He wants us to do in the Bible and also through the impression of the Holy Spirit. The way to tell if it really is the Holy Spirit impressing us to do something is to check and see if it agrees with what the Bible says. The Holy Spirit will never tell us to do something which disagrees with God's Word. He says, if someone does something or writes something which does not agree with the Bible—*"There is no light in them" (Isa. 8:20).*

Lot had light in him. He obeyed God, even though he chose the rich terrain surrounding this area. He was fearful for these men's lives So, he *"pressed upon them greatly; and they turned in unto him, and entered into his house" (Gen. 19:3).* The Holy Spirit must have impressed Lot to welcome them in. This, too, shows us that Lot truly was a man of God. He didn't take no for an answer when God impressed him to do something for Him.

Now let's continue our story. It continues by saying; *"But before they lay down, the men of the city, even the men of Sodom, compassed the house round, both old and young, all the people from every quarter:* saying, *"Where are the men which came in to thee this night? bring them out unto us, that we may know them" (Gen. 19:4–5).* Lot knew what they meant. He knew what would happen! That is why he insisted so hard for them to come stay at his house for the night. When the Bible talks about knowing someone in the manner these men were asking for, it meant they wanted to engage in sodomy with the angels. So Lot went outside to talk with them, saying, *"I pray you, brethren, do not so wickedly. Behold now, I have two daughters which have not known man; let me, I pray you, bring them out unto you, and do ye to them as is good in your eyes: only unto these men do nothing; for therefore came they under the shadow of my roof"* (Gen. 19:7–8).

Lot was willing to let them have sex with his daughters instead of with the men. In the Bible, when it talks about knowing someone in this , it means to have sex with them. Here is a text that shows us this is true. *"And Adam **knew** Eve his wife."* Now notice what happened as a result of knowing her: *"and she conceived, and bare Cain, and said, I have gotten a man from the LORD"* (Gen. 4:1). That's right! They had sex together.

So when Lot offered his daughters to them for sex, it was the kind of sex God created mankind to have. The men became so angry they *"came near to break the door"* (Gen. 19:9). And the two angels reached out and pulled Lot into the house to safety. Then the angels *"smote the men that were at the door of the house with blindness, both small and great: so that they wearied themselves to find the door. (Gen. 19:11).* That's right! These men were so persistent they wore themselves out, trying to find the door even after they were blinded. Isn't that something? That's real determination. Oh, that we would be as persistent to do right.

Then the angels asked Lot if he had more family members, and then they told him why God had sent them to destroy the city. Here are their words: *"Hast thou here any besides? son in law, and thy sons, and thy daughters, and whatsoever thou hast in the city, bring them out of this place: For we will destroy this place, because the cry of them is waxen great before the face of the LORD; and the LORD hath sent us to destroy it"* (Gen. 19:12–13). Lot spoke to each family member, but the Bible says, *"He seemed as one that mocked unto his sons in law And when the morning arose, then the angels hastened Lot, saying, Arise, take thy wife, and thy two daughters, which are here; lest thou be consumed in the iniquity of the city.... And it came to pass, when they had brought them forth abroad, that he said, Escape for thy life; look not behind thee, neither stay thou in all the plain; escape to the mountain, lest thou be consumed"* (Gen. 19:14–17).

His wife disobeyed, and she was destroyed. She *"looked back from behind him, and she became a pillar of salt"* (Gen. 19:26). God had told her not to look back when He rained fire and brimstone down on it, but it appears she did not believe Him. Unbelief in God is what destroys us. Obviously, she loved Sodom more than she loved God. Her heart was with Sodom. Where are our hearts? Does the sin we are clinging to mean so much to us that we will choose to die rather than love and obey God. I would certainly rather go to heaven than die a sinner's death. Our loving God holds out to us the same invitation Lot's family was given. I hope none who read this will choose death over life. Death is a horrible thing—especially the second death. Please, Holy Spirit, speak to every reader who is toying with sodomy. Give them understanding of how much You love them and want them to make an educated choice. Life in heaven with God is so wonderful. Thank You, Lord. Dear reader, I hope you will be in that vast throng when all who love God take that amazing trip to heaven. I love you, friend. And God loves you even more because He has so much love to give.

When God created Adam, he made him *"in His own image" (Gen. 1:27).* They say imitating someone is the greatest form of praise. So when we imitate God and follow His example, we are praising Him. I like that! So, when we do what Jesus did, we are praising Him in the highest manner possible. But! It has to be our choice to copy Him; otherwise, it is force— and force never comes from God—it is always from the devil.

I have noticed that when my mind seems to be in a whirl, it is when I am feeling pressured! If we can't get a thought out of our mind, it is often the devil pressuring us. God never forces or hounds us to do anything. I have found when the Holy Spirit speaks to me, it is like a fleeting whisper. He doesn't bellow at me. Sometimes I wish He would. But He leaves me free to choose whom I want to serve. We will serve someone! If we choose not to serve God, we will be serving someone else. Satan forces everyone he can to serve him. It is my prayer that each person who reads these words will choose to be involved with their Creator—Jesus.

Let's take a moment to look at the creation story again. Here is how man and woman came about.

> Then *"the Lord God"* that's Jesus, *"caused a deep sleep to fall upon Adam, and he slept: and He took one of his ribs, and closed up the flesh thereof; and the rib, which the Lord God had taken from man, made He a woman, and brought her unto the man. And Adam said, This is now bone of my bones, and flesh of my flesh: she shall be called Woman, because she was taken out of Man. Therefore shall a man leave his father and mother, and shall cleave unto his wife: and they shall be one flesh." (Gen. 2:21–24)*

The cities of Sodom and Gomorrah are where sodomy was born. Those towns fathered it. They were situated in a beautiful place, a place to be desired by all mankind. The town featured sodomy. The dictionary says sodomy is "any sexual intercourse held to be abnormal; specifically (a.) bestiality." So I looked this word up, and it is defined as "sexual relations between a person and an animal." So, this would include both men and women. Sodomy is also described as (b) anal intercourse, especially between two male persons." A sodomite is a person who practices sodomy." And to sodomize is to forcibly subject someone to sodomy."

God disapproves of all types of abnormal sexual behavior. Listen to what He says about other sexual sins. He abhors them: *"There shall be no whore of the daughters of Israel, nor a sodomite of the sons of Israel. Thou shalt not bring the hire of a whore, or the price of a dog, into the house of the* Lord *thy God for any vow: for even both these are abomination unto the* Lord *thy God" (Deut. 23:17-18).* The Strongest Strong Concordance, Hebrew -Aramaic Dictionary to the Old Testament says this is 1311 Kaleb "dog; by extension of a person of low status; a dead dog; an immoral person; male prostitute:"

Please do not fail to keep in mind there is no one on this earth who has never sinned. God loves sinners—every last one of them. That knowledge should help all of us feel more comfortable. God does not want anyone to participate in these types of practices. Would you like to know why? It is because God will not remove a person's freedom of choice, even if they say No to Him! And no one else has any business destroying another person's freedom of choice either. That is God's business until the person who wants illicit sex pressures someone like those men pressured Lot. My heart goes out to anyone who is choosing to keep saying no to God and thus is in the process of committing the unpardonable sin.

There is no one more fair than God. He never asks anyone to do something they are incapable of doing. He knows whether you are capable or not, and He accepts that. But! Do you realize, when we grasp the hand of God in faith, He says that union makes it possible for you to win over your desires? I'm sure this verse is probably familiar to you. It says, *"With God all things are possible" (Matt. 19:26).* I know I have used that verse before in this book, but I think it fits this situation perfectly. With God and us together, every one of us can win the battle over every sin if we want to. You have to ask God to help you want to win over this sin, for Satan will push it in your face and make you feel like you can't live without it. Whatever lie the devil harasses you with, just realize what it is—one of his nasty, hurtful lies designed to utterly destroy you. You are too precious for that to happen to you.

Also, God reads everyone's heart and mind. No one can fool God. He is not out to get you. He is the one who created mankind with sexual desires. A deviation is just something that is different from the normal way God created you to be. All sexual deviations come from Satan, the enemy of our soul. He wants us to get hung up on the ideas he places in our minds. Satan does everything he can to pervert our God-given desires. If someone does something, or goes to see something, or talks about something, or acts out something long enough, that something becomes normal to that person because the person has made it their norm. People are comfortable with the things they normally do.

> **"**
> *If someone does something, or goes to see something, or talks about something, or acts out something long enough, that something becomes normal to that person because the person has made it their norm.*
> **"**

The people back then did not come up with those ideas on their own. Satan placed those wrong ideas in their minds. Feelings are strong. It is through our feelings that Satan can destroy us. Don't allow him to win the battle over your sins and make your life miserable. Remember, he is a liar and the father of it. God says so in John 8:44. God has given us a conscience so that we can know right from wrong. It is a beautiful gift. It is none other than the Holy Spirit speaking to us and guiding us into all truth. If we read our Bible, talk to God in prayer, and learn what God's will is for us, then, even if we disobey our conscience, God will continue to speak to us through it. God knows our thoughts. We can't hide anything from Him.

But! If we do not want Him to let us know we are disobeying Him, and we ask Him not to bother us, then He will gradually leave us. He will not force us to be saved. But He will always love us. He is grieved in His heart when we pull away from Him. Thoughts of rejecting God are not our thoughts; they are fed to us through the prompting of Satan. He uses our own selfish desires to destroy us. Really, they are not our own desires; they are actually desires he has placed in our minds. Run from him! It will get worse until he has usurped total control of your will. As he works to destroy our God-given feelings of love, we become weaker and weaker to fight against Him.

Please! At least get down on your knees and ask God for the desire to follow Him. Don't allow Satan to lead you back into sin by yielding to his lies when he says," it won't hurt to do it just this once." That's not true. He knows if you give in to him this time, you will give in again, and again, and again until you are totally unable to obey God. That is a summary of how the unpardonable sin takes place. But! Never give up! God can get you out of those situations, but it's not easy. He dearly loves you. He alone has the power to save you. Ask Him to give you a desire to do His will. A prayer like that is none other than a scream for help. Here is another verse which tells us how God feels about these things.

"And there were also sodomites in the land: and they did according to all the abominations of the nations which the LORD cast out before the children of Israel" (1 Kings 14:24). "And the remnant of the sodomites, which remained in the days of his father Asa, he took out of the land" (1 Kings 22:46). "And He brake down the houses of the sodomites, that were by the house of the LORD, where the women wove hangings for the grove" (2 Kings 23:7). These were places where people went to worship false gods. Who were they? Why, they were worshipping the devil. If we are not worshipping God, we are automatically worshipping the devil. Scary, huh? After all of this with Lot and his family took place, God destroyed those cities. The only people saved were Lot and his two daughters. You can read the whole story for yourself in Genesis 19) Also look up 1 John 2:3–6. God bless you.

15

War in Heaven! Can You Imagine That?

Now let's talk about the war God had with the devil. It happened right in heaven itself—mind you. The beginning of the antichrist was when Lucifer thought he should be equal with God. He thought he had just as much right to be God as the Father, Son, and Holy Spirit had. John tells us a lot about the antichrist. So let's begin with what he has to say. *"Ye have heard that antichrist shall come, even now there are many antichrists; whereby we know that it is the last time" (1 John 2:18)*. Do you notice God says there are many antichrists? He also says **we cannot trust them!** I'm so thankful God gives us faith enough to trust Him. I love Him so much. If you love Him, please feel free to join me and wing a personal prayer to him right now. I'm going to tell Him how much I love and trust Him because of what He is willing to do for us every moment of our life. I know it will make Him extremely happy. We can do this every day because our love for Him changes every day—hopefully, it increases daily. But! Never forget we will have down days. In fact, I had down years, as you saw if you read my other book called *The Lost Thread of God's Love*. Those feelings just show we are human.

John was telling the people way back then to hang on because Jesus would be coming soon. To each generation, it looks like Jesus will come soon. It will seem like it hasn't been any time at all when Jesus comes and wakes us up if we have to go to sleep in death before He comes to take us to heaven. That's because a person doesn't realize how much time has passed when they are asleep. We have to look at the clock to see how long we have slept. It is the same way for a person who is asleep in death. God places the hope of His soon coming in the hearts of people in every generation. Since Jesus has already paid for our sins, He could come anytime. It has been a long time since He died on the cross. But our God of love will not come until every single person who will come to Him has come. He is going to wait as long as there are people who have not heard the good news of salvation. He is waiting until every single person has had the privilege of knowing the wonderful story of salvation and has either accepted or rejected His gift.

Then, when all have heard and taken advantage of the freedom of choice God gives them, and all have made their final choice, He will come and get all who love Him. Jesus will not come and take those who love Him home to heaven as long as there is still one more person who needs to make that decision. Now, that's love for all mankind. So, we need to get busy and let everyone know it's time for Jesus to come and that He is waiting for them. You are that special. Yes! He is anxiously waiting for you to make the most important decision of your life. We can go to Him in prayer right now and pray for those who have not made that most important choice that can ever be made. Ask Him for the guidance of the Holy Spirit and ask Him to send the Holy Spirit to them and us. Each of us needs to decide in our own hearts, too, that we will **not** do anything He does not want us to do. He wants us to give our all to Him and then study our Bible. David said, *"Thy Word is a lamp unto my feet, and a light unto my path" (Ps. 119:105).* And *"Thy Word have I hid in my heart, that I might not sin against thee" (Ps. 119:11).* And we know all the bad things David did. If he can do this, so can we.

What a God. Now that's true love. The kind of love only God has and can give. He is so longsuffering and patient. I just love Him for that. Knowing why He is tarrying lets us know what a special lover He is. And it helps us be willing to wait. We certainly want everyone to come to heaven who will give their whole heart to God. It's well worth the wait. Don't you agree? I'm sure you do. It could be our mom or dad that He is waiting for. Or our brother or sister. We sure don't want to leave them behind. Neither does God. Knowing this should help us be patient.

Then he tells us who antichrist is! Listen! It has something to do with liars. We know who the first liar was, don't we! It was Lucifer, and it includes anyone who walks in his footsteps and agrees with him. And we've all been there and done that. It is a life and death matter that we understand what and who antichrist is. So what do you say we see what God says about him? What do you say we review God's famous war with Lucifer in heaven. It is hard to imagine a war there, but God says there was one. So let's hear it straight from God's Word. It won't lie to us. When the Bible talks about a dragon, it is talking about the devil. And when it talks about stars, it is talking about angels.

Remember how good God was to Lucifer? And the special job God gave him, guarding His holy law! And also, do you remember the fact that God knows everything? Well, God did everything He could to woo Lucifer to Him. He let him know how much He loved Him. He gave him the most important job He could give him. But in Lucifer's opinion, it wasn't good enough. He was obsessed with the desire to be God. He thought he had just as much right to be the Son of God as God's real Son did.

So he caused a war to break out among his angel friends. That war took place in heaven. It went on for a very long time. I'm sure it was very secretive at first. Little snipes behind God's back every now and then. I am sure he probably thought he was getting away with them—even though they took place right under God's nose. Rather naive of him, I'd say! And I'm sure if he thought about it, he knew he was wrong. But he wouldn't listen. He wouldn't admit it. God knew what he was doing. God knew his every thought and desire.

> **“**
> *It is almost time for Jesus to take us home to heaven with Him.*
> **”**

But he just kept getting bolder. He collected a very large number of the angels who took sides against God and believed his lies. They are the angels who are down here on earth now, working with the devil to take control. Our Bible tells us: *"And his tail drew the third part of the stars of heaven, and did cast them to the earth" (Rev. 12:4, first part). "And there was war in heaven."* The angels chose sides. *"Michael"* (Jesus), *"and His angels fought against the dragon"* (the angel who was named Lucifer in the beginning) *"fought and his angels" (Rev. 12:7).* What a mess they have made. The good angels and Jesus won the battle. I say hoo-ray. And our Bible goes on to say that the wicked angels, those siding with the angel God named Lucifer, *"prevailed not; neither was their place found any more in heaven. And the great dragon was cast out, that old serpent, called the Devil, and Satan, which deceiveth the whole world: he was cast out into the earth, and his angels were cast out with him" (Rev. 12:8–9).* That's not good news. That is where he is now, and it is why everything is so terrible on Planet Earth. The good thing is it will soon come to an end. It is almost time for Jesus to take us home to heaven with Him.

God allowed the battle to go on in heaven for a long time, for we know that there was antagonism between Christ and Satan during the time when Jesus was creating our world. It was right after that Lucifer lied to Eve. And we see how the devil had his back up from then on. Also, we know Satan had not been totally barred from heaven clear down to Job's day. But he was probably spending most of his time down here. God still talked with him. Lucifer was still meeting with those wicked angels. Here is a conversation Jesus had with Satan. *"Now there was a day when the sons of God came to present themselves before the LORD, and Satan came also among them. And the LORD said unto Satan, Whence comest thou? Then Satan answered the LORD, and said, from going to and fro in the earth, and from walking up and down in it. And the LORD said unto Satan, hast thou considered my servant Job, that there is none like him in the earth, a perfect and upright man, one that feareth God, and escheweth evil?" (Job 1:6–8).* Satan told God the only reason Job feared him was because He protected him. He accused God of placing a hedge about him, and protecting him, and blessing everything he did, including giving him much cattle.

So God allowed Satan to test Job but with limitations, *"all that he hath is in thy power; only upon himself put not forth thine hand" (Job.1:12).* Thus it became a test for Job. He would prove to all who read God's Word that God was fair to Satan in every way. What a God! He allowed Job to prove his allegiance to Him and be tempted by the devil. But Job was not tempted; he went through the test with flying colors. God allows us to go through tests, too, not because God wants to test us, He knows whether we belong to Him or not, but so others can see our integrity, and through our obedience, come to honor God.

But the devil is always pressuring God and saying God is unfair. The devil claims God is unfair because He unfairly blesses and protects us sinners. Satan contests that the only reason they love God is because He doesn't allow anything to harm them. This scenario we just looked at between Job and God certainly does not bear that out. God allowed Satan to do terrible things to Job, and Job still stayed true to God. Yes! Satan accuses God of protecting His followers unfairly, but it just isn't true. I believe God placed this story of Job in the Bible so that you and I could see how the devil operates and know why terrible things happen to God's people. It really is the only fair way to take care of the sin problem. Cruelty certainly does not happen to anyone because God does not love them, whether they are good or bad. It only happens because God's enemy is jealous of God's Son Jesus and because God loves us.

Job went through terrific pain again, too, because of Satan's selfish, jealous anger against God. He allowed the devil to give Job terribly painful boils *"from the sole of his foot to his crown (Job 2:7).* Why? Because again Satan accused God of over-protecting him, and God said to Satan, he *"holdeth fast his integrity, although thou movedst me against him, to destroy him without cause" (Job. 2:3).* I am sure God goes through this scenario constantly with Satan concerning each one of us. Just think how upsetting this must be for God—a God who loves and does not harm. That's right! God is not the one who harms us. God only allows awful things to come to us because Satan pushes God to prove that we are loving and trusting God. Wouldn't you think Satan would know by now that he is only ruining his own name further and adding more sins to his count? He's just totally rotten to the core and downright evil through and through. He has no conscience at all. He is totally devoid of love for others. He only has selfishness toward himself, and that's not love at all. Then Satan must have whispered in Job's wife's ear, for she gave him some very dangerous advice. The idea had to have come from the mouth of Satan, for it was designed to cause her to lose her eternal life. Those are the kinds of thoughts Satan places in our minds, too. He pits husbands and wives, parents and children, against each other. He is behind every quarrel and all evil things that take place. The thoughts Satan places in a person's mind certainly do match hers. He must have been tempting and goading her. Instead of telling Job to obey the Lord, she told him what Satan told her to say. This is the same scenario we've seen with Adam and Eve and many others. Satan loves to pit spouses against each other. What a shame that we take the bait. It happens over and over. The majority of times, we don't stop to realize our thoughts are being fed to us by Satan. We need to bolt and run into the arms of God.

Listen to what she told her husband to do. She certainly was not helping Him to seek God, for she told him to do terrible, foolish things. Ones, which if obeyed, would have caused him to lose eternal life. God is always willing to forgive if we are truly are sorry. But as a person takes Satan's path, they have less and less desire to do what is right. Satan knows this. That is why he keeps riling us up and telling us God is not fair. It's an extremely dangerous path to be on.

Praise God Job had a wonderful relationship with his Lord. He did not accept her bait! Job certainly was a man of God. She said to him, *"Dost thou still retain thine integrity?"* In other words, do you still think you are better than everyone else? Do you still think you are pleasing God? Oh, how her words must have cut him. Praise God! Despite all the evil she was throwing at him, Job still trusted God. He didn't accept the poor me attitude she urged on him. No, he didn't play the blame game. Instead, he honored God. What a good example his life is for us.

What did she tell him to do? It was terrible! *"Curse God, and die" (Job 2:9)*. Her words plainly show the devil's attitude toward God. That's real hatred. She had to be in the heat of anger toward God to say this. **Curse God**? That" terrible! And the outcome would be that Job would die! That certainly does not show love for her husband either. **WOW!** But notice the contrast between Job and his wife. *"In all this did not Job sin with his lips" (Job 2:10)*. Praise God! He continued to cling to God. Her words certainly were not designed to help him stay true to God. He needed prayer. He needed her sympathy and protection against the wicked one. Instead, she suggested he place himself in more danger. But just listen to his reply, even though he was in severe mental and physical pain. He recognized her plight and tried to help her. Now that's real love and real grit for both for his wife and God. *"But he said unto her, Thou speakest as one of the foolish women speaketh. What? shall we receive good at the hand of God, and shall we not receive evil? In all this did not Job sin with his lips" (Job. 2:10)*. Yes! *"In all this Job sinned not, nor charged God foolishly" (Job 1:22)*.

That should have made her think twice. It is amazing that he could do this for her. God bless him. It's very difficult to stay level-headed when one is in as much pain as he was in. I encourage you to read the whole story for yourself. What I have quoted is only the tip of the iceberg concerning what Satan did to Job. If you haven't read it before, you will be appalled at the things God allowed Satan to do to him. And just think! God allowed this to happen to Job because God would allow Satan to do these same kinds of things to His people all down through the ages. Job was trustworthy. So God can show us in our day what Satan does to all people. Satan is not choosey. He even tries to drown his followers in terrible persecution. That's just who he is—evil to the core—he's a devil through and through.

> **We are living in the last days, just before Jesus comes. It's time to be ready.**

Job clung to God through it all and stayed true to Him. We are living in the last days, just before Jesus comes. It's time to be ready. It's time to be sure we understand what God says to us in His Word. We can't trust people because all of us are struggling to understand God's will. Our Bible tells us, *"There is none righteous, no, not one" (Rom 3:10)*. We must commune with God and back everything we hear with a Bible text. God is the only one we should trust. Job gives us a wonderful example to follow. Read his story and find out how God blessed him after he went through this trial. Remember this verse. It bears repeating. *"Man shall not live by bread alone, but by every word that proceedeth out of the mouth of God" (Matt. 4:4).* It was Jesus who said this when He was being tempted by the devil. We truly need to make Him our example. No one knows better than Him. He experienced the temptations of the devil firsthand. And He loves us so much He died to pay for our sins. May God help us let Him be our guide.

This story about Job is a wonderful testimony of what man can do through the help of God. He placed it in His Word so we would know that Satan will get worse and worse as Jesus' coming gets closer. These stories help us know what to expect and how the devil operates. Truly, we, too, at this time in earth's history, are experiencing the same type of persecution from Satan as they have had in all ages. I am so grateful this story of Job is in the Bible. It really does help us understand what is taking place behind the scenes. We see that the battle is still being fiercely waged. Job's story certainly is an eye-opener. Hang in there! EVERYONE!

Thank You, Lord, for this insight. You are so special. God says these stories pertain to our time just like the things that happened in the time of the children of Israel in the wilderness did.

Now all these things happened unto them for examples: and they are written for our admonition, upon whom the ends of the world are come. Wherefore let him that thinketh he standeth take heed lest he fall. There hath no temptation taken you but such as is common to man: but God is faithful, who will not suffer you to be tempted above that ye are able; but will with the temptation also make a way to escape, that ye may be able to bear it. (1 Cor. 10:11–13)

16

Lucifer's Life after God Totally Kicked Him OUT of Heaven

Tyrus was a great city, the center of trade, but the people who lived there were very evil. They did not honor God—but went the way of the devil. So, in this parable, the writer, who is the prophet Ezekiel, is speaking God's words. They describe both the city and also the one who really was ruling it. The people accepted Lucifer as its ruler. Thus, this prophecy is both about him and also about the literal city of Tyrus. The heart of the figurative Tyrus was lifted up. Ezekiel is basically speaking to the beautiful angel the Lord created and named Lucifer. He said to him, *"Because thine heart is lifted up, and thou hast said, I am a God, I sit in the seat of God, in the midst of the seas; yet thou art a man, and not God, though thou set thine heart as the heart of God"* *(Ezek. 28:2)*.

Yes, Lucifer claimed to be God. Isaiah also prophesied about him after he was kicked out of heaven. Saying, *"For thou hast said in thine heart, I will ascend into heaven, I will exalt my throne above the stars* [angels] *of God: I will sit also upon the mount of the congregation, in the sides of the north:... I will be like the Most High"* (God the Father is the Most High) *(Isa. 14:13–14)*. The devil has never given up his claim to be God, and he never will. Let's go back to what else Ezekiel had to say. Notice! Ezekiel called him Lucifer, the Prince of Tyrus and named him after the leader of that city. Lucifer tricked himself into thinking he had usurped God's throne. He still thinks he will succeed in taking the throne from God. He will think this to the very end. How wrong he is. We are so blessed that God tells us what Lucifer's final end will be.

God said to him, *"Behold, thou art wiser than Daniel."* This tells us that Daniel was extremely wise, but Lucifer was even wiser. For Ezekiel said, *"there is no secret that they can hide from thee" (Ezek. 28:3)*. It was God who supplied Lucifer with this wisdom. This means Lucifer can't truthfully accuse God of making him inferior when he finally lands in the fire of hell, and the human who ruled that region will have no honest reason to complain either.

Let's take a moment and look at some verses that explain what God was talking about when He talked about Daniel's wisdom. God gave Daniel superior wisdom when he was taken captive in Babylon. They say, what comes around, goes around. Interesting isn't it! The king had just destroyed Jerusalem, and he took Daniel and his three friends captive and took them back to Babylon with him. The Bible tells us what Daniel and his three friends were like at that time in their lives.

> *As for these four children, God gave them knowledge and skill in **all** learning and wisdom: and Daniel had understanding in all visions and dreams. Now at the end of the days that the king had said he should bring them in, then the prince of the eunuchs brought them in before Nebuchadnezzar. And the king communed with them; and among them all was found none like Daniel, Hananiah, Mishael, and Azariah: therefore stood they before the king. And in all matters of wisdom and understanding that the king enquired of them, he found them ten times better than all the magicians and astrologers that were in all his realm. (Dan. 1:17–20)*

Also, read Daniel 2:1–49. I think you will find that bit of information interesting.

Now let's go back to talking about Lucifer. God continues to tell us more about this angel. He says; *"With thy wisdom and with thine understanding thou hast gotten thee riches, and hast gotten gold and silver into thy treasures: By thy great wisdom and by thy traffick hast thou increased thy riches, and thine heart is lifted up because of thy riches"* (Ezek. 28:4–5). What was his problem? First of all, he was proud. He thought he had bested God. And God tells him what his problem is. Listen to what God said to Lucifer and the human beings who were ruling that area.

> *Therefore thus saith the Lord GOD;* [That's Jesus! He is the Lord God.] *Because thou hast set thine heart as the heart of God; Behold, therefore I will bring strangers upon thee, the terrible of the nations: and they shall draw their swords against the beauty of thy wisdom, and they shall defile thy brightness. They shall bring thee down to the pit,* [grave] *and thou shalt die the deaths of them that are slain in the midst of the seas. Wilt thou yet say before Him that slayeth thee, I am*

*God? but **thou shalt be a man, and no God,** in the hand of him that slayeth thee. (Ezek. 28:6–9, emphasis supplied)*

It really is only God who can destroy anyone permanently. Isn't it comforting that everything and everyone is in His hands!

God tells us this is what will happen to him in the end. *"Thou shalt die the deaths of the uncircumcised by the hand of strangers: for I have spoken it, saith the Lord GOD" (Ezek. 28:10).* Isaiah adds these words: *"How art thou cut down to the ground, which didst weaken the nations!" (Isa. 14:12).* God was talking about the nations of our world. This battle between God and Lucifer began down here when Adam and Eve were created. Lucifer had his lip out. He wanted to be the Creator. God reserved that right for Himself. It is a huge part of what makes Jesus God.

> **" *There is an ark in which the covenant of God, the Ten Commandments, is kept in that heavenly temple still today.* "**

Now let's go back to the prophet Ezekiel. He gives us God's evaluation of Lucifer. *"Moreover the word of the LORD came unto me, saying, Son of man, take up a lamentation upon the king of Tyrus, and say unto him, Thus saith the Lord GOD; **Thou sealest up the sum, full of wisdom, and perfect in beauty**" (Ezek. 28:11–12, emphasis supplied).* WOW! **He was the wisest, most beautiful angel ever created.** Then the scene changes again, and God is talking about Lucifer when he was in the Garden of Eden. He said, *"Thou hast been in Eden the garden of God; every precious stone was thy covering, the sardius, topaz, and the diamond, the beryl, the onyx, and the jasper, the sapphire, the emerald, and the carbuncle, and gold."* Again, God pointed out to him that he was only a created being. I bet that floated like a lead balloon—knowing how Lucifer is.

We know God reminded Lucifer about the special job He gave him in heaven too, saying, *"Thou art the anointed cherub that covereth; and I have set thee so" (Ezek. 28:14).* Lucifer was one of two cherubs who guarded the Ten-commandment law of God that resides in His holy temple in heaven. Through a vision God gave John, we know that law is still there in God's temple today. Just where it was when Lucifer guarded it long years ago. Let's take a moment and notice that God told Moses how to make a temple for the children of Israel like it for them down here.

There is an ark in which the covenant of God, the Ten Commandments, is kept in that heavenly temple still today *(Exod. 25:9–16)*. God's throne is on the ark that holds His law. His throne is called the *"mercy seat" (vs. 17.)* Isn't that beautiful? It is where we go to receive mercy and experience God's deep love for His wayward children. Listen to God's instructions to the Israelites. *"And they shall make an ark" (vs. 10). "And thou shalt put into the ark the testimony which I shall give thee" (vs. 16).* There were two cherubim who guarded God and His law.

> *And make one cherub on the one end, and the other cherub on the other end: even of the mercy seat shall ye make the cherubims on the two ends thereof. And the cherubim shall stretch forth their wings on high, covering the mercy seat with their wings, and their faces shall look one to another; toward the mercy seat shall the faces of the cherubims be. And thou shalt put the mercy seat above upon the ark; and in the ark thou shalt put the testimony that I shall give thee. And there I will meet with thee, and I will commune with thee from above the mercy seat, from between the two cherubims which are upon the ark of the testimony. (Exod. 25:17–20)*

Lucifer was one of those angels. He was in the temple with God and in the closest possible contact with Him. That means he heard everything God said to those who came to talk with God. This also means he knew God's law backward and forward. He also saw how loving and kind God was as He spoke to all who came to talk with Him. Yes, he saw the fairness of God. But Lucifer did not honor God; instead, he wanted to wrest the kingdom from Him. Remember! Never forget! In chapter one, I used Isaiah 8: 20, and I think it bears repeating. It is the very best guide we have. It comes straight from God. He says. *"To the law and to the testimony: if they speak not according to this word, it is because there is no light in them" (Isa. 8:20).* Those are God's words. The best words ever.

Keep in mind that Satan, or anyone who obeys him, will quote Bible verses to you and often leave out just one word. He came to Jesus and said, *"If thou be the Son of God, command that these stones be made bread" (Matt. 4:3).* Jesus was the Son of God. He didn't have to prove anything. That was one of Satan's nasty tricks to destroy Jesus. Jesus knew who He was. He didn't have to prove anything to Satan. He proved it for us who are under Satan's attack today so God could let us know. *"Man shall not live by bread alone, but by every word that proceedeth out of the mouth of*

God" (Matt. 4:4). That's why *"Jesus was led up of the Spirit into the wilderness to be tempted of the devil" (Matt. 4:1).*

I was greatly upset when I found this out. I will share with you how God helped me with one of those instances in the last chapter of this book. Satan picks at Scripture. Yes! Satan often misquotes the Bible with just one or two words missing so that we won't notice the discrepancy. He loves to misquote Scripture. That is one of the ways He impersonates God and makes it look like he is obeying God. That's called lying. Jesus said to the scribes and Pharisees, *"Ye are of your father the devil, and the lusts of your father ye will do. He was a murderer from the beginning, and abode not in the truth, because there is no truth in him. When he speaketh a lie, he speaketh of his own: for he is a liar, and the father of it" (John 8:44).* Those are very hard words, but they couldn't be more true. Satan never gives up. He doggedly picked on Jesus. He just used his same old tricks. He was trying to wear Jesus down. That's what he does to us too. He knows if he uses the same lie over and over, we just might begin to believe it. It becomes familiar, so we begin thinking may it is true.

So, again He used that very little word with great connotation. That means the word he used was slightly different from the word that would correctly describe it. In other words, the devil veered just a teeny bit from the truth, so the person he was lying to would not realize it was not true. That is the devil's character. He is a liar. Yes, he lied to Jesus, but praise God, Jesus caught it. Again his word was "if"! He had taken Jesus up and set Him *"on a pinnacle of the temple" (Matt. 4:5).* And said, *"If thou be the Son of God, cast thyself down: for it is written, He shall give His angels charge concerning thee: and in their hands they shall bear thee up, lest at any time thou dash thy foot against a stone."* But! Was the devil really quoting this verse? Was every word correct, or was there just a slight variation? Let's look and see!

This is quoted from Psalm 91:11–12. *"For he shall give His angels charge over thee, to keep thee in all thy ways. They shall bear thee up in their hands, lest thou dash thy foot against a stone."* In Matthew 4, the words **"to keep thee in all thy ways"** are not present. It makes a big difference. He was out to make Jesus believe His heavenly Father did not love Him. Wow! But Jesus knew better. He knew the verse. He knew His Father loved Him and would help Him stay true to Him. Jesus knew those His Father would strive to help Him pass the test. I am so glad. The Father will do that for us, too, when we are in the throes of temptation. Yes! We will be tempted. The Father loves us very much, too. We know because He let His Son die for our sins. We must never forget that. It is part of our safety net. God does not control things. He allows people to be their wicked selves. The Father did not keep Jesus from doing what He chose to do either. Neither will He bar the devil from doing his evil work. If He did, He would be removing their freedom of choice. And He would be a controlling God.

It's too bad we have to face such harmful things, but that's the way it is. Remember! It wasn't pleasant for the Father or the Son to have to create a being they knew would become the devil. But once this whole mess is over, everything will be perfect from then on and throughout eternity—forever. Oh, how God must be looking forward to that day. I know, without a doubt, He is anxious for that time to come quickly. I am, too! How about you? I can just smell that sweet heavenly air. Just look at the terrible things happening in our world. All the people who are being mistreated, starving if you please, and with no good place to stay. Fleeing their homes and not being welcomed somewhere else. Oh, how that hurts. That certainly is the devil's doing and has been his doing throughout history. Can we blame it all on the devil! No! Certainly not. Every person on earth has freedom of choice! It is God-given. But Satan blocks it every way he can.

Through prayer and obedience to God's law and with the prompting of the Holy Spirit, we can be like Jesus! Or! We can be like the devil. Each of us daily, moment by moment, is making that choice. So be careful! Know your Bible. Run to it and make sure other people and yourself are telling the truth. Remember! God says, *"Thy word is truth" (John 17:17).* That's right! Every word in the Bible is true. God says He sanctifies us through His truth. That's really important to our salvation. Sanctification is the way God sets us apart to tell the truth. He also says it with these words, *"and thy law is the truth" (Ps. 119:142),* and *"all thy commandments are truth" (Ps. 119:151).*

Never forget, just one word can change truth into a lie, and the devil is good at it. I had to look at those verses very carefully. I didn't expect a whole sentence to be missing. That was a surprise. It shows how very deceitful the devil is. He's working very hard; he knows his time is short. But what is most important is that God is always present to help us. You can't beat that. God is good all time.

17

Jesus Prepared Peter for Following Him and Warned Us about a Problem the Antichrist Would Cause—Come and See What the Problem Was!

Jesus introduced Himself to Peter as the **"ROCK"**—Founder **of His Church**. Yes! Jesus says He is the founder of the Christian Church. Preparing His disciples to raise up churches to teach people the truth about God was uppermost in Jesus' mind. He wanted them to be His missionaries. To do this, they needed to know Him very well. To be able to bring people to a clear understanding of who Jesus was, they must have a correct understanding of who He was and also who His disciples were. Jesus was in the process of choosing His disciples. He had been baptized by John the Baptist and was just beginning to preach, saying, *"Repent: for the kingdom of heaven is at hand" (Matt. 4:17).* He began choosing those He wanted to be His disciples. And He was *"walking by the sea of Galilee, and saw two brethren, Simon called Peter, and Andrew his brother, casting a net into the sea: for they were fishers. And he saith unto them, Follow me, and I will make you fishers of men. And they straightway left their nets, and followed him" (Matt. 4:18–20).* From that time forward, Jesus taught them how to come to Him and bring others to Him.

> **"**
> *Preparing His disciples to raise up churches to teach people the truth about God was uppermost in Jesus' mind.*
> **"**

He taught them to *"beware of false prophets, which come to you in sheep's clothing, but inwardly they are ravening wolves" (Matt. 7:15).* Jesus likened people to fruit trees. Read Matthew 7:16–19. And he said, *"by their fruits ye shall know them" (Matt. 7:20).* Then He told them what made the difference.

> *Not every one that saith unto me, Lord, Lord, shall enter into the kingdom of heaven; but he that doeth the will of my Father which is in heaven. Many will say to me in that day, Lord, Lord, have we not prophesied in thy name? and in thy name have cast out devils? and in thy name done many wonderful works? And then will I profess unto them, I never knew you: depart from ye who work iniquity. (Matt. 7:21–23)*

He trained them well. Jesus was being careful to make sure people did not think one of His disciples was the founder of His new baby church. The antichrist in our day still claims Peter is the founder of God's true church. So listen to Jesus, as He made certain we would know that He, **Jesus, is the founder of His church.** Since Jesus knows everything, even before it takes place, He knew Peter would need this advice. Jesus did this for Peter's protection and ours. That is why He used the word **"Christ"** in the name He gave His Church. That is why we call it the Christian Church! Right after Jesus told Peter who the founder of the Christian Church was, He began teaching Peter who he was. It was then that Jesus voiced these strange words to him! He said, *"I say also unto thee, That thou art Peter" (Matt. 16:18, first part).* It must have sounded very strange to Peter, but Peter loved Jesus and listened.

Jesus did not want Peter to think he was the founder of the Christian Church. That wouldn't have been good for Peter or anyone else. And, of course, God knew there would be a church who would teach that Peter is the founder of His church on earth. God wants all of those people to know Peter is not the founder of God's church. Peter was still in training to be a minister for Christ; before him were many experiences that would make him a fisher of men. Read Chapters 10–13 to see what else He taught them.

So, why did Jesus single Peter out? Jesus was protecting Peter. He looked down through the years of time and saw the problem it would cause if Peter claimed to be the founder of God's first baby church. Jesus also knew what a good witness Peter would turn out to be for Him. And Jesus did not want any roadblocks in Peter's way. Peter was very important to God's new baby church. Jesus knew Peter's heart, and He also knew

Peter's thoughts. Actually, Jesus was aware of everything that would ever happen to Peter, so at that point in time, Jesus informed Peter that he was a stone. Not the Rock foundation of God's church. The Father knew only His Son could accomplish such a feat. I believe Jesus was thinking of us, too, way down here in our day. He wants us to realize that Peter was not the first pope. There were no popes when the disciples raised up churches while Jesus was here on earth. God's true church has never had a pope. Popes were instigated as the church in Rome became corrupted by unsaved parishioners. Many of the pagans were baptized by Roman rulers.

So! With this background, can you picture in your mind's eye Jesus lovingly looking into Peter's eyes and saying, *"You are Peter."* And then, can you visualize Jesus pointing to Himself and saying, *"Upon this rock I will build my church; and the gates of hell shall not prevail against it" (Matt. 16:18,* last part). And can you see the blank look on Peter's face? He probably didn't have a clue as to what Jesus was talking about. If Peter had known, he would have been very excited. For actually, Jesus was telling Peter that Satan would not win the battle over him. That was good. It wouldn't have been good for Peter to know about all of the trouble that would be caused because the church would claim Peter was the first pope. He wouldn't have understood.

I believe the keys Jesus was talking about was some witnessing skills He was going to give him very soon. Jesus was going to trust Peter to give the gospel of the kingdom throughout the then-known world. Peter probably would have been overwhelmed. It was a very important task Jesus was planning to place on His disciples' shoulders. And Jesus was telling Peter that whoever he brought to Jesus would be in God's hands, not his. Isn't that marvelous? What good news it was. But at that moment in time, I am sure Peter had no idea what Jesus was talking about. Can you see the puzzled look on Peter's face? I think I can. God has plans for us, too, we do not know about. He hides them for a very good reason. Someday He will tell us all about it. What a glorious day that will be.

Jesus proceeded by saying, *"I will give unto thee the keys of the kingdom of heaven: and whatsoever thou shalt bind on earth shall be bound in heaven: and whatsoever thou shalt loose on earth shall be loosed in heaven" (Matt. 16:19).* And Matthew 18:18 says the same thing. That must have really bombed Peter out.

Now look at 1 Corinthians 5:4–5: *"In the name of our Lord Jesus Christ, when ye are gathered together, and my spirit, with the power of our Lord Jesus*

Christ, To deliver such an one unto Satan for the destruction of the flesh, that the spirit may be saved in the day of the Lord Jesus." The disciples would be working with church members. They were helping them overcome sinful ways. As they talked with them, they told them what they needed to do to be saved. They needed to stop committing the sins that bound them. The disciples helped them know what to do to become like Jesus.

Peter was not the only disciple who helped rear up God's first churches on earth. The disciples went from city to city, forming new church congregations. I believe Jesus looked down through the corridors of time and saw what people would try to do with His words, and He did not want any of us or anyone in any generation to think Peter was the founder of His church. Yes, these words were placed in our Bible by Jesus Himself for all of mankind. What a lover of our soul He is. The word "bound" #1210 in the *Strongest Strong's Exhaustive Concordance of the Bible* defines the word as "to tie, bind, imprison." God is still the judge, but the gospel is the key to eternal life, and Jesus gave Peter that key so that he could give the gospel to others. The gospel is binding in a way but in a good way. The gospel binds us to Jesus. Jesus was telling Peter He would be binding people to their Savior, Jesus Christ, and to His church. What a wonderful job. And what a huge responsibility. I am sure being called a stone—and then comparing it to a ROCK, was rather shocking and confusing to Peter at first glance.

Bur Peter understood Jesus was just trying to make a comparison between Himself and him. A comparison Peter could understand! And I'm sure Peter did understand! We don't hear him retaliating or complaining and saying to anyone, "Jesus is belittling me." Oh no! Peter understood how important it was that everyone knew who the real founder of the church was. Jesus did not want Peter to get the big head. His temperament could very well have taken him there. Just listen to what Jesus told Peter next.

I checked to see what Jesus had been doing just before He had this conversation with Peter. And I found that two of John the Baptist's disciples had heard John say something extraordinary concerning Jesus. Here is what John said to them as they came near Jesus! *"Behold the Lamb of God!" (John 1:36).* And I again have to say **WOW! For that is a biggie!** When John's disciples heard this, they understood that John was telling them Jesus was the Lamb who would be slain for their sins—their **Messiah**. Therefore, those two disciples followed Jesus and asked, "Where are you staying?" (see John 1:38). And Jesus invited them to, *"Come and see"*

(John 1:39). One of those disciples was *"Andrew, Simon Peter's brother"* *(John 1:40)*. And, of course, Andrew shared that conversation about Jesus being the Messiah with his brother, Peter. Andrew said to Peter, *"We have found the Messias which is, being translated, the Christ" (John 1:41)*.

And the very next Bible verse introduces us to the Rock/stone conversation. Peter didn't murmur. Instead, he probably was experiencing shock and awe. *"When Jesus beheld him, he said, Thou art Simon, the son of Jona: thou shalt be called Cephas, which is by interpretation, A stone" (John 1:42)*.

We are not told how Peter felt at that moment. But if it were me, I certainly would have been in awe. A stone could be a small replica of the Rock. That is what Jesus wanted Peter to be! A replica of Himself. What a compliment! We, too, can be little stones, replicas of the Rock, Jesus Christ. How awe-inspiring is that? All I can say is, "Lord, help me be like You." Interesting! Jesus even gave Peter a name that meant stone—he was not a Rock. That is why I believe, even way back then, Jesus was preparing Peter to witness to all who would listen to him, and people would learn through Peter just who Jesus was. And Jesus did ask Peter to bring people to Him! That was Peter's mission! As he and the other disciples told people Jesus was the Messiah, they banded together into the very first Christian Church under Jesus' leadership. What a privilege! And have you thought about it? Everyone who follows Jesus' example has that same privilege that Peter had.

> **Christian is a word that means Christ-like. So, when you say you go to the Christian Church, you are saying you are like Jesus and a member of His church.**

Christian is a word that means Christ-like. So, when you say you go to the Christian Church, you are saying you are like Jesus and a member of His church. Can you imagine that? Jesus knew what lay ahead for Peter. Actually, some of it concerning Peter is still in our future. I believe Jesus asked Peter who He was so He could prepare him for the trials that lay ahead of him and for us. He knew Peter would swing between boldness and fear. And that he would boldly cut off a man's ear to stick up for Jesus when He was in thick of persecution. Jesus knew people would misuse these verses and claim Peter was the first leader of His church. God wanted to protect Peter from this. Jesus also wanted to let us know He was the only One who could fulfill that service in His church. Neither Jesus nor His Father ever put one disciple above another. We need to remember who we are! Only created beings—not God—not the "Rock." And that includes every single person on earth who has ever been born.

Jesus knows what will happen to us clear down in our day. Jesus knows our thoughts, too! Here are a few of the recorded instances the Bible gives us to let us know Jesus can read our minds. Look at this verse. It is talking about the righteous and the wicked, those who will be alive when Jesus comes. God says, *"For I know their works and their thoughts" (Isa. 66:18).* And do you remember this example of Jesus knowing someone's thoughts in an earlier chapter? *"And, behold, certain of the scribes said within themselves, This man blasphemeth. And Jesus knowing their thoughts said, Wherefore think ye evil in your hearts? For whether is it easier, to say, Thy sins be forgiven thee; or to say, Arise, and walk?" (Matt. 9:3–5).*

Yes, Jesus knew Peter's heart. He knew Peter would be obedient to Him and do what He asked Him to do. But Jesus also knew Peter would have problems. Peter was impetuous. Remember! This is the Peter who would lie and refuse to admit he knew Jesus. Why would Peter lie? For two reasons! One was because he was afraid of getting killed. Jesus knew it would happen to him after he became His disciple. It happened just before Jesus' crucifixion. Jesus knew when they wanted to kill Him, Peter would reason within himself, I am Jesus' disciple, so they might kill me. Also, at that time of his walk with Jesus, he wasn't really converted. He hadn't developed a close enough relationship with Jesus yet. Read Luke 22:32 for proof. Also, Peter was very excitable, and often he got himself into deep trouble.

You see, Jesus knew people would be claiming all sorts of things about Peter. So He proceeded to help Peter know what His will was for him, and Jesus also helped Peter know himself. Listen, as Jesus reveals Peter's future to him. Listen as Jesus prepares him to be one of the charter members of His new baby church on earth.

The main thing Jesus pressed upon Peter's mind was that he would **not** be the founder of the new Christian Church. Jesus reserved and claimed that title for Himself. This was something Jesus thought Peter needed to know, or He wouldn't have instructed him on it the way He did. Jesus knew it would be essential for Peter to understand this very important issue. Why? Because Jesus knew Satan would be buffeting Peter on it.

The Holy Spirit pricks our consciences too, and helps us with things He knows will happen to us. Also, He shows us our sins so that we can go to God the Father and have them forgiven. Peter, just before Jesus' death, was very needy. He needed forgiveness. Without it, he could not do the work Jesus wanted him to do. Jesus wanted Peter to be able to help get the Christian Church up and running. What Jesus did for Peter that day is what love is all about. We don't always understand it. Sometimes love has to be tough. But I see nothing but loving guidance for Peter in these verses. That's what love is all about—love guides people—love helps people understand the things they wouldn't understand unless God taught them. The Bible helps us understand what God's love is all about. It is a rescue plan for saving us from our enemy, Satan. Jesus was nurturing and enlightening Peter.

Jesus is no longer on this earth, but the Holy Spirit and the Bible are. We need to read and study our Bibles every day. Jesus prepared Peter for the work He wanted him to do from the very first time He came in contact with him. His guidance to Peter was specially tailored for the work of letting us know about both our salvation and Peter's. How do we know? Because God has a plan for each one of us. Remember what Job said after God tried him? Read the whole chapter for yourself. (see Job 23: 10). Also remember! Job vowed, *"Though he slay me, yet will I trust him" (Job.13:15).* Both Job and Peter trusted God and understood that the bad things sometimes came to them because of their mistakes, as in Peter's case, and always because of Satan's persecution as in Job's case.

These very things alert and tell us there is a battle going on between Christ and Satan. So Jesus was preparing Peter for that battle. And the first thing Jesus did was identify Peter as a stone, not the Rock. Jesus said, *"Thou art Peter," Strong's Concordance #4074, (Matt. 16:18).* So I looked up the name *"Peter"* in my concordance, and according to the *Strongest Strong's Concordance*, the word "Peter" has the designative meaning of "rock" or an "individual" stone, in other words, "rock, stone." It reminds me of the saying, He's a chip off the old block. Meaning we look like our dad. No one can mistake us as being the child of someone else. I like that! How about you?

Well! Just consider what Jesus went through to save you. Our journey will look like His. Satan will see to that. It's not God causing all of the trouble, it's Satan, and possibly, partly our allegiance to him. Please notice that the number for the word "Peter" —#4074— is different from the number given for the word "Rock"—#4073—used for Jesus. Take special note that the writer of these Bible verses used the word "Rock"(#4073) when He talked about Jesus compared to #4074—the word Jesus used for "Peter" that meant stone. Jesus Himself, when speaking to Peter, said that the "Rock" (#4073) was Himself. Jesus used the word that tells us He was talking about Himself. He said, *"Upon this rock [#4073] I will build my church" (Matt. 16:18).*

Can you picture in your mind Jesus pointing His finger at Himself when He said this? Paul verifies further, without a doubt, that Jesus was speaking of Himself when He said to Peter, *"Upon this rock [4073] I will build my church."* Paul didn't even stop there. He goes on to say Jesus wanted Peter to know for sure the Rock (#4073) was Jesus! He was the one the children of Israel were following in the desert. For he goes on to say,

> *"Moreover, brethren, I would not that ye should be ignorant, how that all our fathers were under the cloud, and all passed through the sea; And were all baptized unto Moses in the cloud and in the sea; And did all eat the same spiritual meat; and did all drink the same spiritual drink: for they drank of that spiritual Rock [#4073] that followed them:"* then Paul adds the final clincher by saying,

> *And that Rock [4073] was Christ."*
> *(1 Cor. 10:1–4)*

Yes, Jesus has been on this earth as our Rock ever since He created it. He became the founder of the Christian Church. No man (notice I used a lower-case "m") is the founder of it. Only the Man, Christ Jesus, is the founder of God's Church on earth. Isn't that heart-warming? There are men who claim to be Christ on earth. That must be why Jesus took time to link it to the crossing of the Red Sea. So we would know it was the same Rock that followed the children of Israel in the desert. *"I will publish the name of the LORD: ascribe ye greatness unto our God. He is the Rock, his work is perfect: for all his ways are judgment: a God of truth and without iniquity, just and right is he" (Deut. 32:3–4).*

God also prepares every person today to do the work He wants them to do when we are willing. Yes! Us today! What a privilege that we can be a chip of that amazing Rock, Christ Jesus. It is done the same way as it was done for all of Jesus' disciples. Only now God does it through the guidance of the Holy Spirit. The Holy Spirit was given to the disciples on the day of Pentecost, just before He went to heaven. It is the Holy Spirit who has done the work of guiding God's people right up to our day. That is part of the Holy Spirit's job in bringing us salvation. The Spirit will always guide us if we ask Him to.

Listen to what Jesus said to the people of His day. *"If ye then, being evil, know how to give good gifts unto your children:*

> *How much more shall your heavenly Father give the*
> *Holy Spirit to them that ask Him?"*
> (Luke 11:13)

Jesus isn't living here on earth with us now. He can't be with us physically as He was with the disciples, so Jesus and His Father provide us with another comforter and guide—the Holy Spirit. Just as He did for His disciples when He left this earth. Jesus said, *"And I will pray the Father, and he shall give you another Comforter, that He may abide with you forever"* (John 14:16). "But the Comforter, which is the Holy Ghost, whom the Father will send in my name,

> *He shall teach you all things,*
> *and bring all things to your remembrance,*
> *whatsoever I have said unto you." (John 14:26)*

What a blessed promise this is. It can soothe our fears today if we trust and obey Him. It must have really soothed the disciples' fears when He told it to them as He left to go to heaven right before their eyes. What a glorious promise. God always keeps His promises. Unfortunately, that does not mean we won't be persecuted. It means the Holy Spirit will be with us when Satan is sending people to persecute us. He will see us through. We just need to keep holding God's hand. Soon it will be over—and Jesus, His Father, and all of the holy angels will come to take us home with Them.

"

We just need to keep holding God's hand. Soon it will be over—and Jesus, His Father, and all of the holy angels will come to take us home with Them.

"

18

Who Is Antichrist? The First Antichrist Has Many Imitators

He's real! We need to know who he is so we can recognize him when he is deceiving us. Even our plain, ordinary dictionary tells us who he is. My Webster's dictionary gives me at least some idea of who antichrist is. Here is what it says: (1) One who denies or opposes Christ; specifically: a great antagonist expected to fill the world with wickedness but to be conquered forever by Christ at his second coming. (2) a false Christ" ("Antichrist." *Merriam-Webster.com Dictionary*, Merriam-Webster, https://1ref.us/1ss, accessed January 10, 2022).

So what is an antagonist? It is "one that contends with or opposes another ("Antagonist." *Merriam-Webster.com Dictionary*, Merriam-Webster, https://1ref.us/1st, accessed January 10, 2022).That fits well. I'd say that's a pretty good general description, even though it is just basic. At least it aims us in the right direction and does not disagree with the Bible. That's good! Now we can go to our Bibles, and God will pinpoint exactly who that being is. There are only five references in the Bible for that word. Let's look at them. Just remember as you read this verse that it is John who is writing. He was the youngest and one of the firstJesus chose. And the last one to leave this world after Jesus died and paid for our sins. So that's a long time ago. He says, *"Little children, it is the last time:"* That's right! He thought he was living in the last days of earth's history. How wrong he was: *"and as ye have heard that antichrist shall come, even now are there many antichrists; whereby we know that it is the last time" (1 John 2:18).* Isn't that interesting? So, according to him, there were already antichrists in the world. He said there were many of them way back in his day. Today, there are many, many more.

Every generation has thought they were living in the last days just before Jesus will come. I think it's because there has always been strife. Ever since Eve sinned, there has been sinfulness on this earth. I am sure God has wanted all generations to think Jesus is coming soon so people in every generation would get ready for Him to come. Jesus wants everyone who has ever been born to be saved. There have always been wars and strife. This is not God's doing—but humanity's. It's that way because of the devil's anger. He wants to destroy everything and anything God created.

The Bible says things will be that way when Jesus comes back to rescue the people on Planet Earth. This means every generation will feel the need to prepare for that great event. It gives them a desire to get ready to go home with Him. Probably without that feeling of urgency, a lot more people would not get ready for His coming.

Remember! Jesus, when He was on earth, didn't know when He would be coming back to get us. For John quotes Jesus as saying, *"But of that day and hour knoweth no man, no, not the angels of heaven, but my Father only" (Matt. 24:36).* Also realize that when Jesus said this, He was on earth in the form of a man. Isn't it amazing that He didn't even know how long it would be before He would come back to get those who love Him? Later, He said, *"Watch therefore: for ye know not what hour your Lord doth come" (Matt. 24:42).* We need to be ready all the time. One never knows what the next day will bring. This day you are living could be your last. You could be killed by a storm or auto accident.

Jesus isn't looking for just fair-weather friends. He wants real friends, ones who really love Him and aren't just out to get what He can offer them. I don't blame Him! Do you? True love really does beget love. And He truly loves us. Just look what He went through to save us. Remember, God says sin will never rise up again. What a beautiful promise that is.

John warns us, saying,

> *Beloved, believe not every spirit, but try the spirits whether they are of God: because **many false prophets** are gone out into the world. Hereby know ye the Spirit of God: every spirit that confesseth that Jesus Christ is come in the flesh is of God: and **every spirit that confesseth not that Jesus Christ is come in the flesh is not of God: and this is that spirit of antichrist**, whereof ye have heard, that it should come; and even now already is it in the world. (1 John 4:1–3, emphasis supplied)*

Isn't God wonderful? He gives us good instructions on how to recognize the antichrist because He loves us so much. After all He went through to save us, why wouldn't He warn us about His and our enemies?

John says if someone doesn't believe Jesus came down here and was born in human flesh, they are antichrist. In other words they are against

Christ. John walked and talked with Jesus. They loved each other very much. He knew Jesus was honest. He knew Jesus was a real, live, Holy Being, born in human flesh. Jesus' mission was to pay for our sins. He is the real thing! Not just some impersonator who claims to be Christ.

The antichrist makes out like He is God. But He is a liar. Jesus obeyed His Father's commands; antichrist will not. That means we need to know what God's commandments say. We must ask the Holy Spirit to interpret them for us. He alone is able to do this. God is very clear about how we can show Him we love Him. Antichrists want that power for themselves so that they can steal the salvation God offers us. Stick close to God every moment.

John also says, *"And this is love, that we walk after His commandments. This is the commandment, That, as ye heard from the beginning, ye should walk in it. For many deceivers are entered into the world, who confess not that Jesus Christ is come in the flesh. This is a deceiver and an antichrist" (2 John 6–7).*

The original antichrist was Lucifer. He is still the leader of the antichrists we have today! He is still trying to steal God's power, and glory, and everything he can from us especially our salvation. He does it through deceit and lies. Remember, he was the first liar, so this makes him the father of lies. Do you remember what Jesus said in John 8:44? Look it up. When Jesus came to this earth, He let people know about the antichrist through a parable. It gives us a good description of who antichrist is. In it Jesus said, *"He that soweth the good seed is the Son of man" (Matt. 13:37).* That's Jesus! He became the *"Son of man"* so that He could save us. The seed is the gospel of Jesus Christ. That's the vibrant truth—His Holy Word. Through Jesus' death and actions while on this earth in human flesh, He sowed the seeds of truth.

The devil even tries to mess with our thoughts. He knows if he can get us thinking wrong thoughts, he has won that particular battle. Thoughts are like a row of dominoes that have been lined up. You touch the first one in the row, and they all tumble down. Satan listens to our words and then watches our actions. Thus he knows pretty well what we are thinking. So all he has to do is place a thought in our mind, entice us with an evil we are hankering to do, and then take note of our actions. In that way he will know what we choose to do. Then he will reap an act from us. It's as simple as that: think a thought, reap an act, and you have put the devil in charge of your thoughts and actions. God says, *"Blessed is the man that endureth temptation: for when he is tried, he shall receive the crown of life, which the Lord hath promised to them that love him. Let no man say when he is tempted, I am tempted of God: for God cannot be tempted with evil, neither tempteth he any man" (James 1:12).* Jesus became human flesh. He faced every type of test we will ever have to face. He won those battles with the devil. In our sinful flesh, we fall short. We can't do what He did. He did it for us.

> **" Jesus became human flesh. He faced every type of test we will ever have to face. "**

Paul quotes Jesus as saying, *"My grace is sufficient for thee: for my strength is made perfect in weakness" (2 Cor. 12:9).* We must place our feet on the path He took. No! It's not an easy road, but the Holy Spirit is there to help us be meek, loving, and gentle like Jesus—even to our enemies. Remember! An enemy is just someone who is being tempted by the devil. Pray for them. Treat them like a brother or sister. But don't walk in their footsteps. Get away from them if they tempt you, for if they are tempting you, they are a servant of Satan and do not want to be saved.

Then Jesus told them who the weeds were. He called them tares. He said, *"The tares are the children of the wicked one" (Matt. 13:38).* Jesus doesn't leave us wondering what wicked one He is talking about. He plainly says, *"The enemy that sowed them is the devil" (Matt. 13:39).* He is the great deceiver (see Rev. 12:9). He is the first and original antichrist. He is the one who deceives the whole world. He even deceives the other antichrists. Yes! Those who become antichrists chose to be deceived by Satan, the original antichrist. He is the father of every last one of them. He will never admit that Jesus is the One and only true Son of God. He still contends that he is God's Son, too. Not just son, but God's Son. He still has his lip out, and it will be out until the day God destroys him in the fires of hell.

Yes! God tells us those fires will be prepared for the devil and his angels. Not for people! But all who reject God and turn away their ears from hearing His Word will end up there unless they learn to truly love Him. Someone who has that kind of love is not out to get what they can get. They recognize Jesus for who He is and truly fall in love with Him. They admit they are sinners. They ask Him to forgive the sins they have committed against Him. That's what Jesus died for—to save mankind. He loves every single being He ever created just because that's who He is.

God is LOVE! John pleads with us, and I repeat his words. Why? Because repetition cements God's words in our minds. He says, *"Beloved, believe not every spirit, but try the spirits whether they are of God" (1 John 4:1).* Why does John counsel us this way? *"Because many false prophets are gone out into the world"* (1 John 4:1). A prophet is someone who gives us a message from God or a message from Satan. There are true prophets, and there are false prophets.

Satan, too, claims his messages are from God. That makes him a false prophet. He is frantically telling us things that are not true. John tells us how we can know whether a person is from God or from Satan. If we love God and reject untruths, believing only those things that are written in our Bible and doing the things John mentions, then we have God's Spirit in us. *"Hereby know ye the Spirit of God: Every spirit that confesseth that Jesus is come in the flesh is of God: and every spirit that <u>confesseth not</u> that Jesus is come in the flesh is not of God: and this is that spirit of antichrist, whereof ye have heard that it should come; and even now already is it in the world" (1 John 4:2–3).* Jesus says people who refuse to admit He was born down here in the flesh have the spirit of antichrist. They do not believe what God tells them. They do not believe Jesus is the Savior of the world. They don't believe He came and died for their sins. They don't accept Him as their Savior. In this verse, John tells us antichrist has already come. He was still here on earth when Jesus was here. There were people who didn't believe in Jesus. They didn't believe He was God. They didn't believe His death had paid for their sins. These are all lies of the antichrist. There are many lies and many antichrists.

Their lies about God are changing all the time. That's how they can deceive so many people. They just keep giving them a new twist. But they are still lies and do not agree with what God says. The changes expose the lies because God never changes (see Mal. 3:6). It's imperative that we read and believe what the Bible says for ourselves. Ask the Holy Spirit to help you. He will give you understanding as you read His Word and compare all the verses on each subject. God never changes. (see Isa. 28:10,13).

Paul goes on to say: *"For by one Spirit"* (He is talking about the Spirit of the Father, and of Jesus, and of the Holy Spirit) *"are we all baptized into one body, whether we be Jews or Gentiles, whether we be bond or free; and have been made to drink into one Spirit" (1 Cor. 12:13).* Later, Paul said, *"There is neither Jew nor Greek, there is neither bond nor free, there is neither male nor female: for ye are all one in Christ Jesus" (Gal. 3:28).* God treats everyone alike.

Do I hear grumbling? This doesn't mean there will no longer be both men and women. I have a friend who says she loves Jesus. But she has decided she does not want to go to heaven because there will be neither male nor female there. This is none other than a lie of Satan, antichrist number one. He is twisting God's words. She does not want to go to heaven because there will be no sexuality there. Is that really what God is saying in those verses? No! God also says, *"Now I know in part; but then shall I know even as I also am known" (I Cor. 13:12).* Who knows! Maybe women will even give birth in heaven to unborn children conceived on earth. Remember! He says, *"Eye hath not seen, nor ear heard, neither hath entered the heart of man, the things which God hath prepared for those who love Him" (1 Cor. 2:9).*

What is the problem? Trust! It is a faith problem. Why? Because she doesn't trust God. You must trust someone or something to have faith in them. That means she is trusting God's enemy. We all have issues like this. She's not a bad person just because of her mixed-up feelings. She's just human. That's the way we all are. Certainly, she's not the only one Satan picks on with this question. It is also a lack of love for God. Other things are more important to her—to all of us. God impressed me to visit a lady I had met at a friend's house. She was sick unto death. I persevered! Finally, I found out where she lived, and I went to see her. She, too, was worried that we would be very different in heaven. She was concerned she might not recognize her loved ones there. So I shared the verse above with her and made an appointment for my pastor to visit her.

The next day she called me. She was in the hospital, dying. I had prayer with her over the phone, and she died right while I was on the phone with her. I believe I will see her in heaven. It gives me goosebumps just thinking about her being lost. If I hadn't persevered, she might have. That's up to God. He knows whether she loves Him or not. We must trust God. Remember, we are saved via God's grace. Grace is love for sinners. You can't buy it or bargain for it. The other factor in this equation is faith. Faith is believing in something you can't even see, feel, hear, and humanly trust. That's what salvation through Christ is all about. Faith is the act of believing God is telling us the truth, whether we can figure it out or not. If we understand something, then we don't have to take it by faith. It's our own knowledge, not God's. We can't trust ourselves. None of us are trustworthy. *"By grace (God's love) are ye saved through faith;… not of works, lest any man should boast" (Eph. 2:9).*

Grace—God's undeserved love devoid of man's works = faith (total trust in God)

Faith in one's self is not faith at all. Those thoughts sound like an anti-christ thing to me. What do you think? I say this because of something Paul said. I consider this one of the most beautiful verses in the Bible. See if you agree! Paul said, *"Eye hath not seen, nor ear heard, neither hath entered into the heart of man, the things which God hath prepared for those who love Him" (1 Cor. 2:9).* It takes faith to believe those words.

It is Satan himself who places worries as those two people had. How cruel to attack someone on their deathbed with worries like that. I had only seen her once while I was at a friend's house and did not know she was so sick. I am so glad I was able to give her hope and show her in the Bible that she will be known in heaven just like she was down here on earth. It was something Paul wrote. He said, *"For now we see through a glass, darkly; but then face to face: now I know in part; but then shall I know even as also I am known" (1 Cor. 13:12).* Our families and friends will know us the same way they do here on earth. I can't imagine God not making it that way. Of course, we will want to recognize and know our family members and friends.

It is our enemy who wants us to think we won't be able to recognize our family. God created families. Why in the world would He want to destroy family life in heaven. It's just another lie of Satan. He wants us to think heaven won't be the beautiful place God says it will be. I hope to go to heaven with her and see the joy on her face as she sees family members and friends. Thank You, Holy Spirit, for letting me talk to and encourage her and give her hope. Satan placed sad thoughts in her mind so he could cause her to dislike and distrust God. He tries to get us to want the earthly things we crave. Stop and think for a moment. God made us male and female. He made us to love others.

There are many things we do not understand. And that's O. K. If God wants us to understand and we have asked the Holy Spirit to help us, then He will have the Holy Spirit reveal it to us if it is good for us to know at that time in our life. He just might be testing us. He must test us. If we knew the answer to everything, we wouldn't need faith. Faith is believing in things we do not understand or know. It is *"The substance of things hoped for, the evidence of things not seen" (Heb. 11:1).* Remember! We are saved through faith. So it is extremely important that we **do not** go by the premise that "seeing is believing." That statement definitely is not from God.

Those were just thoughts that matched her own selfish desires. The deceiver, Satan, told her sex is more important than God. Whew! I hope she has come to that conclusion and understands that it is the devil trying to deceive her so that she will lose out of heaven. Unfortunately, it looks like he did a pretty good job. I was so astonished—I didn't say a word. I love her dearly. She is so precious. She will always be a precious daughter of mine. I will never stop loving her and praying for her. Thoughts like she had are definitely from antichrist, the enemy of our soul, Satan. He brings those kinds of thoughts to all of our minds. He is such a trickster. He makes us believe they are our own desires, but really, they are desires he wants us to have. So he places them in our mind. And it is a rejection of God. I know! He has done it to me over many issues. I will never stop praying for her.

Anytime we make a choice such as this, we are resisting the Holy Spirit and rejecting Christ. Actually, we are putting our wants ahead of God's love. Remember! Satan hates God. That is his number one reason for lying to us. If he can deceive us and cause us to lose out on companionship with our Maker in heaven, he has attained his goal. He has hurt both God and us. I don't know if she ever stopped to realize that she was putting her wants ahead of the wants of our wonderful God's wants. We are choosing to walk down the path with Satan, and we are turning away from God when we put our wants first, ahead of and in place of His. Jesus died to save us from instances like these. God is out to bless us and make us happy. He made families. He has a family. Thoughts like those are designed to make us turn away from God. He is trying to steal all the glorious things God has promised her.

> **We are saved by having faith in what God has and is doing for us.**

It is Satan himself who places thoughts like this in our minds. I am talking about thoughts he uses to try to get us to want sinful, earthly things. He tries to make us feel like it is something we just can't give up. But we are choosing to have antichrist in our heart when we do not trust God. We are saved by having faith in what God has and is doing for us. His plans are bigger than our wildest dreams. Believe what God says. Ask the Holy Spirit to help you trust God.

I used to think I didn't want Jesus to come until I had children. Notice! Satan tailors all of his enticements to match our wants. Hers was a desire for sex; mine was a desire to have children. That's related to sex. God created us with sexual desires. That is why Satan toys with it so much. Those little tykes really meant a lot to me. And that really was a lot like the girl I was just talking about. But now that I am older, I see it for what it was—a shove from the devil to make me feel like something I wanted was more important to me than loving God. Satan knows we can't have both. In fact, if you have sex, you are bound to have children. Duh!

Today, I see it for what it is—a temptation Satan whispered in my ear. It is my prayer she will see it that way, too. I don't suppose Satan has told her what will happen to him if she continues to believe his lies. Or that he will have to burn in hell for her sin if she begins trusting and obeying God. He should be running scared—but he's too wicked to do that. He has committed the unpardonable sin. God means everything to me now. But as long as we are here on this earth, we are susceptible to Satan's attacks on us. The only way we can survive those attacks is through much prayer and real, unselfish love for the One who loves us so much—that is our triune God. Each one of Them is available every moment if we want Them to be with us.

Every moment, we must choose to follow the prompting of the Holy Spirit, no matter where it leads us. He went through every trial we will go through. God help each one to be willing to go through the pain Satan heaps on us so we can have the reality of following Him no matter what other people or the devil does to us. We are only following in His footsteps feebly. How sad that so many refuse to accept the pain Satan heaps on us and thus make all of God's pain worthwhile. How sad He must feel that so many refuse to follow Him and tell Him thank you. Never forget that He promises to see us safely through all the hell Satan puts us through. He loves us very much, no matter what juncture we are at in this life.

When we understand things like this, then he will help intercede for those who are going through temptations like we have been through. Sometimes prayer alone is the best route to take when helping someone. Then it is God who speaks to them. He knows them much better than we do. He knows their joys and their sorrows. He knows their heart and whether they love Him or not. He will plead with them if we ask Him to. And He will do it just right! Isn't He wonderful? Sometimes when we put our two cents in, we mess everything up. In fact, we are often obeying Satan and don't even know it unless God is prompting us to help them.

Salvation needs to be between them and God unless they come to us for help. When they ask us what we think, then they are asking for help. Then, it is their choice. That is what it needs to be. That's our time to fervently pray for the help of the Holy Spirit to tell us what to say to them. It's important! Pray for their protection against the wiles of the devil. Always test what someone says with the Bible because if what they say does not agree with God's Word, it is totally untrue. Even just one wrong word can make the whole thing false.

I can't imagine why anyone would want to imitate the devil, but many do. Some know they are imitating him, but many do not. God will help both groups, but the innocent group has something on their side. They don't really want to imitate the devil, so it will be easier for them to change, but the ones who know they are disobeying the Lord and don't want to change will be more difficult. But it can be done! Bow your head with me if you wish. Dear Lord, help each of us to have a clear picture of You! Your law gives us that special picture. Change our hearts into ones that want to do your will. Thank You, Lord, for answering each person's cry for help, for turning them away from destruction, and for showing us that we are all in this dilemma together. One is not better than another.

The Ten Commandments Written by God's Own Finger (Commandments 1–5)

"And the LORD delivered unto me two tables of stone written with the finger of God" (Deut. 9:10).

I

Thou shalt have no other gods before Me. (Exod. 20:3)

II

Thou shalt not make unto thee any graven image, or any likeness of any thing that is in heaven above, or that is in the earth beneath, or that is in the water under the earth. Thou shalt not bow down thyself to them, nor serve them: for I the LORD thy God am a jealous God, visiting the iniquity of the fathers upon the children unto the third and fourth generation of them that hate me; and shewing mercy unto thousands of them that love me, and keep my commandments. (Exod. 20:4–6)

III

Thou shalt not take the name of the LORD thy God in vain; for the LORD will not hold him guiltless that taketh His name in vain. (Exod. 20:4–6)

IV

Remember the sabbath day, to keep it holy. Six days shalt thou labour, and do all thy work: But the seventh day is the sabbath of the LORD thy God: in it thou shalt not do any work, thou, nor thy son, nor thy daughter, thy manservant, nor thy maidservant, nor thy cattle, nor thy stranger that is with thy gates: For in six days the LORD made heaven and earth, the sea, and all that in them is, and rested the seventh day: wherefore the LORD blessed day, and hallowed it. (Exod. 20:8–11)

V

Honour thy father and thy mother: that thy days may be long upon the land which the LORD thy God giveth thee. (Exod. 20:12)

The Ten Commandments Changed In the Catechism (Commandments 1–5)

The Ten Commandments—changed by the church in its catechism—they did not change Bible—that's good! God never gave man permission to change His ten-commandment law ANYWHERE!

> Jesus said, *Think not that I am come to destroy the law, or the prophets: I am not come to destroy, but to fulfil. For verily I say unto you, till heaven and earth pass, one jot or one tittle shall in no wise pass from the law, till all be fulfilled. Whosoever therefore shall break one of these least commandments, and shall teach men so, he shall be called least in the kingdom of heaven: but whosoever shall do and teach them, the same shall be called great in the kingdom of heaven.* (Matt. 5:17–19)

Jesus was talking about the dotting of the i or the crossing of a t. He does not even want simple things like that to be changed or removed from His law.

I

I am the Lord thy God; thou shalt not have strange gods before Me.

*God never mentioned strange gods in His law; in doing so, they are destroying His law. Notice also, that their version of His law does not cover other gods. There are other gods, which God accepts, but, He does not accept them to take His place or be placed ahead of Him because He is **always** first, last and best in everything.* Look up Revelation 22:12–15, 1 John 3:24, Revelation 21:27, and Revelation 22:7–12.

II

Thou shalt not take the name of the Lord thy God in vain.

Notice that the second commandment, which talks about bowing down to graven images is totally deleted from God's holy law by them, in the catechism. They do not change it in the Catholic Bible. But! The catechism is the tool they use to teach God's law to their parishioners. The children are taught from it. They may never check it against the verses in the Bible, which is God's True Word.

(Note: **"You Shall Not Make For Yourself a Graven Image . . ."** 2129 The divine injunction included the prohibition of every representation of God by the hand of man. Deuteronomy explains: "Since you saw no form on the day that the Lord spoke to you at Horeb out of the midst of the fire, beware lest you act corruptly by making a graven image for yourselves, in the form of any figure ..." [https://1ref.us/1sq, accessed January 10, 2022]. However, it seems to be a part of the first commandment because they specify as the second commandment:

Article 2

THE SECOND COMMANDMENT

You shall not take the name of the Lord your God in vain.)

III

"Remember the sabbath day, to keep it holy. Six days you shall labor, and do all your work; but the seventh day is a sabbath to the Lord your God; in it you shall not do any work" (https://1ref.us/1sp, accessed January 10, 2022). *Take note that this is the fourth commandment in God's law, but they have given it third place. And they delete most of the commandment. And their command totally sidelines the reason why God wants us to keep the seventh day of the week holy. That is because God uses the*

> **❝**
> *No one can change the solemnity of the seventh day of the week.*
> **❞**

200   *The Devil Made Me Do It*

fourth commandment to let us know which day of the week God made holy. No one can change the solemnity of the seventh day of the week. Man chang- ing it to a different day of the week just blasphemes God—it does not change the day or the solemnity of it. The holy command itself states that the seventh day of the week is "the Sabbath of the Lord thy God." That is the only day that is His Sabbath. When He created our world, He made that day holy, blessed it, and set it apart for us to worship Him on (see Gen. 2:1–3).

IV

Honor thy father and thy mother.

The fourth commandment should be here—the Sabbath command. It is (see Exod. 20:8–11) in the Bible. This is the sabbath command in the Protestant Bible.

V

Thou shalt not kill.

The Rest of the Ten Commandments Written by God's Own Finger (Commandments 6–10)

VI

Thou shalt not kill. (Exod. 20:13)

VII

Thou shalt not commit adultery. (Exod. 20:14)

VIII

Thou shalt not steal. (Exod. 20:15)

IX

Thou shalt not bear false witness against thy neighbour. (Exod. 20:16)

X

Thou shalt not covet thy neighbour's house, thou shalt not covet thy neighbour's wife, nor his manservant, nor his maidservant, nor his ox, nor his ass, nor any thing that is thy neighbour's. (Exod. 20:17)

The Rest of the Ten Commandments Changed in the Catechism (Commandments 6–10)

VI

Thou shalt not commit adultery.

VII

Thou shalt not steal.

VIII

Thou shalt not bear false witness against thy neighbor.

IX

You shall not covet your neighbor's house; you shall not covet your neighbor's wife, or his manservant, or his maidservant, or his ox, or his ass, or anything that is your neighbor's (https://1ref.us/1so, accessed January 10, 2022).

X

You shall not covet ... anything that is your neighbor's... (<u>https://1ref. us/1sn</u>, accessed January 10, 2022). Yes! It is a big deal that these commands are out of sync with the Bible.

> **66**
>
> *I encourage everyone to read the Bible.*
>
> **99**

Doing something like this causes confusion. The only command that is in sync with God's Word is the first one. There is so much left out that people do not get a true picture of God's holy law, which will never be done away with. The Bible says, *The grass withereth, the flower fadeth: but the word of our God shall stand for ever (Isa. 40:8).* Everyone needs to have a correct copy of God's law, so they know what God wants them to do.

This is what is in their catechism. It is not changed in their Bible. But the catechism is what is used. They never used to encourage their parishioners to read the Bible, but now they do not discourage them from reading it. That is good. I encourage everyone to read the Bible. It is the most important book a person can read because every word in it came from God, either a direct quote of what Jesus said or from a vision God sent to one of His prophets. That, too, is a big deal!

Signs and Symptoms That Tell Us Who Is NOT the Antichrist

1. They will be obeying all of God's ten commandments as recorded in the Bible.
2. They will accept Jesus Christ as the Son of God and as their Redeemer.
3. They worship God—the Father, the Son, and the Holy Spirit.
4. They have the spirit of love.
5. They give freedom of choice.

Signs and Symptoms Which Tell Us Who IS Antichrist

There is a church whose leader proudly claims attributes that belong only to God, which is the essence of what it means to be antichrist.

1. They have changed God's ten-commandment law.

    > Command # 1 Exodus 20:3
    > *Command # 1 a. (Deut. 5:7–9)*

2. Yes! That church leader claims, "We hold upon this earth the place of God Almighty." —Pope Leo XIII. Jesuit History (https://1ref.us/1sr, accessed January 10, 2022). This is what antichrist is: to put oneself in the place of God.

    a. Christ on earth.

    b. He is proud that he is antichrist.

3. No leader of any earthly church can be Christ on earth.

    > Command # 1 **Exodus 20:3**

    > **NO ONE can take God's place. No man except Jesus is God.**

    That is why Jesus became a man—so He could offer us salvation.

4. Another sign is: they are a persecuting power—when they feel the need to be.

    No one knows how many people were killed during the Dark Ages.

5. They are a controlling power. Our true God does not control us.

He leaves us free to choose whether we want to worship Him or some other god. Who do you choose to serve?

Let's take another look at antichrist!

19

So! Who Is Antichrist? Let's Look and See!

First of all, it is someone who is against or place of Jesus.
We know who the first antichrist was. It was Lucifer, now called Satan, the serpent, the devil, and any other name you can come up with that describes him. Do you realize he is a created being? And do you know what the term "man" means? It means he is merely a created being - made of dust. That's how Jesus made us. *"And the LORD God formed man of the dust of the ground, and breathed into his nostrils the breath of life; And man became a living soul" (Gen. 2:7).*

Do you realize when the words *"the LORD God"* are used in this Bible verse, it is talking about Jesus, the One who created us? I think it is very important to know and remember this. As you will see, it is a distinguishing mark of Jesus. *"And out of the ground the LORD God [Jesus] formed every beast of the field, and every fowl of the air" (Gen. 2:19).* That's right! Do you realize the animals were created out of dust, too? And they were given the same breath of life God gave us.

> **"**
> **The devil has ruined every living thing God created.**
> **"**

"Every beast after his kind, and all the cattle after their kind, and every creeping thing that creepeth upon the earth after his kind, and every fowl after his kind, every bird of every sort. And they went in unto Noah into the ark, two and two of all flesh, wherein is the breath of life" (Gen. 7:14–15). And do you realize the animals can be good or bad, too? Yes! They have a conscience. They are sinful, too.

We once took in a stray kitten. It appeared that a male cat had sodomized him. The poor little thing was bleeding from his rectum. That cat knew he was being mean. I am sure you have seen the same kind of animal be opposites, one loving and the other mean.

205

Both humans and animals cave to sin. The devil has ruined every living thing God created. Why? Because he is antichrist. Yes! He is against Christ. He succeeded in getting Christ killed. He would love to kill him again. But the closest he can come to that is to grieve God by killing created beings He formed. *And it repented the LORD that He had made man on the earth, and it grieved him at his heart. And the LORD said, I will destroy man whom I have created from the face of the earth; both man, and beast, and the creeping thing, and the fowls of the air; for it repenteth me that I have made them. And behold, I, even I, do bring a flood of waters upon the earth, to destroy all flesh, wherein is the breath of life, from under heaven; and every thing that is in the earth shall die. (Gen. 6:6–7, 17)*

Just look what man has done to every living thing.

The dust of the ground is what all created beings on earth were made from. Every angel, including Lucifer is just a created being like we are. Here is the verse that says Lucifer was created. The Bible talks about the prince of Tyrus, and it has a dual application. It is talking about a prince and also about the devil. And the Lord gave Ezekiel this message to give Lucifer: *"Thus saith the Lord GOD; Because thine heart is lifted up, and thou hast said, I am a God, I sit in the seat of God, in the midst of the seas; yet thou art a man, and not God, though thou set thine heart as the heart of God: Behold, thou art wiser than Daniel; there is no secret that they can hide from thee" (Ezek. 28:2–3).* Let's look at that statement concerning the devil. It will help us find his roots and see how rebellious he was toward God.

God said to him, *"Thou wast perfect thy in ways from the day that thou wast created, till iniquity was found in thee" (Ezek. 28:15).* Notice this verse says he was created. So, what caused Lucifer to be so proud? God tells us what happened to Lucifer via the prophet, Ezekiel. He says, *"Thine heart was lifted up because of thy beauty, thou hast corrupted thy wisdom by reason of thy brightness" (Ezek. 28:17).* That's right! Lucifer was proud. God is the same yesterday, today, and forever, so we know God would have told Lucifer what pride would do to him. He would not be a loving God if He did not warn Lucifer. So we know He told him just what He tells us. God says, *"Pride goeth before destruction, and a haughty spirit before a fall"* (Prov. 16:18).

Let's look at other created beings and see what pride did to them. No one is without danger of this happening to them. We should not look down our noses at our enemies. That is not the action of a child of God.

We need to obey God, love our enemies, and do good to those who hate us. Jesus tells us to: *"Love your enemies, do good to them that hate you, Bless them that curse you, and pray for them which despitefully use you" (Luke 6:27–28).* Read the rest of the chapter for yourself. It is Jesus telling us how to live and how to treat others. There can be no better instructions on how to live our life. We are to be different from those who do not love God and disobey Him. We are to be like Jesus—loving and kind while continuing to obey God and not take part in their evil ways. Lead them to Jesus if they are willing. Then you will have gained another friend for both you and Jesus. If they do not become a friend of Jesus and cling to their sins, then we must distance ourselves, or we will get caught up in their sins.

God balances it out with verses like this: *"Trust ye not in a friend, put ye not confidence in a guide: keep the doors of thy mouth from her that lieth in thy bosom* [your wife]. *For the son dishonoureth the father, the daughter riseth up against her mother, the daughter in law against her mother in law; and a man's enemies are the men of his own house. Therefore I will look unto the Lord; I will wait for the God of my salvation: my God will hear me" (Mic. 7:5–7).* God, alone, is trustworthy. It's too bad, but that's the way it is.

And just look at these verses which God gave to Obadiah the prophet. They tell us who God is talking about. *"How are the things of Esau searched out.…* All the men of thy confederacy have brought thee even to the border … and prevailed against thee" (Obad. 1:6–7). This is what often happens to those who are proud and sure of themselves. They do not trust the ones who can save and protect them from the wiles of the devil. They are walking in the devil's footsteps. And he will lead them to destruction.

Esau was one of those who was walking in Satan's footsteps. (Read the whole chapter. It is short). It helps us understand that God is talking about evil people versus righteous ones, and it lets us know how dangerous it is to refuse to treat others right—even our enemies. We are all in danger of doing the same things. Jesus told the multitudes:

> *But I say unto you, Love your enemies, bless them that curse you, do good to them that hate you, and pray for them which despitefully use you, and persecute you; That ye may be the children of your Father which is in heaven: for he maketh his sun to rise on the evil and on the good, and sendeth rain on the just and on the unjust. (Matt. 5:44–45)*

The devil and his workers are very persuasive and devious. *"We wrestle not against flesh and blood, but against principalities, against powers, against the rulers of the darkness of this world, against spiritual wickedness in high places" (Eph. 6:12)*. We read what we can do about this problem in Ephesians 6:13–24.

It is God Himself who places an enormous amount of animosity between His children and the children of the devil. Let's take a moment and read again what God told the devil He would do to him after he led Eve into sin. Remember also that the devil did not look like an enemy to Eve. He deceived her. He is out to deceive us, too. Jesus said, *"I will put enmity between thee and the woman, and between thy seed and her seed; it shall bruise thy head, and thou shalt bruise his heel" (Gen. 3:15)*. God gives us enmity so we can hate evil. God's enmity is far different from hatred. He wants us to hate their sins but love them.

No one wants to face the fires in hell that the devil's angels are going to face. And the truth is we don't have to. That is the purpose of the enmity God gives us. He helps us hate evil. That enmity is such a beautiful gift. The devil faces extinction in the fires of hell, and so do those who honor and trust him. God will destroy him and his followers when everyone has made their final choice to either follow God or the devil. God can't be more fair than that.

Look what Joshua told the people in his day. Read the whole chapter. He includes all people, Both before and after the flood. He said to them,

> *Now therefore fear the LORD, and serve Him in sincerity and in truth: and put away the gods which your fathers served on the other side of the flood, and in Egypt; and serve ye the LORD. And if it seem evil unto you to serve the LORD, choose you this day whom ye will serve; whether the gods which your fathers served that were on the other side of the flood, or the gods of the Amorites, in whose land ye dwell: but as for me and my house, we will serve the LORD. (Josh. 24:14–15)*

20

The History of Compromise—Man's Compromise That Is!

Compromise in the church is nothing new. Satan, the arch antichrist, has used it throughout all of history to destroy God's people. In His Word God has traced the evidence of the compromise of His people with pagans from the very beginning of time on this earth. We can trace it from Noah's day clear down to our day. At the time of the flood, God placed His finger on why He was grieved about creating mankind. Yes! God pinpointed the culprit. Since they were deceived, they felt their religion was right! So, of course, they taught their children to worship that way. Yes, compromise came into being through something they probably thought shouldn't cause any trouble at all.

But God had told His children what would happen, and they married the pagan women anyway. They knew better. They disobeyed God. They sinned and chose to honor their own selfish desires rather than honor God. Just see what it did to His people! Also, notice who it was that instigated it. Who did God say was at fault? He said, *"The sons of God saw the daughters of men that they were fair" (Gen.6:2).* He said it was because godly men married non-Christian women, i.e., pagans.

Why was that a problem?

Their pagan wives brought their ungodly religious practices right into their homes.

That's right! And isn't that what you would expect? *"And they took them wives of all which they chose" (Gen. 6:2.)*

That's right! It was the sons of God who initiated the compromise.

Oh! I am sure Satan whispered in their ear and caused the pagan woman to look more beautiful than their own women. But! Satan can't bend us if we refuse to allow our thoughts to wander into forbidden territory. That's when God said, ***"My Spirit shall not always strive with man"***(Gen. 6:3). That day is almost upon us. God will not strive with mankind after people have made the permanent choice to not follow God. There is a day coming when all who will have made their final choice. Then Jesus will come. He's waiting! Are you ready?

The next time God brought up this subject was when they were on their way to the promised land. He was reminding them again and for the same reason. He repeated the admonition: *"Neither shalt thou make marriages with them; thy daughter thou shalt not give unto his son, nor his daughter shalt thou take unto their son" (Deut. 7:3).*

God knew better!
Even the slightest deviation
from obeying God
is very dangerous
and it is
a sin.
Why?
For they will turn away thy son from following me,
that they may serve other gods:
so will the anger of the LORD be kindled against you,
and destroy thee suddenly. (Deut. 7:3–4)

Yes, it probably looked like a simple little compromise—but it was anything but simple. It was deadly to their spiritual connection with God.

> **"**
> ***The mission of God's people with a non-believer in this life is to introduce them to their wonderful God.***
> **"**

Still, today, God does not approve of His people making best friends with those who do not believe in Him. The mission of God's people with a non-believer in this life is to introduce them to their wonderful God. Basically, God said the compromise began with their failure to keep themselves separate from the things of the world. Their sin was the mingling in marriage of Christian men with non-Christian women. It seemed so simple. It came across as a very innocent act. But it wasn't. God said, don't do it. If you do, you will lose your love for Me. You see, God says obedience to Him is how we love Him. When we disobey His commands, we are not loving Him; we are pleasing ourselves. God knows what sin will do. Mankind has been sinful ever since Eve disobeyed God in the Garden of Eden. Man needs God to survive. It was the same thing as bringing pagans into the church with all of their non-Christian beliefs and practices.

Even the slightest deviation
from obeying God
is very dangerous
and it is
a sin.

21

He's Coming Soon! Are We and Our Loved Ones Ready?

Acording to the Bible, the coming of Jesus is very soon. If you love Jesus, or even if you don't, I would be surprised if you do not feel like something big is in the air. Just look at what is happening everywhere in this world. Everything is at a feverish pitch. At the top of the list is greed.

Do you know what God says about that? Read the whole chapter of James five. It tells the rich men to *"howl and weep" (James 5:1)*. Why? Because they cheat the workers they hire to harvest their fields (see James 5:4–5), and they have *"condemned and killed the just" (James 5:6)*. **Wow!** We see it in government, too.

It's happening every day all around us. Refusing to take care of the earth is in the same category. God gives us this eye-opening verse. See if you don't think it describes our day—right now. God said, *"The nations were angry, and thy wrath is come, and the time of the dead, that they should be judged, and that thou shouldest give reward unto thy servants the prophets, and to the saints, and them that fear thy name, small and great; **and shouldest destroy the**m **which destroy the earth"** (Rev.11:18, emphasis supplied).*

They have refused to heed the warning signs of the weather scientists. Countries are losing their livelihood because people in high-up places refuse to believe the scientists concerning global warming. God says those people will be destroyed. They don't want to obey because it would destroy their huge incomes. Greed is rampant everywhere. Just consider how many of the leaders of our country are affected. God will take care of that problem when He comes. I say, come, Lord Jesus! What do you say? God cites another problem that is becoming more and more rampant in our day. People have lost track of what real love is. They foster sexual immorality and accuse those who are loving and friendly of infringing on their rights even if they only touch them in a normal way when they them-selves are really acting inappropriately. It has always been a problem. It is not something new, but it is getting worse daily. James brings it to our attention and then states the reason such actions exist.

Just look at his questions. He asks:

From whence come wars and fightings among you? come they not hence, even of your lusts that war at your members? Ye adulterers and adulteresses, know ye not the friendship of the world is enmity with God? whosoever therefore will be a friend of the world is the enemy of God. (James 4:1, 4)

God sites still another problem that is causing trouble. One must honor another person's wishes when it comes to touching. And people are learning to take note of such things. But! Not everyone has been brought up the same way. And I dare say there are thousands of people who have been mistreated by sexual deviates. They, especially, will be wary of touch contacts. Their rights do need to be honored. But there is a difference between godly affection, i.e., called love, and someone pushing themselves onto someone. There needs to be a happy medium. We need to make our wishes known and gently let someone know if they have crossed that invisible line. Not get irate and yell at them or take them to court. Read 2 Thessalonians 1:3–12. It's scary! What used to be normal is now way out in left field.

God tells us to love one another, and true love never steps on anyone's toes. It honors their wishes. No one should ever be touched if they do not want to be. Those who like to give friendly hugs should not be ostracized, either, for their loving ways. Just remember, there are others who feel unloved if someone is not loving toward them and gives them a caring hug. We just need to live by the golden rule and not expect others to act as we act. I was raised by loving grandparents. I don't remember them hugging me, but they did not scold me or treat me mean.

Dear, precious, burdened people, God hears your cry. Yes, the cry from both groups. He knows your pain. But God does not tell us we won't have pain in this world. Remember! Every one of Jesus' disciples suffered persecution. They were killed for being a follower of His. Satan will see to it that every follower of Jesus will suffer some kind of harassment. He delights in harming God and His followers. But just look at this wonderful promise God gives those who love and obey Him. He promises us victory over Satan. All of the horrible things that are coming on the world are caused by him. His days are numbered.

There are very few prophecies that have not been fulfilled about Jesus coming. Our hope is through looking at the life of Christ and following in His footsteps. He went through the things many of His true followers will have to go through. He died for our sins. He paid for our iniquities. Only the perfect human could do that. That's why He, the Son of God, became totally God and totally man. He did it so He could pay for our sins. The only way He could pay for our sins was to be human (like us) and sinless at the same time.

All of us are sinners—every last one of us. Not one person is better than another. God does not grade the sins—big or little. Sin is sin. Just as the big sin (in our way of thinking) is sin, so is the little sin in God's eyes. Sin is a lack of love for another being—created beings included. Even the animals and all other creatures suffer because of sin, and they, too, are sinful. Satan has tampered with them, and so have people. They have anger, deceit, and even sexual cruelty. I once saw a kitten being sodomized by a grown male cat. We rescued that baby and protected and adopted him.

It is time for Jesus to come. Why is He waiting? It is simple! Our God is a God of love. I am going to let you listen to Peter, and then I will give you my take on it. He says, *"Knowing this first, that there shall come in the last days scoffers, walking after their own lusts"* (lusts are the things we shouldn't have that we desire), *"And saying, Where is the promise of His coming? for since the fathers fell asleep, all things continue as they were from the beginning of the creation" (2 Peter 3:3–4).*

And Peter says they are not just ignorant! What is his reason for saying this? Listen as he speaks:

*For this **they willingly are ignorant** of, that by the word of God the heaven were of old, and the earth standing out of the water and in the water: Whereby the world that then was, being overflowed with water, perished: But the heavens and the earth, which are now, by the same word are kept in store, reserved unto fire against the day of judgment and perdition of ungodly men. (2 Peter 3:5–7)*

So, Peter says people will always be scoffing and saying that God says it is time for Him to come and that it is just like it always was. And it is! For those who die! You see, when people die, they don't know anything. Death is like it is when we are asleep. We don't hear, see, or know what is going on around us. So when Jesus comes in the clouds and wakes them up from the sleep of death, it will seem to them like Jesus came and woke them up the very next moment after they died. It will seem to them that they took a momentary nap. That's the way it will be for every single person who dies before Jesus comes to wake us up and take us to heaven.

Consider how God took care of evil when it got so bad just before the great flood took place. It didn't take long for the devil to almost totally destroy all righteousness. God is not going to do something like that again. Just as He did then, He will allow evil to ripen. And this time, He is going to come to take those who love Him home to heaven with Him. Satan has not yet filled his cup to the brim. But he is filling it fast. He is gaining more and more moments of punishment time. Our God is not a God of vengeance. He is a God of love and justice. But He will display vengeance toward those who destroy those who love Him. He will save them.

How do we know we love Him and His children? John, that great lover of Jesus, tells us simply. *"By this we know that we love the children of God, when we love God, and keep His commandments. For this is the love of God, that we keep his commandments: and his commandments are not grievous"* *(1 John 5:2–3)*. And how do we become overcomers and become children of God? It is by reading and learning God's will, believing him, and obeying Him once we learn what His will is through what He commands us to do in His law.

And how can we do that? It is only accomplished via God's loving assistance, through the power of the Holy Spirit, and by exercising the faith He gives us. Remember! John says, *"For whatsoever is born of God overcometh the world: and this is the victory that overcometh the world, even our faith"* *(1 John 5:4)*. Paul says, *"Now the just shall live by faith: but if any man draw back, my soul shall have no pleasure in him. But we are not of them who draw* back *unto perdition; but of them that believe to the saving of the soul"* *(Heb. 10:38–39)*.

Praise God for this insight. He is telling us to have faith. It is Satan who whispers doubts in our ears, and often he does it through our loved ones and friends who are well-meaning. He is speaking in their ears, too. Often we, our friends, and our loved ones obey the wicked devil and don't even know it. That is why we need to read the words of God from an accepted version of the Bible that has not had God's words changed. As we read our Bible and ask for the guidance of the Holy Spirit, our perception of the truth will increase. Then the Holy Spirit will bring us to repentance. Read the whole third chapter of Second Peter. He ends the chapter with this warning to His followers: *"Ye therefore, beloved, seeing ye know these things before, beware lest ye also, being led away with error of the wicked, fall from your own steadfastness. But grow in grace, and in the knowledge of our Lord and Saviour Jesus Christ" (2 Peter 3:17–18).*

I wrote this book because I want you, my brothers and sisters, to know things about God you may not be aware of. Every word you are told from anyone must be backed up with God's Word; He is the only one we can trust. I love all of you. Jesus says, when He comes in the clouds to take us home to heaven with Him, it will be just like it was before the flood in Noah's day. What were those people doing? They were just living their normal, daily lives. They were *"eating and drinking, marrying and giving in marriage, until the day that Noah entered into the ark" (Matt. 24:38, NKJV).* They didn't expect any unusual events to take place. In the days of the promised second coming of Jesus, many will not expect Jesus, His Father, and all of the heavenly angels when They come to take the righteous home with Them.

God does not want it to be that way. He wants everyone to know about it. He wants everyone to go home with Him. But there is a price to pay. We must love God. Only those who love Him will go to heaven. God's people have always been persecuted by those who are following the ways of the wicked one. Each person is free to pick their own final fate. The only requirement is to love God. That shouldn't be hard. God promises to be with us.

I encourage you to look for those who are obeying God's commandments. Remember! God says He will never change His law. They will be glad to help you understand the hard passages in your Bible, and so will the Holy Spirit. But! You must read and study, comparing verse with verse, on each subject. God tells us everything we need to know. We must study it to make sure what they are telling us agrees with what God says in His Word. He has the final, honest answer to every question. That part is so easy and uncomplicated. Just love Him with all your heart. Even a child can do that.

Jesus said to the scribes and Pharisees of His day,

Why do ye also transgress the commandment of God by your tradition? For God commanded, saying, Honour thy father and thy mother: and, He that curseth father or mother, let him die the death. But ye say, Whosoever shall say to his father or his mother, It is a gift, by whatsoever thou mightest be profited by me; And honour not his father or his mother, he shall be free. Thus have ye made the commandments of God of none effect by your tradition. Ye hypocrites, well did Esaias prophesy of you, saying, This people draweth nigh unto me with their mouth, and honoureth me with their lips; but their heart is far from me. But in vain they do worship Me, teaching for doctrines the commandments of men. (Matt. 15:3–9)

Jesus, the Son of God, corrected them Himself. This is what those who disobey God's law are doing when they deliberately refuse to obey God's commandments and teach others to do the same. It is a perfect law, straight from God's own hand and mouth. Remember, He wrote it with His own finger. God has never changed His law—to change it would be to mar it. It is a perfect law. God will never change it. God Himself says He never changes. Listen to this beautiful promise. It is for all of us.

And I will come near to you to judgment; and I will be a swift witness against the sorcerers, and against the adulterers, and against false swearers, and against those that oppress the hireling in his wages, the widow, and the fatherless, and that turn aside the stranger from his right, saith the LORD of hosts. For I am the LORD, I change not; therefore ye sons of Jacob are not consumed. (Mal. 3:5–6)

Malachi was talking about paying tithe, but it pertains to anything God has told us to do.

We are not saved by keeping God's law, but we keep it because we are saved. Obeying God's law shows God we love Him. That's important. God appreciates being loved. He yearns for our love. Remember! He is like us. He made us in His image. He likes to receive love just as we do. He likes loving us. His very character is love. I think it's neat that when we obey His law, we are loving God. The Bible also teaches that *"A man is not justified by the works of the law, but by the faith of Jesus Christ, even we have believed in Jesus Christ, that we might be justified by the faith of Christ, and not by the works of the law: for by the works of the law shall no flesh be justified"* (Gal. 2:16). If we could become sinless just by obeying God's law, Jesus wouldn't have to die to save us from our sins. But when Jesus died for us, He took our sins from us, and we became justified.

Yes, we became sinless. He removed them from us. How humbling that Jesus and His Father agreed for this to happen. And what do we become through this transaction? You'll be surprised. *"Now then we are ambassadors for Christ,… For he hath made him to be sin for us, who knew no sin; that we might be made the righteousness of God in him"* (2 Cor. 5:20–21). So, what does obeying God's law do for us? It shows God and others that we love Him. That's why Jesus said if we love Him, we will keep His commandments. That's what His commandments are all about. He says, show me you love Me. That's what those bear hugs are all about that I have been talking about. I'm sure you want God to know you love Him whether you like bear hugs or not. Those commandments are extremely important. They decide whether we get life or death. They are the laws of heaven—God's government. If you read each command, you will find that each one tells us one special way to love God and love our fellowmen. Isn't that beautiful? So, may I ask, why wouldn't we want to obey them?

Jesus showed us He loved us when He died on the cross for our sins. Now! That's a big deal. Certainly, we can keep ten commands. If we can't face hardship to be His child, then we don't really love Him. He doesn't like it when we have to face danger to be His child either, but He can't treat us differently than He treats Satan. If He did, He would be an unfair God. He has to do it to keep freedom of choice. It is the only way to keep love alive. It was the only route God could take. Heartily, I say, thank You, Lord, for going through so much for me.

You see! The devil has even deceived himself into thinking he will win this battle—the battle between good and evil, the battle between himself and Jesus. He will never be willing to give up his murderous actions toward us. He wants to take as many of us with him as he can into hellfire. Every time we mess up and get confused, the devil is hilariously happy. But not for long! If you love Jesus, with God's help, you will be willing to face Satan's music and show God how much you love Him. But! Obeying God must be from the motive of our love. It must not be from fear of punishment or what you can get out of your obedience. It must be because you truly love God.

The truth will set you free. Free of sin. I pray that each of you will be in that group, with those who are either raised from the grave when Jesus comes or are among those who will be alive when He comes and will rise to meet Him in the air. Satan and his angels are telling many lies about Jesus' coming. Jesus warns us about them. So let's quickly look at a few. First of all, those who love Jesus and have died

> **God wants us to know the truth about death.**

before His coming will be raised to life and will be the first ones to rise up into the clouds.

God says, *"But I would not have you to be ignorant, brethren, concerning them which are asleep, that ye sorrow not, even as others which have no hope" (I Thess. 4:13).* Paul is talking about those who love Jesus and are asleep in the grave. God wants us to know the truth about death. It is one of the lies Satan tells us. God wants us to know this so we won't believe the devil's lies. This lie is a nasty one. It really hurts people at one of the most vulnerable times in their life—when they are mourning over a loved one. The majority of Christians do not understand what really happens when a person dies. That is why I am telling you this.

22

God Pictures His Church as a Virtuous Woman

"And there appeared a great wonder in heaven; a woman clothed with the sun, and the moon under her feet, and upon her head a crown of twelve stars" *(Rev. 12:1).*

And God pictures the church which houses the

antichrist as a Harlot,

and the churches who are following her,

as the Harlot's Daughters.

"And there appeared another wonder in heaven; and behold a great red dragon, having seven heads and ten horns, and seven crowns upon his heads" *(Rev. 12:3).* Scholars consider the dragon to be both the devil and pagan Rome. Paganism is a type of false religion. Remember! Satan wanted to be worshipped.

Before we go any further, I encourage you to bow your head in prayer with me and ask the Holy Spirit to be with us and give us love and understanding. God counsels us on this very serious subject because it is a matter of life and death. He is not pointing His finger at any one of us. Rather, He is telling us these things so we will understand the truth of what is happening as a result of the devil's work. God is not putting anyone down, and neither am I. He wants us to understand the truth concerning the war between Christ and Satan, and I am going to try to share it with you.

Do you know who the harlot and her daughters are? You will be surprised. Keep in mind, every one of us has a choice to make whether we want to follow antichrist or God. God will always maintain our freedom of choice, but remember—it's not God who kills—it is sin that kills. God wants everyone to be saved. In the end, it is our choice—whether we follow the Lamb, Jesus, or follow the serpent, called the devil and Satan.

From the very beginning of our world, there has been a battle going on between Christ and Satan. And between God's church and the churches which are innocently bowing to Satan's wishes. Yes! I said innocently. Let's look at God's church first. In the beginning, God had a church in heaven. And, yes, it is still there. It was the temple where God allowed Lucifer to officiate as one of His covering cherubs. Remember! Lucifer is the one who started all of the trouble in heaven right in that heavenly church. The same is true clear down to our time. There are people who love God and are in God's church, but many of those churches have been polluted by Satan despite what the reformers like Martin Luther did to bring them back in line with biblical teaching. God has done all He can to warn His people, but the enemy is blinding the eyes of the people of God.

The first church God set up on this earth was His church in the garden of Eden when He set apart the seventh day of the week for them to worship. It is the same seventh day of the week the church in heaven worshipped on back then and still worships on today. Satan polluted the early church through sun worship. Remember? It got so bad God had to destroy mankind with a flood. Only eight people believed and worshipped God on His holy seventh day. Every single person on earth was invited to get into that ark, but they refused and made fun of those who obeyed God. It has always been that way on this earth, and it will continue to be that way until Jesus comes to take us home to heaven with Him.

Then God gave the Jews the heavy responsibility of telling the world about God's holy day. The Jewish faith was the same church God gave Adam and Eve in the garden. They just weren't called Jews yet. After the flood, God asked Abraham to evangelize the world. But again, most of the people failed to worship the true God. There really are only two gods: Christ, the true God of heaven, earth, and all of the other worlds God has created; in other words—everywhere—and Satan, the god of this world. Then, when Jesus came to this earth as a baby, via a Jewish girl, the Jews failed to accept Jesus as the Messiah. But they still kept God's Sabbath day that He had created—the seventh day of the week. Many Jews are beginning to accept Jesus as their Savior today. They have a group called Jews for Jesus. It is important that we know the difference between the followers of Jesus and the followers of antichrist.

The biggest difference is Jesus' followers accept and obey all God's ten commands in God's law. God's true church accepts the seventh-day Sabbath as their day of worship. The churches who are following the antichrist do not keep God's chosen day of worship holy; rather, most of them have innocently adopted the first day of the week as their sabbath. God only called one day of the week "Sabbath." It was the seventh day of the week, and it still is His day of worship.

Then, after Jesus' crucifixion, Jesus had His disciples set up His church, the Christian Church, on earth. It is still His church today. That true church still keeps holy the seventh day, the Sabbath. In fact, that church still keeps all of the commandments of God. It is the remnant of the people who were in the Christian churches the disciples started. God says, *"Here are they that keep the commandments of God, and the faith of Jesus"* (Rev. 14:12). But what is the faith of Jesus? God says, through John, *"And I fell at his feet to worship him. And he said unto me, See thou do it not: I am thy fellow servant, and of thy brethren that have the testimony of Jesus: worship God: for the testimony of Jesus is the spirit of prophecy"* *(Rev. 19:10)*. What God's true prophets wrote was always true. We can trust their prophecies. They will always guide us to keep all of God's commandments—every last one of them. God's true church had a prophet. She died, just like all of God's prophets have. She kept God's seventh-day Sabbath holy till her dying day. God's true Church has had prophets down to our day.

John says, *"And the dragon"* (that's the devil), *"was wroth"* (angry with the woman, i.e., the true church), *"and went to make war with the remnant of her seed."* John is talking about the end-time church, *"which **keep the commandments of God, and have the testimony of Jesus Christ** (Rev. 12:17, emphasis supplied).* When you go to the fabric store to buy cloth, a remnant is the last little bit left on the bolt.

God's remnant people is the end-time church here on earth at the end of time. To us it seems like our church has been here for a long time, but it really hasn't. It has only been a couple of hundred years. God tells us what it will be like in the days just before He comes. Notice that Matthew begins talking about the days just before Jesus comes, saying, *"But pray ye that your flight be **not in the winter, neither on the sabbath day"*** (Matt. 24:20–31, emphasis supplied).* Do you think Jesus would tell us to pray about something that is not important? He considers keeping His special day holy right up to the day He comes to take us home with Him very important. It is the one command most people are disobeying. And I think we should be praying that we don't have to flee in the winter or on His special holy day. Since Jesus tells us to pray about it, I think we'd better be doing it. Doing what God asks us to do shows Him we love Him. Nothing could be more important than that. Do you think God would tell us to pray that we won't have to flee only the Sabbath if He didn't think it was important? I don't!

And He says, *"For then shall be great tribulation, such as was not since the beginning of the world to this time, no, nor ever shall be. And except those days should be shortened, there should no flesh be saved: but for the elect's sake those days shall be shortened"* (Matt. 24:21–22, emphasis supplied). Do you know who the elect are? They are those who choose to obey God's law. God elects His end-time followers and considers them His children. He invites every person to be one of His elect. It's very easy. Why wouldn't we want to obey His laws of love—the Ten Commandments. They tell us how to love Him and our fellow human beings. Jesus tells us in these next verses how He will come. Yes! It is Jesus talking. He says not to believe someone if they tell you to go somewhere to find Him. Remember, He says His feet will never touch this earth. His coming will be extremely visible with trumpets blaring, and the brightness of angels such as we have never seen. But people will be lying about it, or Jesus wouldn't have told Matthew to write and tell us what it would be like. If it wouldn't be a problem, Jesus wouldn't have warned us about it. He says,

> *Then if any man shall say unto you, Lo, here is Christ, or there; **believe it not**. For there shall arise false Christs, and false prophets, and shall shew great signs and wonders; **insomuch that, if it were possible, they shall deceive the very elect**. Behold, I have told you before. Wherefore if they shall say unto you, Behold he is in the desert; go not forth: behold, he is in the secret chambers; believe it not.* (Matt. 24:23–26, emphasis supplied)

It would be very dangerous to go. It would be none other than Satan in disguise, trying to get you to obey him. Stay away! I find that very scary.

Jesus gives these verses to us to protect us. He knows those things are going to take place. It is very dangerous to go to séances. That is what this verse is talking about. They are getting answers from the devil.

Jesus also tells us what will happen to the unrighteous—those who are not obeying His commandments. Paul said way back in his day, *"For the mystery of iniquity doth already work: only he who now letteth"* (it is God who lets people be wicked—yes, He lets them choose whether they want to serve Him) *"will let, until he be taken out of the way"* (2 Thess. 2:7). Then Jesus painted a very beautiful word picture of what it will be like when He comes back to earth. He says, *"For as the lightning cometh out of the east, and shineth even unto the west; so shall also the coming of the Son of man* be" *(Matt. 24:27)*. I like watching the lightning streak across the sky. It's beautiful and scary at the same time! It fills one with awe at its brightness and power.

Now, let's go back to talking about the churches. Remember! The disciples went around starting churches. One of those churches was in Rome. When that church was set up, it was virtuous. But it became corrupt through pagan practices. This came about through the battle of antichrist—Satan; via his followers. I encourage you to read Revelation 12:1–17. It depicts what took place in heaven between God's angels and those who worship Satan, the beast.

Now let's look at verses that depict the illicit church. Another name for that church is "Babylon." Here is a quick review of the characteristics of the beast. Fornication is the comingling of false doctrines with false religions. God pictures His church as His bride. God's bride is a church that will stay true to Him. It will honor and obey Him to the very end of time by keeping all of His loving commands. Here is how the Bible describes her. *"And there appeared a great wonder in heaven; a woman clothed with the sun, and the moon under her feet, and upon her head a crown of twelve stars: And she being with child cried, travailing in birth, and pained to be delivered" (Rev. 12:1-2)*. God depicts His church that stayed true to Him as a pure woman. Jesus was born into the true church. He is the child of Mary and the true church that was keeping all of the commandments of God—including the seventh-day Sabbath. Jesus was the baby Mary travailed with—the Son of God. That church will come through the controversy safely. It is too bad she rejected her Savior for so long.

If the church you are attending is not keeping all of God's commandments, it is not being true to God. Most people are not in the true church. They are in churches God says are daughters of the false church. Why are they in the false church? Because they think they are obeying God. They do not know they are disobeying Him. He wants them to come out of those churches, or better yet, God wants their whole congregation to return to Him and keep His seventh-day Sabbath holy. Here is His command. *"Come out of her, my people, that ye be not partakers of her sins" (Rev. 18:4)*. Until they wake up and realize Satan has been tricking them, they will fail to change. They are called daughters of the church depicted by a great red dragon, the devil. Because of the devil's lies, deceit, and trickery, they have accepted false doctrines. The main doctrine they accept is Sunday-keeping. They do not realize Sunday observance came into God's church through the devil.

God calls these churches harlots. Why? Because they do not show God they love Him by believing Him. Jesus explains it. He says, *"If ye keep my commandments, ye shall abide in my love; even as I have kept my Father's commandments, and abide in his love" (John 15:10).* Jesus always kept the seventh-day Sabbath. He is our example. You can't go wrong following Him. The daughters of the great harlot do not know they are disobeying God. That's because the harlot herself has blinded them through her activities with Satan. The false church has been desecrating God's fourth commandment through paganism, the devil, and his deluded followers.

The third church is the one that God pictures as a great red dragon. Let's look at it now. As we have already learned, the dragon represents Lucifer, the serpent, devil, Satan. How did these false teachings get started? As we have learned, the devil is very deceptive, deceitful, and a pro at lying. He is the one who made up these lies. Star is another name for angels. God tells us in His Word, the Bible, that *"His tail drew the third part of the stars of heaven, and did cast them to the earth: and the dragon stood before the woman which was ready to be delivered" (Rev. 12:4).* That is how we got evil angels down here on earth. They were deceived by the devil. *"And the great dragon was cast out, that old serpent, called the Devil, and Satan, which deceiveth the whole world: he was cast out into the earth, and his angels were cast out with him" (Rev.12:9).*

On the one hand, can't you just see the angels who stayed true to God? The ones who were not kicked out of heaven, clapping their hands and praising God because those wicked angels would no longer be in heaven. They had won the battle. But on the other hand, I can also see them grieving because they know what we on the earth will face and how much harder their work will be, taking care of us. How grieved they are when we believe Satan's lies. But on the other hand, how elated they must be when we successfully win the battle over evil. I sure am looking forward to talking with my guardian angel, and I'm sure you are, too.

Then Jesus came as a baby. Boy! Did the angels who guarded Him have their work cut out for them. What a blessed privilege it was—to protect Jesus as much as they could. But they were not able to keep all of the devil's hatred from harming Him. This was done just so God could show heaven, the other worlds, and earth how truly wicked the devil is. Thank You, Father, Holy Spirit, and you, holy angels, for protecting our Lord the best you could. The devil is in a frenzy right now. Isn't that exciting? The Christian church that Jesus' disciples erected at Rome began as a virtuous woman, but its holiness didn't last long. Let's look and see why one of the Bible verses calls that city a whore. When the disciples began planting churches, they set up many. But the one they set up in Rome had problems right away. You see, Lucifer heckled that church. He was determined to make it his church. It was situated in an area where Satan and those who obeyed him could easily cause conflict. That church became the mother of harlots. In other words, she caused members of that church to chin with people who were worshiping the devil.

Actually, they were deceived by the big red dragon himself. They are still deceived by him today. Just look at all the sexual abuse that has been going on in that church. He corrupted the new baby church in Rome that the disciples raised up. Satan, the dragon, via Satan's followers, brought sun worship into that new baby church through the people the devil had tricked. The pagans violated that church through the worship of the sun. Constantine and the sun worshipers corrupted it. They turned the members from the worship of God to the worship of Satan and his sun worship. They worshipped on Sunday in place of, and instead of, the true Sabbath of the Lord. God loved those sun worshippers. He wanted to save them. But He would not force them to love Him. Love cannot be forced. When forced, it is not love but is control.

Remember, Lucifer had the bigs in heaven. So why not bow to the largest star in the heavens. Thus he happily worships that large star to this day. The church in Rome still honors Satan's chosen day of worship. It is amazing how true these words are. For truly, we see leaders of that church fostering physical, sexual, and spiritual abuse through its priests today who claim to be Christ on earth.

There is a drastic contrast between God's commandment-keeping church and the church whose priests claim to be Christ on earth and also tell its worshippers that the priest is the one who forgives people's sins on earth. No man can take Jesus' place as our sin-bearer. No man is God. No man can forgive our sins. Only the man Christ Jesus and His shed blood washes away our sins. Today, it is not difficult to see what church is the true church. Just look at the atrocities taking place within the false church. Many of its leaders do not realize they are obeying Satan. I pray they will ask God to forgive their sins and will begin obeying God, and coming out of Babylon, and forsaking that church. Many are beginning to come out of her. But they do not realize they need to change their day of worship. That's why I am writing this book. I want to tell as many of my brothers and sisters as I can about the lies Satan is feeding them. Many of them are not aware they are disobeying God. They were taught as children that the church they go to is the true church.

God loves them, and I do, too. I want everyone to understand God's will for them. He is patiently waiting for them to see that church for what she is. God says, in her was found the blood of prophets and of the saints Recall the Dark Ages when God's church was in deep trouble while all those great men, Martin Luther, and many others who each brought back one truth and started new churches that changed and kept God's word. The Baptist church brought back baptism by immersion, as Jesus was baptized instead of sprinkling like the mother church taught. These are the same Christian churches of our day, but they failed to change and keep the fourth commandment. Satan is so devious! He is the one who ruined God's true church and turned it into a whore.

Those are words God used—not mine. They are aimed at getting people's attention. Yes! At rescuing His children. I think it bears repeating that God says, *"Come out of her, my people"* (Yes, there are many of God's true worshippers still in that church. God is waiting for them to come out of her. This includes her daughter churches, too. Many of them, too, do not realize they are dishonoring God. He is saying to them, too, to come out.), *"that ye be not partakers of her sins, and that ye receive not of her plagues. For her sins have reached unto heaven, and God hath remembered her iniquities" (Rev. 18:4–5)*. Ask the Holy Spirit to give you understanding. Join God's church that is keeping all ten of God's commandments. Better yet! Get your whole church to accept this truth. There are many people of God on television preaching the truth. You can find them on Roku. A couple of my favorites are Pastor John Carter and Pastor Doug Batchelor, and many more. God loves you, and so do I. Pastor Carter makes things so understandable.

Just look at these words John penned concerning the mother church and her daughter who are innocently obeying her.

> *How much she hath glorified herself, and lived deliciously, so much torment and sorrow give her: for she saith in her heart, I sit a queen, and am no widow, and shall see no sorrow. Therefore shall her plagues come in one day, death, and mourning, and famine; and she shall be utterly burned with fire: for strong is the Lord God who judgeth her.* (Rev. 18:7–8)

These words bring to my mind how this church burned the saints at the stake back in the Dark Ages.

May God bless you, dear loved ones of God—my sister, my brother. The next great event will be Jesus coming in the clouds of heaven to take us home with Him. I am looking forward to taking the wonderful trip to heaven with you. Won't that be a blessed and fun time? I hope each of you will take it. Pray for me that I will stay true to the Lord during the hard times that are even now beginning to come on the earth. None of us are safe from the devil's sly lies. But all of us can read and understand God's law. God never makes things hard, but His enemy, the devil, certainly does. Flee from him! God bless you. Remember! There is no sin God is not willing to forgive, except the one we refuse to ask Him to forgive. What do you say, dear reader, that we take that trip to heaven together? I'd love to meet you. Hope you feel the same way about me. Your sister in Christ.

23

Are We Obeying God or Antichrist? Hope You Enjoy the Test

This test will give you positive proof of whether you are obeying:

God

or
antichrist.
Are you checking to see if
what you are being told
agrees with what God has to say about it?
I certainly hope you check me out.
No man is perfect—but God is.
We all make mistakes. No created being knows everything.
Thus!
There is always room for improvement and growth.
But we must be sure we are growing more like Jesus—not more like
some human being.
But we can know God's will via His ten-commandment law.
Also remember! God has said:
"Man shall not live by bread alone,
But on every word that comes out of the mouth of God" (Matt. 4:4, NASB).
So!
What are the leaders of your church telling you?
Are they teaching you to have faith in God and believe His Word alone?
I believe that even though I have already used many of these verses, I
should use them again
with this purpose in mind.
To get a complete picture of what God is telling us, we must compare
Scripture with Scripture.
One verse builds on another, as it paints the whole picture.
Repetition cements the words of God in our minds.

And we need those words cemented in our minds for the hard times
ahead of us.
We can never hear God's words too much or too often.
For a brother or sister might be innocently misquoting a verse,
or they could be facing temptations, and are being tricked by the devil,
too.
We've all been there and done that! So, rely on God's Word alone.
The Bible is chock full of affirmation and instruction.
And it says,
"If they speak not according to this word,
there is no light in them" (Isa. 8:20).

That's Right!
If what is being told to you
is truly what God said, it will
Always
Agree with the Bible.

This verse tells us how God says we are to test what people say, and
remember, these are God's words telling us this. If the Bible says it, it
is God saying it! And, of course, God is always right. He is God. He is
the rule-maker. God alone is the only one we can truly and totally trust.
And it is only through faith that we learn to trust Him. All faith is, is total
trust. When we believe every word He says and consequently obey Him,
then we trust Him. So! We need to check to see whether we are obeying
the commandments of God. If we aren't, we are not walking in Jesus'
footsteps. For the Ten Commandments are part of the Word of God. In
fact, those commands are the laws of God and of heaven. We need to pray
for ourselves, our family, our friends, and all mankind. If they are being
taught error, they probably do not realize it. Even the one who is teaching
them may not know they are teaching error. All of us have been misled
many times in our life. No matter what church we attend, all of us are still
sinners and have been misled by Satan. Yes! Even pastors, priests, popes,
and masters, are sinners; and have been misled.

Remember, God says through John, *"Believe not every spirit, but try the*
spirits whether they are of God: Because many false prophets are gone out
into the world" (1 John 4:1).

Also!

The Bible we use should be an authorized version of the Bible, not a version documented by a specific denomination or a paraphrase of some church, committee, or person. Our authorized versions were assembled by a combination of men from different faiths to make sure the Word of God was kept pure when it was translated into the various languages.

When I say this, I am not talking about pastors who insert their own thoughts and ideas on particular subjects to help their parishioners study their Bible. They are not forming a new Bible or altering the words of the Bible—they are merely including their own study notes and ideas that they like to use.

I am talking about churches that change the words of the Bible and make it their own. Just one word changed makes it not the true, pure word of God. Yes! One changed word can ruin the whole Bible. It's a big book. How can you be sure those words are the only ones which have been changed? The Jehovah's Witnesses have their own Bible, the Latter-day Saints have their own, too, and the Catholic Church used to have their own version, too. They still have one they favor. You may be thinking, "But there are so many versions. How do we know which one is right?" Well! Even true versions may have some mistakes in them. Either from errors the copiers made or errors by the translators themselves—but if they are honest mistakes, they will be caught. I am only talking about the men who translated the Bible from Hebrew and Greek, and other languages. There were very few errors, and they were made by mistake, not design. There is a huge difference between an honest mistake, which will be corrected when the writer catches it, and a deliberate change because they thought God meant something else. God makes no mistake. It was not the purpose of the original translators, who translated our Bible into other languages, to change God's Word to suit their understanding. But we all know, when humans do things, there are bound to be honest mistakes.

Our God made sure that no terrible mistakes occurred when the original, honest translators did their work under the inspiration of God. Yes, even true versions of the Bible sometimes do have errors, but not deliberate errors. If you are interested, there is a book called *So Many Versions?* by Sakae Kubo & Walter F. Specht, Zondervan Publishing. It pinpoints the errors they know about. If you are concerned about errors being in the Bible, you would probably find that book interesting. It is a good guideline for deciding which version you want to use.

The Bible is written by the method of repeat and enlarge. One tells one prophet to write something, and then He inspires another prophet to add more knowledge to that subject in another book of the Bible. These were holy men of God, and they were writing under the inspiration of God. If we can't believe the Bible, then there is nothing we can trust, and we are in a deplorable condition. I ask, "What other book has been written by a lot of different people, covering so many generations, coming from so many walks of life, and prophecies that have come true so far?" Amazing, isn't it? And the answer is "none." No, none of them can substantiate their claims like the Bible has.

A majority of the prophecies have been fulfilled. Prophecy tells us what is going to happen in the future. Some of the most exciting events are still in the future, such as the second coming of Jesus to this earth. That's called the blessed hope. It is prophesied to happen when the people of this world are in great distress. Praise God; His Word has shown itself to be reliable time and time again. We need to accept all of the Bible as true and ask God to help us understand the verses we are having trouble with.

Ask the Holy Spirit to guide your mind as you read. Don't get upset if you can't seem to get an answer from God. Remember! He tells us to say, *"Thy will be done" (Matt.6:10).* He promises to send the Holy Spirit to us. God knows what is best. Sometimes He does not answer us the way we want Him to because He is testing us to see if we will obey Him. We have to go through tests like that because the devil accuses God of being unfair. And also because tests like that help us grow spiritually. That is if we choose to serve God no matter what happens to us as a result of our obedience. I got bitten by a pit bull for that reason; God gave me great faith through that experience. God always leaves the choice to us. Look at Timothy's take on it.

He says, *"All that will live godly in Christ Jesus shall suffer persecution" (2 Tim. 3:12).* The devil makes sure of that. We must remember all of these things are in God's hands. He will not allow Satan to make you suffer more than you are able to bear. God offers a way out so you can stand Satan's persecution. Remember Esther, Job, and the three Hebrew boys in the burning fiery furnace.

Look at this beautiful promise!

"From a child thou hast known the holy scriptures,

which are able to make thee wise unto salvation."

How does that happen? It happens

"through faith which is in Christ Jesus"

(2 Tim 3:15).

I totally thank the Father that He was willing to make Jesus

"to be sin for us, who knew no sin;

that we might be made the righteousness of God in him"

(2 Cor. 5:21).

God bless you, fellow Christian.

TEACH Services, Inc.
P U B L I S H I N G

We invite you to view the complete
selection of titles we publish at:
www.TEACHServices.com

We encourage you to write us
with your thoughts about this,
or any other book we publish at:
info@TEACHServices.com

TEACH Services' titles may be purchased in
bulk quantities for educational, fund-raising,
business, or promotional use.
bulksales@TEACHServices.com

Finally, if you are interested in seeing
your own book in print, please contact us at:
publishing@TEACHServices.com
We are happy to review your manuscript at no charge.

www.ingramcontent.com/pod-product-compliance
Lightning Source LLC
Chambersburg PA
CBHW070347090426
42733CB00009B/1320